THE
STEEL
CRISIS

Roy Hoopes

THE JOHN DAY COMPANY

NEW YORK

HD
9516
.H6

For Thomas David Hoopes,
whose arrival prompted an increased
interest in the President's efforts
to hold prices down

Acknowledgments

I wish to thank the many people—in the Administration and in the steel industry—who took time out from busy schedules in order to discuss with me the hectic week of April 9th, 1962.

In addition, many people helped me along the way. They include: Edgar Baker, Samuel C. Brightman, Wallace Carroll, Mary Clynes, Dixon Donnelley, Barbara Gamarekian, Thomas Geoghegan, Andrew Hatcher, Frank Holeman, John Jacobs, Edith Midgett, John Munhall, III, Richard Mooney, Alan Otten, Charles Rayner, William Reddig, Albert Roland, Paul Sarbanes, Hugh Sidey, John Sweeney, and Thomas Schroth.

I also wish to thank my mother, Mrs. Lydia C. Hoopes, Mrs. Pat Schroth and my wife, Cora, for expert assistance in the preparation of the manuscript.

Finally, thanks to my editor, Robert Hill, and my agent, Perry Knowlton, for editorial counsel, and, above all, patience.

Contents

APPENDICES

PART I

A SUDDEN TEMPEST
IN APRIL

CHAPTER 1

Tuesday, April 10: Roger Blough Disturbs the Calm

> I wouldn't bet on any price increase this year . . . I'm not optimistic, because price shading and discounts are just as prevalent as before, so I don't think the climate is here.
> —*Steel executive, quoted in the* Wall Street Journal, *April 9, 1962*

The week of April 9, 1962, began calmly enough in Washington. The weather was beautifully springlike and much of the talk around town, as elsewhere around the country, centered on the baseball season which was to open Monday. The international climate was also relatively mild. Since the Russian resumption of nuclear testing the previous fall and the West's decision to resume testing, the topic uppermost in many people's minds was strontium-90 which was expected to come down in increasing amounts with the spring rains. When the new baseball season or strontium-90 began to lag in a conversation, the subject of automation was sure to come up. The President himself had discussed it at a press conference only a few weeks before, saying that he considered it the major domestic challenge of the 1960's. And, of course, the state of the economy. People everywhere, from the New Frontiersmen in Washington to the men on the assembly line in Detroit, were talking about business conditions. There had been a lot said of a price rise in the steel industry, but just two weeks before, the union and the industry had agreed to a "noninflationary" contract, and it was generally assumed that the price line would be held at least for another year. The last steel wage contract had been signed on the previous Friday, and now that the threat of a strike was out of the way, many people were becoming more optimistic, and some were going so far as to predict a pretty good year—even for the steel industry. In the April issue of *Fortune,* which had been on the newsstands about a week, an article on the Bethlehem Steel Corporation said that the company's 1962 prospects were excellent—providing there was no strike and orders held up. "Unless the steel industry goes to pot, which it won't," said Controller Frank Brugler, "Bethlehem isn't going to plateau out. We're going to make more money than ever." And on Monday the *Wall Street Journal,* in a report from Pittsburgh, had said that most steel producers doubted there would be a general price boost in 1962.

All in all it looked as if the White House might enjoy a relatively calm week. The President's schedule was light, the high points being the opening of the baseball season, the arrival of the Shah of Iran and his wife, who were coming on a state visit, and a weekend review of the Atlantic Fleet off the North Carolina coast. Monday afternoon the President went out to Washington's huge new Memorial Stadium and launched the baseball season with a respectable heave that no one was able to catch. Then he settled back to enjoy the game, which featured an interrupting shower during which Kennedy chatted with Umpire Hank Soar in the latter's locker room, and a much publicized foul tip off the bat of Washington's Willy Tasby which started a great debate as to whether the President's friend Dave Powers had ducked or stood firm when the ball headed in Kennedy's general direction. Later, pictures showed Powers standing firm. The President himself was a little worried about his own reaction, but after he saw the pictures he felt relieved. "Everett Dirksen was ducking even lower," he quipped, with the typical Kennedy smile. Washington defeated Detroit 4 to 1, and considering that the hapless Senators were to win only 60 games all season, it was a pleasant afternoon for the 49,000 hometown fans.

On Tuesday, President Kennedy prepared for another relatively quiet day. In the morning he had breakfast with Democratic Congressional leaders, and later saw Julius Holmes, U. S. Ambassador to Iran. He also sent an extended unemployment compensation bill to Congress and issued jointly with Great Britain a statement giving Russia one last chance to accept a safeguarded treaty banning nuclear tests before the Western powers resumed their atmospheric testing later in the month.

The afternoon looked even more peaceful. Outside the White House a crowd was gathered to watch Caroline, helped by her mother, ride her pony Macaroni. A man in a blue suit emerged from the White House, and a voice shouted: "That's the President!" "No it's not, but it's a Kennedy," said another. It was, in fact, Attorney General Robert Kennedy who had just had a conference with his brother.

The rest of the day promised such quiet that the President thought he might have time for a nap and a little relaxed reading. However, there was one point he wanted to clear up. A rumor had been going around that one of the steel companies was getting ready to raise prices, so early Tuesday afternoon the President called Secretary of Labor Arthur Goldberg to ask about it. Goldberg gave him a definite negative answer, saying that he got the opposite reading—as far as he knew, no steel price increases were anticipated by anyone.

Later the President was to recall an incident which had occurred the previous weekend and wonder whether it had not been significant. On Saturday, April 7, by prearrangement, he had telephoned union and management leaders in the recently completed negotiations on the steel contract, congratulating them on the signing of the contract. When he reached R. Conrad Cooper, a vice-president of U. S. Steel and the company's chief negotiator, and said "This is the President," he got in return only a surprisingly cold "Yes, sir." As Kennedy later described this conversation, Cooper did not have more than a dozen words to say, and these were spoken in flat, distant tones. Mr. Kennedy is reported to have given more than one mimicking account of the conversation, and later said that he had been puzzled by the reaction to his friendly congratulations.

Still, every straw in the wind pointed to Big Steel holding the price line; that afternoon the White House Associated Press wire had carried a story from Wilmington reporting the remarks of Bethlehem Steel President Edmund F. Martin to a group of reporters after a stockholders' meeting. "There shouldn't be any price rise," Martin was quoted in a somewhat garbled account of his remarks. "We shouldn't do anything to increase our costs if we are to survive. We have more competition—domestic and foreign."

The afternoon of Tuesday, April 10, was equally tranquil in New York. The weather was mild and sunny—especially on Wall Street where the specter of a steel strike, averted by the recently announced agreement between labor and Big Steel, seemed to be letting in a little more sunlight than usual. That very afternoon the lead article in the monthly survey of the Morgan Guaranty Trust Company—whose top members also sat on the board of United States Steel—was being printed. It read, in part: "To a business community eager for good news, the labor agreement in the steel industry has provided the brightest word in recent weeks . . . If it proves to set a pattern for other industries, the bargaining outcome could encourage investment spending by easing apprehensions over a further profits squeeze in industry generally, and over a period of time could help the competitive position of U. S. goods in world markets."

Almost everyone in the business community seemed to feel that business was in for a period of quiet, if sluggish, stability with perhaps even a chance of a pickup in the last two quarters.

They reckoned without a handful of men gathered early that same afternoon in a paneled room at 71 Broadway, New York, home of United States Steel. The men were members of the 12-man executive committee of the board of directors. It was an interesting committee, and considering the national tempest it was about to stir up, its composition is significant. From U. S. Steel there was Roger Blough, Chairman of the Board; Leslie B. Worthington, President; Robert C. Tyson, Chairman of the Finance Committee; Enders M. Voorhees, Cleo F. Craig and Clifford F. Hood. Committee members from outside the company were Henry T. Heald of the Ford Foundation; John M. Meyer, Jr., Senior Vice-President of the Morgan Guaranty Trust Company; Alexander C. Nagle, Director of the First National City Bank of New York; C. Jared Ingersoll, Chairman of the Muskogee Company; Arthur A. Houghton, Jr., President of the Steuben Glass Company; and Joseph P. Spang, Director of the Gillette Company. Three members of the committee were absent, but the key men—Blough, Worthington and Tyson—were there.

The committee had met to consider a decision made the previous Friday by U. S. Steel's operations policy committee, composed of the top ten executives of the company. The decision had been unanimous—to raise the price of steel approximately 3½ percent. Since only four votes were needed in addition to those of Blough, Worthington and Tyson— who were members of the operations policy committee—little opposition was expected and it is presumed that none materialized. The executive committee approved the decision, and the company's public relations department was given one hour to prepare and release the statement announcing the increase.

When the meeting broke up at around 3 P.M., Roger Blough placed a telephone call to the White House. Presidential Appointments Secretary Kenneth O'Donnell, who screens incoming visitors and some phone calls, was not at his desk just outside the President's office, so the call was taken by one of O'Donnell's secretaries. "I would like to see the President this afternoon on a very important matter concerning steel," said Mr. Blough, adding that he was about to board a plane for Washington. The message was given to O'Donnell when he returned to his desk; when Blough called after arriving in Washington, he was told that he had an appointment with the President for 5:45 P.M.

Obviously, Roger Blough's ability to pick up the telephone and get an appointment with the President of the United States within a matter of hours was not merely attributable to the fact that he was chairman of the board of U. S. Steel. As chairman of the business council, an advisory committee of top businessmen which serves the Government, he was a frequent visitor in Washington, and was often seen at the White House.

In addition, Blough had also played a role in the recently completed negotiations between the steel industry and the labor unions. Consequently it is not surprising that he should get an appointment with the President on such short notice, an appointment which O'Donnell was able to handle without clearing it with the President. Still, when Kennedy decided to check his calendar that afternoon with his secretary, Mrs. Lincoln, he was surprised when she said: "You have Mr. Blough at a quarter to six."

"Mr. Blough!" exclaimed the President.

"Yes," said Mrs. Lincoln.

The President was baffled. With the business council presumably quiet and the steel contracts not only agreed to but signed, why should Roger Blough want to see him? Just to make certain, the President checked with O'Donnell, who confirmed the Blough appointment. Neither of them could guess what it was Blough wanted to talk about; there was nothing to do but wait.

Roger Blough is a tall, distinguished-looking and somber man who used to be a high school teacher, and as chairman of the board of the nation's largest corporation, is rarely given to levity. However, as he entered the White House just before his scheduled appointment with the President he appeared almost jolly. In fact one of the White House aides said that "he bounced in like a man who was about to cut steel prices." Blough was ushered into the President's office almost immediately, and with a bare exchange of amenities, the President offered him a seat on the sofa to his right as he seated himself in his much publicized rocking chair.

"Perhaps the easiest way I can explain why I am here," said Mr. Blough, "is to give you this and let you read it."

He handed the President a four-page mimeographed document. It was a press release containing a statement by Leslie Worthington which at that moment was on its way to newspaper offices in New York and Pittsburgh. (See Appendix A.) The President began a hasty reading of the document; as he read, his apprehension quickly turned to anger. Briefly, the statement made the following points:

● That United States Steel had decided to raise its prices by an average of 3.5 percent—or three-tenths of a cent per pound;

● That the company was forced to take this action because since the last overall price increase in 1958 it had been faced with increase in costs totaling about 6 percent—despite cost reductions which had been realized through the use of more modern equipment;

● The net result had been a "profit squeeze" which had reduced profits to the lowest level since 1952;

• Due to this loss in profits, less money had been available for the modernization of equipment necessary to enable the steel industry to compete with foreign steel products and steel substitutes produced at home. "Only by generating the funds necessary to keep these facilities fully competitive," Worthington's statement said, "can our company continue to provide its customers with a dependable source of steel, and to provide its employees with dependable jobs."

When the President finished, he looked up coldly and said: "I think you have made a terrible mistake." He then asked Mrs. Lincoln to summon Arthur Goldberg "immediately!" While they were waiting for Goldberg, the President reviewed for Blough his efforts in the recent wage negotiations to persuade both sides to reach a noninflationary agreement. The President did not lose his temper and Blough listened silently.

Secretary Goldberg covered the four blocks from the Labor Department to the White House in a matter of minutes. He had hardly passed through the door of the President's office when he launched into an argument against raising the price of steel.

The President interrupted him. "Wait a minute, Arthur," he said. "Read the statement. They've raised the price. It's already done."

Goldberg was stunned. Then he lost his temper. What was the point of the meeting, he wanted to know, since the decision to raise prices had already been made? Blough replied that he had felt it a matter of courtesy to inform the President personally. Goldberg shot back that it was hardly courteous to announce a decision of such magnitude and then confront the President with an accomplished fact. A fairly heated discussion followed in which Secretary Goldberg lectured Mr. Blough at some length, stressing four points in particular:

1. He argued that the price increase would be a great dis-

service to the nation because it would jeopardize the entire economic policy of the Administration. The whole country has a stake in stable prices—consumers, labor and business.

2. The price increase would also be a disservice to U. S. Steel because it, too, had a stake in the stability of our economy.

3. The increase would be a severe blow to the whole future of collective bargaining. Because of what everyone felt were the Government's successful efforts to restrain the unions in the recent negotiations, no union could now be asked by the Administration to show restraint in its wage demands. Goldberg also stressed the fact that his own position was completely undermined and that he personally could no longer approach any union head with a request to restrain his demands.

4. Finally, Goldberg said, the move appeared to be a deliberate double cross of the President, because while the Administration was encouraging the labor unions to hold back their demands Blough had never once given any indication of his intent to raise prices after the negotiations had been completed. It was Goldberg's contention that Blough had been completely lacking in candor in his private talks with President Kennedy and that candor is owed to the President of the United States.

There were no invectives or threats, and neither the President nor Goldberg asked Blough to rescind the price rise. Roger Blough quietly defended his company's action, but it was obvious that he had not come to the White House to negotiate or ask for advice. A price rise in steel by the nation's largest steel producers was now a matter of fact. And in a few hours—as the President and Secretary Goldberg well knew—the other steel companies would probably be announcing similar rises.

At 6:35 P.M.—fifty minutes after he had entered the President's office—Roger Blough left. Although he looked far from jolly now, he was nevertheless determined to stick with the price rise in the cost of steel. If he had known what the next three days would bring, he probably would have looked even more somber. For without fully realizing what he had done, Roger Blough had just touched off a series of events which, in the words of *Fortune,* would "reverberate for years to come through the political and economic life of the U. S." He had also set in motion a 72-hour chain of action which would strike the nation like a huge bolt of lightning, illuminating just for a flash the sources of power in the most powerful economic system the world had ever developed.

Once Blough had left the President's office, the President exploded. He paced up and down angrily, muttering heated phrases and making little effort to restrain his language. One aide said he had never seen the President so angry. From time to time he would flop into his rocking chair when he wanted to talk. "That rocking chair should have had a speedometer," said one staff member later, describing the President's reaction.

Some of the presidential aides had been standing outside the door, waiting to attend a regular prepress conference briefing scheduled for 6:15 P.M. When Blough left, they began to wander in. They included Andrew Hatcher, Acting Press Secretary for Pierre Salinger, who was on vacation; Ted Sorensen, the President's Chief Counsel, and McGeorge Bundy, a special White House assistant for foreign affairs. It was decided to hold a council of war right then and there, so the three members of the Council of Economic Advisers were also called. The chairman, Dr. Walter Heller, came hastily from his office in the Old State Department Building across the street. Dr. Kermit Gordon followed in a few minutes. James Tobin could not join the council until later that evening.

The President continued to seethe. He felt that he had

been deliberately double-crossed, that the office of the Presidency had been affronted, and the national interest ignored. As he paced up and down he recalled a fight which his father, the first chairman of the Securities and Exchange Commission, had had with steel executives in 1937. "My father always told me that all businessmen were sons of bitches," he burst out, in a now famous remark, "but I never believed it until now." [1]

It was obvious that the President intended to fight, but at

[1] After this explosive statement was published by *The New York Times* on April 23, 1962, Publisher Orvil E. Dryfoos wrote President Kennedy, apologizing for having printed it. However, the quotation was widely circulated and it did cause considerable resentment, not only in the business community but elsewhere. In considering this remark, it must be remembered that it was made in private in the company of his closest male associates. As is well known, the club-room and locker-room conversations of the nation's business leaders would not always bear public repetition either. Neither, for that matter, would the closed-door official conversations of past Presidents. President Eisenhower, for instance, was widely quoted in a similar remark (also directed at businessmen) during a Cabinet meeting when he was shown the "ground rules" for conduct in a conspiracy as set down by one of the men involved in the electrical industry antitrust conspiracy case. Eisenhower said: "The only thing those sons of bitches forgot to warn them about was: 'Don't take notes.' " (See *The Great Price Conspiracy*, John Herling. Washington, D.C.: Robert B. Luce Associates, 1962, p. 80.)

However, President Kennedy's remark was not quoted with complete accuracy. He explained a month later when asked about it at a news conference. "The statement which I have seen repeated as it was repeated in one daily paper is inaccurate," said the President, surprising reporters with his explanation of *which* part of the remark was inaccurate. "It quotes my father as having expressed himself strongly to me, and in this I quoted what he said and indicated that he had not been, as he had not been on many other occasions, wholly wrong.

"Now, the only thing wrong with the statement was that as it appeared in the daily paper it indicated that he was critical of the business community and the phrase was 'all businessmen.' That is obviously in error, because he was a businessman himself. He was critical of the steel men, and he worked for a steel company himself, and he was involved when he was a member of the Roosevelt Administration in the 1937 strike, and he formed an opinion which he imparted to me, and which I found appropriate that evening.

"But he confined it, and I would confine it. Obviously these generalizations are inaccurate and unfair, and he has been a businessman and the business system has been very generous to him. But I felt at that time that we had not been treated altogether with frankness, and therefore I thought that his view had merit. . . ."

that moment, with his usually curbed temper unleashed, no one could have predicted his first move. Everyone present was certain of one thing, however: there would be *action*. As *New York Times* Columnist James Reston was to write two days later: "The Kennedys do not like to lose. They do not like to be double-crossed. And when they think they have been double-crossed, brother, hand me down my steel shillelagh."

The President, in fiery language, first asked if the Administration had received a formal commitment from Big Steel about a price freeze. The answer was no, that during the negotiations in which government pressure was being exerted on the unions, the question of an industry price freeze was so taken for granted that no formal commitment was considered necessary. The government representatives had looked upon the price freeze as a gentlemen's agreement. It would just not have been proper to ask for a commitment. Besides, in the opinion of at least some Administration aides, a pledge in itself might have been a violation of the antitrust laws.

Someone remembered that David McDonald, President of the United Steelworkers' Union, who had done most of the bargaining for the unions, ought to be called. It was feared that McDonald would be made to look stupid before his union, and the White House group felt that McDonald should know that the Administration was just as shocked as he would be. Secretary Goldberg put through the call to McDonald, who took the news pretty calmly. Actually, McDonald knew something was in the wind, even if he did not know precisely what it was at the time he received his call from the White House. That afternoon, while at Pittsburgh's Forbes Field watching the Pirates win their opener against the Philadelphia Phillies, 6–0, McDonald was visited in his box by Conrad Cooper, who had been the steel company's principal negotiator during the wage talks. Conrad asked

McDonald to meet him at 5:30 that afternoon at the Penn-Sheraton Hotel where negotiations were continuing on the B-List—clerical workers, ore miners, ore boat crews and other categories of steel employees. McDonald went to the hotel that afternoon and waited until 5:55. Cooper did not appear. Shortly after McDonald left, Cooper telephoned the hotel anxiously trying to locate McDonald. He finally reached McDonald and arrangements were made to meet at 7:30 P.M. When they did get together, Cooper told McDonald, who had by this time heard about the price increase from the White House, that he had known about the possibility of a price increase but could say nothing about it until after the announcement was made. Cooper said the action was in no way intended to reflect upon the labor settlement.

McDonald told the White House that he felt that his good faith was well known by his union and that he would probably ride through the shock all right. Later that evening, McDonald issued a statement saying that he was "surprised, troubled and concerned" by the announcement. He added that the decision was U. S. Steel's alone. "We had no understanding and no discussion with the company on prices," McDonald said.

As soon as the President began to simmer down, White House telephone wires started to hum. A call went out to Attorney General Robert Kennedy, and for some time the President and his brother discussed U. S. Steel's move, dwelling longest on the antitrust aspects of the price increase if— as assumed—the other steel companies followed U. S. Steel's lead. Before the conversation was completed, it was agreed that the Justice Department would announce an antitrust investigation, and later that evening a spokesman for Robert Kennedy issued a statement saying: "Because of past price behavior in the steel industry, the Department of Justice will take an immediate and close look at the current situation and any future developments." The spokesman also noted that in the past when one steel company had raised prices, the others usually followed suit.

Secretary of Defense Robert McNamara was also called, and the implications to the national defense effort were discussed in detail. The possibility of putting a ceiling on the price the Government would pay for steel was considered, although the impracticality of the idea later became obvious. During the meeting a call also came in from Secretary of the Treasury Douglas Dillon, who was on vacation in Florida. Another call went out. This one from the President to Senator Estes Kefauver at his home in Spring Valley, a Washington suburb. Kefauver was just getting ready to go out for the evening—to the White House, in fact. Would the Senator, the President wanted to know, make a public announcement of "dismay" at the action taken by U. S. Steel and consider a Senate investigation by the Senator's powerful antitrust and monopoly subcommittee of the Senate Judiciary Committee? The Senator would. (Later that evening Kefauver issued a public statement registering shock at the action by U. S. Steel and stating that "Whether other steel companies slavishly follow United States Steel's proposal will determine whether there is any real competition in the steel industry." He added that he would follow the steel price picture closely, and said, "I have ordered the staff of the subcommittee to begin an immediate inquiry into the matter . . .")

About this time, statements being issued by other steel companies began coming in over the wire. Most of them were cautious: a spokesman for the Jones & Laughlin Steel Corporation said the firm would withhold comment on the price rise "until we have had a chance to study the matter"; a Bethlehem Steel spokesman said there would be no immediate comment. However, a statement about to come from Republic Steel in Cleveland would show which way the wind was blowing: "Republic certainly needs a price increase," said its President Thomas F. Patton (within a few hours after U. S. Steel's announcement), "and will review the reported action of United States Steel immediately. Since our last price increase in 1958," Patton added, "Republic has incurred substantial cost increases which have resulted in a severe squeeze on its profits, despite the fact it has invested tens of millions of dollars in capital improvements and conducted vigorous cost-reduction programs. By reason of these facts, Republic's earnings have not been sufficient to pay a reasonable return to its stockholders and to contribute adequately to the costs of financing its capital improvement which is so essential in keeping plants and properties modern and competitive."

Meanwhile, the group still assembled in the President's office had no doubt that Republic as well as the others would soon decide the time had come to correct their "profits squeeze," and the discussion now centered on what might be done to prevent the other companies from following suit. It was generally agreed that the first thing to do would be to make an economic rebuttal to the case presented by U. S. Steel. By the time the group broke up at around 8:00 P.M., some basic decisions had been reached, the most important of which was that an effort would be made to roll back the price increase. At the moment, the men assembled did not really have much hope that it could be achieved, and at least one member of the group was absolutely convinced that the steel industry would hold firm.

It was also decided that Sorensen, Goldberg and Heller would gather material for a statement which would be made the following day at President Kennedy's already-scheduled press conference. In addition, other material of a more economic nature would be assembled in a long-range effort to prove that a price rise in steel was unjustified.

Goldberg and Heller decided to pool the resources of the Labor Department and the Council of Economic Advisers in order to get the job done in the shortest possible time. Goldberg called Hyman L. Lewis, Economic Chief of the Bureau of Labor Statistics, and asked him to assemble a crew. Lewis eventually reached three members of his Bureau—Peter Henle, special assistant to the Commissioner of Labor Statistics; Arnold E. Chase, Chief of the Division of Prices and Cost of Living; and Leon Greenberg, Chief of the Productivity Division. The mission was described and the three men were instructed to meet Dr. Heller in the Old State Department Building.

One reason the meeting was discontinued was that the President had to dress for the annual White House reception for Congressmen and their wives at 9:45. Ironically enough, just before the last year's White House reception for Congress, President Kennedy had been confronted with Cuba and the Bay of Pigs. All that Tuesday the bad news had trickled in, and as 9 P.M. approached, the staff had to virtually push the President out of his office to get him into his white tie and tails. This year it was black tie, and once again the staff had to urge him to get ready. "I think we're going to call off Congressional receptions," he said. "Last year it was Cuba—now this." This remark would no doubt have been highly endorsed by the authors of a recent Air Force study which found that the ability to quip under pressure was the mark of a leader, but it was going to come back to haunt him by helping to give currency to the idea that the steel crisis was the Administration's "domestic Cuba"—an angle which more than one newspaper would play up the following morning.

At the reception, the President appeared quite relaxed. The party was spread out over three rooms, so it was hard to tell just how often he slipped off for private consultations; besides, most everyone's eyes were on the First Lady, who, according to a Washington *Post* society reporter, "was radiant in the floral appliquéd white satin Givenchy dress she had worn in France for the DeGaulle dinner at Versailles."

However, there was plenty of steel talk in the air. At one point the President had a long discussion with Vice-President Lyndon Johnson and later another with Senator Albert Gore of Tennessee. The President also had long talks in the Red Room with Andrew Hatcher, and another with Secretary Goldberg. By midnight the party began to break up; the President retired for the night at 12:08.

For many members of the Administration, it had been an evening of concentrated telephone calling. Secretary of Commerce Luther Hodges, for instance, had stayed home that evening with his wife, who was ill. At about midevening he was called by William Ruder, then Assistant Secretary of Commerce for Information, who told him of the price rise. Hodges went to work immediately, phoning colleagues and businessmen who might be helpful in the struggle ahead. Although he usually retires early, he was on the phone until well after midnight.

For other members of the Administration the night of April 10 lasted well into the morning hours. The task force assembled by Goldberg and Heller had begun to put together some figures early in the evening. Dr. Heller himself had had to leave to attend a black-tie dinner being given by the German Ambassador in honor of Professor Walter Hallstein, President of the European Common Market. Heller arrived at the dinner quite late, and when he left around midnight, went directly back to his office. With him came another dinner guest—George Ball, Undersecretary of State. Heller's two colleagues, Dr. Gordon and Dr. Tobin, were already there. These men and the task force worked until about 2:45 P.M., at which time the members of the task force left to bring up to date a fact book on steel which had been put out by the Eisenhower Administration two years previously. It was to be a "White Paper" showing that the steel price increase was unjustified. The rest of the men stayed on, discussing various aspects of the situation and what to do about it until 4 A.M.

After the meeting in his office broke up, Dr. Heller finally made it back to his home in the Virginia suburbs, only to find that he was not completely through with steel for the day. Waiting for him was a copy of U. S. Steel's statement announcing the price increase; it had been delivered to his house about 10 o'clock that evening. Attached to it was a handwritten note on a small piece of blue note paper from the Sheraton Carlton Hotel. It read:

DEAR WALTER, I discussed the enclosure with the President briefly late today and I thought you would like a copy. I hope to discuss it with you sometime soon. ROGER.

"Roger" was of course Roger Blough, who had returned to New York that evening. He had joined his wife at a friend's home for dinner during which the principal topic of conversation was the steel price increase and Washington's reaction to it. Blough says that at that time he had no idea of what was to come, but that he did not sleep well that night. "If I'd had any inkling of the furor of the next three days," he said later, "I am sure I would not have slept at all."

CHAPTER 2

Prologue to a Major Domestic Crisis

In the last analysis, however, the steel industry can be internationally competitive only by braking the rise of its wage costs. This is why the current wage negotiations, which will determine costs over the next few years, are so important. If steel wages rise sharply, the industry will have no choice except to lift prices, and so render itself more vulnerable to foreign competition than ever. If, however, wage costs can be held well within the level of the national productivity advance, say 2 per cent a year, the prospects for the American steel industry are good.

—*Gilbert Burck in* Fortune, *April 1962*

When Roger Blough walked into the President's office that Tuesday afternoon, he touched off—in the words of the Washington *Star*—"an economic-political drama such as has not held the national stage since the early days of the New Deal." For 72 hours the Administration and the steel industry were locked in a test of power which not only shook the nation but riveted the attention of the entire world on the United States.

To understand completely the struggle between President John F. Kennedy and the nation's largest corporation, it is necessary to know something about the events leading up to the crisis. Attention must also be given to the deteriorating profit situation in the steel industry, as well as the timing of the price rise, coming as it did so soon after the major steel companies had signed a wage contract with the steelworkers' union. A flashback will put Roger Blough's action—and more importantly, the President's—in proper perspective.

Much has been written about John F. Kennedy's self-possession, his calm and detached manner in dealing with public events. One biographer has even suggested that the President's apparent lack of compassion might prevent him from being the great President he wants to be, because he does not seem to *feel* the problems of his time; he treats them as so many issues to be debated and attacked, with victories neatly tabulated on one side of the ledger and defeats on the other. There is perhaps some truth to this assessment, although it is still far too early to tell whether the President's self-possession and sense of detachment is a liability or an asset. However, he does have a dispassionate approach to most of the crises he faces, and perhaps the best measure of the blow which he had been struck was the anger with which he reacted.

In the President's eyes, the country could not afford to wait for public opinion to turn against the steel companies. Long before public opinion would have any real effect, another round of inflation would be under way. Nothing could hold back the labor unions in any industry now, and when the steel wage contract again came up for negotiation, there would certainly be a strong wage demand on the part of the union and possibly even a crippling steel strike before the contracts were signed.

Maintaining price stability and holding back inflation was the rock on which the President's entire economic program, both at home and abroad, had been built. And the key to wage and price stability in the United States is the steel industry. It is the principal underpinning of the whole economy, and not merely because it provides jobs for 569,000 workers and accounts for $14 billion in annual sales. Its output of 100 million tons of steel a year—a quarter of the world's production—is the starting point for hundreds of other industries, from the manufacturing of bobby pins and nails to the construction of skyscrapers and ocean liners. The average house may contain as many as four tons of steel in its construction and equipment. Obviously the price of steel—the basic ingredient of so many of the nation's manufactured products—has a great deal to do with the price of our finished products. The giant of the steel industry, of course, is United States Steel Corporation. Of the 76 million tons of steel produced by the top eight companies in 1961, nearly one-third was produced by U. S. Steel.

Since World War II, the steel industry has been the bell-wether of consumer prices. From 1945 to 1958, the price of steel went up regularly, and other prices followed shortly thereafter. From 1945 to 1950, the wholesale price of steel went up 66 percent, while consumer prices rose 37 percent. Since 1950, steel prices have risen even faster—61 percent, as compared to 20 percent for consumer prices. Because of concern over the continuing inflation in recent years, the Government has exerted tremendous pressure on both industry and labor to hold back wage demands and prices, and since 1958, at the urging of both the Eisenhower and Kennedy administrations, the steel industry had held the price line.

Developing simultaneously with the problem of inflation has been the equally serious problem of economic growth. During the last decade, U. S. economic growth, as measured in terms of the rise in the Gross National Product, has been less than 3 percent a year. At the same time, the economic growth of our principal competitors for international markets, such as Japan and the nations of the European Common Market, has been the phenomenon of the postwar world. For instance, in the same decade, annual economic growth has averaged 8.5 percent for Japan, 7.5 percent for Germany, and 5.8 percent for Italy. Ironically, much of the economic success of these countries can be attributed to our financial aid.

One result of the economic lag in the United States has been the inability of U. S. industry to raise capital with which to modernize plant and equipment. And gradually over the years as the equipment in many of our basic industries has become more and more obsolete it has become increasingly difficult to compete with foreign producers. This has created an industrial crisis which has been particularly acute in the case of steel. In 1960, American steel production was 10 percent higher than in 1954, but in the same period the six nations in the European Common Market increased their steel production 66 percent; in 1960, the U. S. share of the world's steel trade was 17 percent, while today it is around 7 percent. One of the main reasons for the deterioration of the U. S. position is the cost of our steel, which is about 24 percent higher than the steel produced abroad.

The crisis has been compounded for the U. S. Government because at the same time it has been facing the problem of a lagging economy it has also been facing a crisis in its balance of payments. One way the Administration has tried to correct its balance-of-payments crisis has been to stimulate conditions of trade so as to encourage more exports. The United States actually has a favorable balance of trade—in 1961, exports exceeded imports by $5 billion—but this excess is more than offset by the dollars we spend abroad on our overseas commitments, mostly defense installations and foreign aid. Consequently it is generally agreed that if we are to maintain our immense overseas operations we must increase our balance of trade to a point where it is even more favorable than it is.

Of course, the Government and big business agree on this point, but they disagree on the best method of achieving a more favorable balance of trade. The steel industry argues that it must have a price increase in order to raise its profits so that more capital will be available for modernizing its production facilities; this in turn will make its operation more competitive with companies which already have modern equipment—and presumably will then permit it to lower prices. There can be little debate over the fact that U. S. industry in general and the steel industry in particular have been suffering a "profit squeeze." Although the actual dollar value of profits has remained high in the postwar years, profits have not increased at anywhere near the same rate of growth for the economy as a whole. For instance, in 1950, total corporate profits after taxes were $22.8 billion; in 1961, profits were an estimated $23 billion. But in this same period our Gross National Product had increased 45 percent. And the profit picture in the steel industry has been particularly acute; as measured in profits per dollar of sales, steel industry profits declined from 8 percent in 1950 to 5.7 percent in 1960.

The reason for this "profit squeeze" has been due primarily to taxes, increased costs and a sluggish economy. The President agrees that something must be done to improve the situation, but argues that a price increase is the wrong solution; that in addition to contributing to another damaging round of inflation, it would also increase the prices of our goods in the world market place, thereby making American industry less—not more—competitive. Already the competition of foreign steel companies—even before the $6-a-ton price increase—was having a serious effect on our balance-of-payments problem, as the following *Wall Street Journal* figures on exports and imports show. The units are in net tons and the total in thousands:

YEAR	EXPORTS	IMPORTS
1956	4,348	1,336
1957	5,348	1,445
1958	2,823	1,676
1959	1,677	4,357
1960	2,980	3,333
1961	1,989	3,145

As foreign steel imports increase and U. S. Steel imports decrease, the balance-of-payments crisis becomes more and more acute—and as one European steel executive says: "Even Peru is exporting some steel now. Imagine! Peru!"

The President has not been unaware of industry's need for increased capital; for some time the Administration had been considering ways in which industry might be encouraged to put more money into modernizing its equipment. Two methods designed to increase expenditures on plant and equipment—both of which U. S. industry knew about—were under consideration at the time U. S. Steel announced its price rise. They were: (1) an investment credit which the Kennedy Administration had asked Congress to provide the year before, but which was still in the Senate Finance Committee at the time of the steel price controversy; and (2) a liberalized schedule for depreciating plant and equipment costs, which was to be announced soon in the Treasury Department's new guidelines for determining how fast a corporation may write off its plant and equipment. (In addition, within the Administration there was also much discussion of tax relief, which eventually was translated into the Administration's tax proposals of 1963.)

The President had made it clear that he was willing to consider almost any suggestion for helping industry meet foreign competition *except by raising investment capital through widespread price increases*. If there was one thing his Administration was wedded to it was price stability, and the President and his staff knew that any large increase in either wages for the steelworkers or prices for the steel companies would probably touch off another round of inflation.

Actually the President's concern with inflation goes back a long way. James M. Burns, in a precampaign biography of Kennedy, said that he was always "agin inflation." For instance, while in the House of Representatives he opposed dismantling wage and price controls following World War II, and he voted for President Truman's requested price-and-wage-control legislation after the Korean war broke out. He also openly fought the many pressure groups which tried to obtain exemption from the wage-price controls after the Korean war.

However, the point too often overlooked—at least by businessmen—is that John F. Kennedy has always been just as concerned about big labor's excessive wage demands as a cause of inflation as he was about high prices. If in recent years there has been a relationship between the price of steel and consumer prices, it is equally true that there has also been a relationship between steel industry wage increases and the price of steel. As the chronology on the following pages shows, since World War II wage increases in the steel industry invariably have been followed by an increase in the price of steel.

This did not necessarily mean that Kennedy agreed with the steel industry's position that increased labor costs were the primary reason for increased prices, but he was firmly convinced that at a time when price stability was essential to maintaining the leadership of the free world, business and labor were equally responsible for helping to maintain price stability. As a result, in Kennedy's economic thinking there gradually emerged the concept that the public interest must also be considered in management-labor disputes. As early as 1959, he said to a United Automobile Workers audience: "I am concerned that there should be some representative of the public view in connection with major union-management negotiations," although he added that this did not mean that the public representative should be given a veto.

Chronology

Steel prices have risen sharply since World War II, usually on the heels of wage increases. These have been the developments in the steel industry since late 1945.

1945

Sept. 11—Only nine days after V-J Day, the United Steelworkers announced they would seek a 30 percent pay rise.

1946

Feb. 15—After a month-long strike, Steelworkers won an 18½-cent hourly raise. Steel companies raised prices by $5 a ton.

1947

April 20—U. S. Steel and Steelworkers agreed on new contract providing a 15-cent hourly pay boost.

July 29—U. S. Steel raised prices a range of $5 to $10 a ton.

1948

Feb. 19—Most steel producers raised prices by $5 a ton.

Feb. 24—Commerce and Justice Departments were asked to investigate the latest hikes by President Truman, following (by three days) announcement of Congressional investigations.

March 13—Justice Department found no illegal collusion in steel price rises.

July 16—Steelworkers and companies agreed to a 13-cent hourly pay boost.

1949

Nov. 11—After a strike, U. S. Steel signed a new contract with Steelworkers. It was one of the last companies to do so. Contract provided no pay increase, approximately 10 cents hourly in fringe benefits.

Dec. 15—U. S. Steel increased prices by $4 a ton. Other companies soon followed.

1950

Nov. 31—Bethlehem, U. S. Steel agreed to a 10 percent wage boost of some 16 to 18 cents an hour. Steel prices went up $5.50 a ton.

1952

March 20—Wage Stabilization Board recommended a 19-cent hourly pay increase, but steelmen objected.

April 3—Talks between Steelworkers and major producers broke down. Union prepared to strike.

April 8—President Truman seized the steel mills.

June 2—Supreme Court voided the Truman seizure.

July 24—Strike ended with Steelworkers winning wages and fringe benefits of some 21.4 cents an hour. Companies raised prices $5.20 a ton.

1953

June 12—Union and industry agreed to a nine-cent package hourly increase in pay.

June 16—Republic Steel announced price boosts from $5 to $10 a ton. Next day, U. S. Steel hiked its prices $3.40 a ton.

1954

June 29—U. S. Steel, Steelworkers signed two-year pact providing fringe benefits and a nine-to-ten-cent hourly pay boost.

1955

July 1—After a strike lasting only several hours, most major steel companies signed a year's contract calling for a 15-cent hourly raise for Steelworkers. United States Steel promptly raised its per-ton price by $7.50; other big companies soon followed.

1956

July 26—After a strike, the Steelworkers won package benefits from 41 to 45 cents an hour. A three-year contract was signed.

Aug. 6—Quickly followed by other companies, U. S. Steel jumped its prices $8.50 a ton.

1957

June 27—U. S. Steel hiked its price $6 a ton.

1958

Feb. 27—Senate anti-trust subcommittee announced a study of steel price policy, claiming the industry's June-July boosts were unjustified.

July 30—Republic, Jones & Laughlin, and National Steel companies hiked prices $4.50 a ton. Sen. Kefauver, anti-trust subcommittee chairman, threatened an investigation.

Aug. 6—U. S. Steel raised prices an average $4.25 a ton. John W. Gwynne, Federal Trade Commission chairman, told Senate subcommittee his agency found no price-fixing in companies' action.

1959

March 26—President Eisenhower asked both sides in coming steel negotiations to arrive at contract which would not necessitate a price boost.

1960

Jan. 4—After Vice-President Nixon helped mediate dispute, Steelworkers won 40-cent hourly package pay increase, 30-month contract. There was no price hike.

1962

April 6—Ten of 11 major steel producers signed new two-year contract providing no wage increase, about 10 cents an hour in fringe benefits, and provision for possible reopening of contract after one year for talks on wages, pensions, and insurance. President Kennedy hailed pact as non-inflationary.

April 10—U. S. Steel announced a rise in steel prices of $6 a ton.

April 13—Under heavy pressure from the Administration, big steel firms—including U. S. Steel—rescinded price boosts.[1]

After the 1960 election, President-elect Kennedy called for a series of task force reports to serve as guidelines for the New Frontier. The task force on economic conditions was credited solely to Dr. Paul A. Samuelson, and the importance to Kennedy's economic adviser of controlling inflation can be seen from the final section of Dr. Samuelson's report, which was subheaded: "Direct Attack on the Wage-Price Spiral." After a lengthy discussion of the use of fiscal and monetary policies as economic weapons, Dr. Samuelson concluded that

[1] Reprinted by courtesy of the *National Observer*.

if wages and prices continued to rise before a high level of employment was reached, then fiscal and monetary policies would be unable to promote the desired economic growth.

"What may then be needed," wrote Dr. Samuelson in his closing paragraph, "are new approaches to the problem of productivity, wages and price formation. Will it not be possible to bring government influence to bear on this vital matter without invoking direct controls on wages and prices? Neither labor, nor management, nor the consumer can gain from an increase in price tags. Just as we pioneered in the 1920's in creating potent monetary mechanisms and in the 1930's in forging the tools of effective fiscal policy, so may it be necessary in the 1960's to meet head on the problem of a price creep. This is a challenge to mixed economies all over the free world and it is not to be met by government alone."

Thus from the start it was the policy of the Kennedy Administration to try to bring labor and management together in an effort to arrive at wage and price levels which would best serve the national interest—*without invoking direct controls*. And the firm adherence to this policy led directly to the clash with Roger Blough.

Of course, a dedicated opposition to inflation was hardly an origination of the Kennedy Administration. During President Eisenhower's eight years in office, he, too, repeatedly spoke out against the dangers of inflation, and at times gave the impression that it was the most dangerous threat facing the country, including Communism. And Eisenhower also brought pressure to bear on both the steelworkers' union and the steel industry to check the wage-price spiral. During the steel wage negotiations of 1959, he called for "statesmanship" by both sides and said: "While this is a matter between the steelworkers and the steel companies, the whole public is affected by everything they do." In the costly steelworkers' strike of 1959–60, Vice-President Nixon was finally forced to intervene, and although the much-publicized settlement he achieved called for a 40-cent package increase for the steel-workers over a two-and-a-half year period, the companies refrained from raising prices.

Despite President Eisenhower's efforts to hold the price line, there was a slow but steady creep of inflation during his Administration. President Kennedy was determined to stop this, although at times during his first year in office it appeared to some that he did not really plan to do much more than Eisenhower had done to combat inflation—which was mostly talk. But even with his determination to hold back both wages and prices, the new President could hardly have been described as antibusiness.

"Whatever it was that Joseph P. Kennedy told John F. Kennedy about businessmen—or some businessmen," wrote *Newsweek's* Kenneth Crawford in an excellent summary of the new President's attitude toward business, "the father didn't prejudice the son against the business community. The son entered the White House predisposed to accept the business community's own ideas about the proper relationship between government and private enterprise. He appointed an Eisenhower Republican his Secretary of Treasury. He announced that it would be his aim to balance the Federal budget, fight inflation, stand by gold as the medium of international payments, encourage economic growth, and depend upon free collective bargaining to regulate industrial relations. True, he had some ideas about extension of social services and reduction of unemployment that business didn't like. But these were not central to the problem of maintaining a cooperative relationship between business and government. His orthodoxy in economic and fiscal matters was so firmly fixed that he was the despair of some of his academic advisers. By and large, business was happily surprised by the new President's amiability. It was particularly pleased with his apparent determination to continue the Eisenhower policy of trying to stabilize wages and prices—particularly wages."

After Congress had recessed in 1961, the new Administration began an earnest campaign to explain itself to business. Secretary Dillon addressed the bankers in San Francisco; Secretary Hodges addressed businessmen in Hot Springs; Secretary Goldberg addressed the Illinois Chamber of Commerce in Chicago; and the President himself spoke to the National Association of Manufacturers. The message was always the same: the Kennedy Administration is for a sound dollar and a balanced budget and against inflation; we expect business and labor to maintain a reasonable level of prices and wages, to consider the total economy and not just self-interest. The President did not always get a wild reception at his appearances before business groups, and neither was the AFL–CIO very enthusiastic when he told delegates that he expected them to be moderate in their wage demands.

Although the new President had appointed a former counsel for the AFL–CIO as his Secretary of Labor, Arthur Goldberg soon let it be known that his loyalty was to the President and the public interest. One of the first things Goldberg did on taking office was to urge the establishment of his long-cherished advisory committee on labor-management policy, composed of 7 labor leaders, 7 prominent businessmen and 7 distinguished private citizens. "It would be lacking in realism," he said, explaining the committee's function, "to believe that twenty-one men could transform the character of American industry and labor. This is just a beginning. The important thing is to make both sides realize that they must act out of the public interest, and that, as the representative of the public, government must concern itself in the process." The committee actually has done very little except issue reports and position papers, but it has, by focusing public attention on prices and by the threat of action, tried to discourage price increases.

However, the Administration was soon to take much stronger action in its efforts to hold the price line. Under the terms of the 1960 contract, wages and other employment costs were scheduled to increase on October 1, 1961, and in August rumors began to spread that a steel price rise was coming. On August 22—the date which in Roger Blough's opinion the steel controversy actually began—Senator Albert Gore and several other liberal Senators urged on the floor of the Senate that the President use the power of his office to prevent any rise in the price of steel. Gore also suggested that if the steel companies did not comply, the President should direct the Federal Trade Commission and the antitrust division of the Department of Justice to take action against them. "To my knowledge," Roger Blough said later, "this is the first time any President has been publicly called upon to exercise control without authority of law—over the price of an entire industry—and initiate or participate in a whole series of administrative and legislative actions of a punitive nature if that control were not accepted."

The following month the President wrote a letter to the heads of the twelve major steel companies,[2] urging them not to raise the price of steel. He said that in his opinion the industry could "look forward to good profits without an increase in prices." In support of this statement, he used figures prepared by the Council of Economic Advisers. The President also made this significant comment:

> I recognize, too, that the steel industry, by absorbing increases in employment costs since 1958, has demonstrated a will to halt the price-wage spiral in steel. If the industry were now to forego a price increase, it would enter collective bargaining next spring with a record of three and a half years of price stability. It would clearly then be the turn of the labor representatives to limit wage demands to a level consistent with continued price stability. The moral position of the steel in-

2 U. S. Steel Corp., Bethlehem Steel Corp., Republic Steel Corp., Jones & Laughlin Steel Corp., National Steel Corp., Youngstown Sheet & Tube Co., Armco Steel Corp., Inland Steel Co., Kaiser Steel Corp., Wheeling Steel Corp., Colorado Fuel & Iron Corp., McLouth Steel Corp.

dustry next spring—and its claim to the support of public opinion—will be strengthened by the exercise of price restraint now.

Roger Blough looked upon the President's letter as an attempt to predetermine prices of the steel industry—"an unprecedented move in the history of our country in peacetime." On September 13, he replied to the President:

> ... we in United States Steel cannot forecast the future trend of prices in any segment of the steel industry and have no definite conclusions regarding our own course in the foreseeable future ...

Blough later said that this was the first of many occasions when U. S. Steel indicated that it was making no commitment to holding the price line.

All of the steel companies replied to the President's letter, and most of them took the position that his figures were too optimistic and that, because of the need for increased profits with which to modernize their equipment, they could not guarantee to hold prices down. One of the most interesting replies came from Joseph L. Block, Chairman of the Board of Inland Steel. He said it could be easily documented that profits in the steel industry compare unfavorably with profits in industries generally and that the prospects for profits on new facilities are so low as to discourage risk capital from being attracted to such ventures. "However, if it is deemed in the public interest that prices be frozen," Block continued, "then it would seem to me that it is also in the public interest for employment costs to be frozen for a year beyond the expiration of the current labor contract on June 30, 1962."

Despite noncommittal replies from the steel companies, the industry did not increase prices in 1961, although in his annual report of the following March, Roger Blough emphasized that the "influences" of the market place, rather than pressure from the President, caused U. S. Steel to refrain from raising prices.

With steel companies, regardless of their reasons, having refrained from a price increase, the Administration then turned to the unions. At the fourth Constitutional Convention of the AFL–CIO in Miami in December 1961, Arthur Goldberg, while asserting that the Administration did not favor a "single-wage policy," emphasized that "wage increases should be earned by increased productivity." This increase in productivity was to be the basis for the Council of Economic Advisers' suggested "guideposts" for governing labor's wage demands—and according to government economists, productivity was estimated at that time to be increasing at an annual rate of around 3 percent. As applied to the forthcoming negotiations with the steel industry, the "guideposts" meant that labor should keep its wage demands within a limit of 12 cents an hour for the first year of any contract to be negotiated.[3]

Needless to say, the delegates in Miami did not take kindly to Goldberg's remarks, and they refused to accept responsibility for holding back prices by adopting a policy of wage restraint.

At the same time, Secretary Luther Hodges was reporting that after a year of diplomacy and soft talk, the giants of the business world still remained hostile to the Kennedy Administration, and if the leaders in American industry continued to hold the price line, it would not be out of any desire to cooperate with the Administration.

Nevertheless, the Administration continued to pursue its goals. The first move was to call for an early settlement of the steel wage contract which was to expire on July 1, 1962. As early as November and December, 1961, Secretary Gold-

---

[3] It should be emphasized here that the steel industry did not accept the Administration's figure of 3.5 percent as an accurate measurement of the annual productivity increases. (See Chapter 8.)

berg had meetings or telephone conversations with David McDonald, Conrad Cooper, Joseph Block and Roger Blough. At meetings with steel company executives, Goldberg specifically raised the subject of the upcoming steel talks, stressing that:

1. the President hoped for an early settlement in order to prevent stockpiling by steel consumers;

2. the President hoped the settlement would be a modest one which would prevent another wage-price spiral;

3. he was willing to use the good offices of the Administration, providing that both sides would cooperate.

Having received assurances that the steel industry did not object to the good offices of the Administration in general and the Secretary of Labor in particular, Goldberg, who was then in Miami for the AFL-CIO convention, contacted McDonald and repeated the President's wishes. McDonald indicated his general sympathy with the President's position, and within a few days Cooper and McDonald were in communication regarding the possibility of an early negotiation.

In late January, McDonald, Blough, Cooper and Goldberg met with the President at the White House. Again, the purpose was to discuss the possibility of an early settlement. Prior to this meeting, the President had received a memorandum from Walter Heller suggesting that if a wage increase could be held to 2.5 to 3 percent, an increase in the price of steel would be unnecessary. At the White House meeting, the President urged the importance of a noninflationary settlement, and of an early settlement because of the threat of stockpiling. Roger Blough said he was agreeable to accelerating the negotiations, and he stressed the poor profit situation of his company. Blough insists that he made it plain he would not be involved in any negotiations in which prices were discussed, but, according to Administration sources, at no time did he take exception to the President's remarks about price increases. McDonald stressed the problems of the steelworkers but said he was willing to co-operate in speeding up the negotiations.

On February 6, Secretary Goldberg, on behalf of the President, sent telegrams to the steelworkers and to the industry urging them to commence negotiations, which they did on February 14th, marking the first time in 26 years that bargaining had begun at such an early date. The very fact that it agreed to an early meeting was, in some ways, a concession on the part of the union. One of its strongest negotiating weapons is a last-minute strike threat if its major demands are not met. In addition, union demands, when they were finally revealed, were considered the most moderate in years— a security package, not a wage increase, amounting to approximately 17 cents an hour. As a result, there was considerable optimism for an early, noninflationary settlement, and the four-man industry negotiating team added weight to this optimism by commenting that while the union demands, on the face, "cannot be considered moderate in any sense," the "varying degrees of emphasis appear to indicate a more moderate approach" than in the past. The team added that this was appropriate "in light of the serious problems now facing the steel companies and the nation."

The union demands were, indeed, moderate, but just in case the union was inclined to forget the seriousness of the problems facing the nation and the steel industry, Arthur Goldberg continued the Administration's crusade for a "responsible" and noninflationary settlement. In a steady stream of speeches, television appearances and interviews, Goldberg pressed the Administration's case, with the emphasis on union restraint during this period. In fact, only three days before the wage talks opened, Goldberg had appeared on the CBS program, *Washington Conversations*, sounding almost like a steel company executive. "The steel union ought to know," he said, responding to a question from Paul Nivens about a wage increase, "that the steel industry has its own problems. The industry is more competitive, both at home and abroad; profit margins have to be preserved; and profits have to be available for necessary modernization and expansion of the industry. So I would hope that after all these years of collective bargaining each of the parties can recognize the other party's problems and arrive at a settlement which will be noninflationary and compatible with the national interest."

On the 23rd of February he gave a speech before the Executive Club in Chicago which he described as a "definitive" summation of the Kennedy Administration's labor-management philosophy. His main point was that conflicts between labor and management were intolerable because of the Soviet threat and because of the new competition posed by an economically united Europe. He stressed again the importance of the government's "guideposts." Neither labor nor management greeted this speech with much enthusiasm, but in Miami, where the AFL-CIO executive committee was in session, George Meany virtually exploded. He told reporters that Goldberg had overstepped proper bounds, that the Secretary's position was "infringing on the rights of a free people and a free society." Considering that Goldberg had said much the same thing before, Meany's explosion came as somewhat of a surprise.

In addition to his public statements, Goldberg also made numerous direct contacts, in person and by telephone, with both sides in the steel negotiations, in a continuing effort to bring about a settlement which would be in the national interest. But despite his efforts, the talks proceeded slowly in February, and on February 24th, the negotiations recessed. Although both union and management spokesmen discounted reports of a stalemate, in Florida, George Meany said that the negotiations had made "no progress whatsoever."

In the February 26th issue of *U. S. News,* Roger Blough said in an "interview" that employment costs in the steel industry had risen about 12 percent over the last three years. He added: "And you're asking me how long can that continue to increase and how long it can be borne without some kind of remedy. I would give you the answer that it's not reasonable to think of it as continuing. In other words, even now there should be a remedy. If any additional cost occurs, the necessity for the remedy becomes even greater." This quotation is extremely important because it was later suggested that this was about as plain as anyone could make it that something would have to be done about the price of steel, and that therefore the price rise in April should hardly have come as a shock to the Administration—and certainly not to the business community. In fact, *U. S. News and World Report* was later to insist that Blough's statement in its February 26th issue clearly indicated that U. S. Steel planned to raise its prices.

The wage talks were finally resumed—only to suffer a complete collapse on March 2nd over the size of the cost of the proposed contract. At this point, Goldberg contacted Blough and they met to discuss the contract. Blough complained that the 17-cents-an-hour cost of the benefits demanded by the union was not acceptable because it was clearly inflationary. Goldberg inquired as to whether the steel industry would resume negotiations along more realistic lines if the union was agreeable. Blough replied that the industry would. Goldberg then met with McDonald and told him flatly that the union was asking too much. He then suggested that the union reduce its demand substantially, and said, frankly, that the union could not expect what it had been asking if price stability was to be preserved. McDonald then agreed to resume negotiations, on a more realistic basis.

On March 14th the talks resumed, and on the same day Leslie B. Worthington gave a speech in which he stressed that American industry must obtain higher profits if the

United States was to meet the challenge of world trade. A week later, in a story about U. S. Steel's annual report, the *Wall Street Journal*—commenting on the fact that the steel industry figured it had absorbed an increase in employment costs of 12 percent since 1958—said that "most steel users look for prices to head upward after the conclusion of current steel labor negotiations." The *Journal* added, however, that Roger Blough was noncommittal.

Agreement between the steelworkers and the industry was finally reached near the end of March, and the negotiators signed the formal contract on April 6. Under its terms, the steelworkers were to receive a job security package costing from 10 to 11 cents an hour—well within the Government's "guideposts." The contract could be reopened on thirty days' notice any time after April 20, 1963. The Administration was delighted and in telephone calls to both Conrad Cooper and David McDonald, President Kennedy praised them for "high industrial statesmanship" and said that the agreement was "obviously noninflationary and should provide a solid base for continued price stability."

Blough said later that "this remark troubled me, since I had repeatedly told him that cost increases were basically the cause of this nation's recent inflation and that a price rise was long overdue . . ."

If Blough meant that he felt he had made it as clear as he could that a price rise was inevitable, then it is obvious that not only the Administration but almost the entire business community and interested segments of the press had missed the signals. The relief and jubilation with which the steel settlement was received throughout the business community is difficult to imagine, considering the hostility soon to dominate the atmosphere. *Life* magazine printed a picture of a beaming Cooper and McDonald under a brief text which read: "Never in the generally bitter and sometimes bloody history of relations between labor and steel had an agreement been so rapturously received" (because there would be no steel strike and because the agreement was noninflationary). "Everybody seemed happy," wrote Scripps-Howard columnist Pete Edson. "Government, labor management and the whole business community all broke into spring songs of peace and continued uninflated prosperity." *U. S. News,* which later helped lead the business community's revolt against the Administration's labor-management policies, glowed that a "steel settlement—free of an increase in cash wages—is expected to have a big effect on business sentiment. The point is made that a major union in a basic industry, for the first time since World War II, has recognized broad public interest in a new contract."

In short, the business community could hardly restrain its applause for the Administration's having used its good offices to hold the union's wage demands to a "moderate" level, discourage a steel strike, and bring about an early noninflationary settlement in the industry. Of course, the steel industry had given no commitment that it would hold the price line, but many people, including most businessmen, assumed that labor's restraint would be followed by no increase in the steel prices for at least six months to a year. Obviously the White House assumed this, and the settlement was considered not only a major victory for the Administration, but a long stride toward a historic transformation in labor-management relations. The President viewed it as such, and was frankly quite proud of the achievement—his staff possibly even more so. One Administration spokesman was quoted as saying that its ability to bring labor and management together without a strike and without a damaging build-up in inventory "shows we knew what we were doing when we got the parties together early."

The temptation on the part of the New Frontiersmen to do a little crowing was understandable. With Berlin and Cuba pressing them on the international front and troubles with

Congress continually plaguing them at home, here at least was one bright spot. With steel wages agreed to without an inflationary rise in prices, full attention could now be given to the measures necessary to step up the lagging economy. A boom was not exactly just around the corner, but at least American goods would still be able to compete in the international market place as well as they had been. Holding the price line did not mean that things would suddenly get better, but at least they would not get worse. Maybe by next year, if the President could get the bulk of his economic program through Congress, the long-expected business recovery—which many economists said was only waiting for a steel settlement without a costly strike—would be getting up a full head of steam and our economic growth would be heading back to normal. At least, those were the President's hopes.

But suddenly, on a Tuesday afternoon in April—only three days after the last major steel wage contract had been signed—Roger Blough and United States Steel shattered everything. In the President's eyes, they had, in one quick action, wrecked his entire economic program. As the *Wall Street Journal* said: "Wage-price stability in steel was intended as the graven image of a total program of stability; the Kennedy sculptors unveiled it as a finished masterpiece—and then suddenly it was shattered." Although a price rise and another round of inflation were bad enough, the shattering of their "masterpiece" meant more than that. American goods would now have less chance of competing with the goods of the Common Market countries and with our other international trade rivals; our balance-of-payments crisis would become even more critical; the net result—both at home and abroad—would be a more sluggish economy, a continually lagging rate of growth, and continued high levels of employment which automation was already making a serious problem regardless of what the economy did. Especially serious, in the eyes of the President, was the impact the price rise would have on the dollar. To European bankers concerned about the soundness of the dollar, the Treasury Department had long been pointing out the stabilizing influence of the anticipated steel wage settlement, plus the general stability of the consumer price index as signs of general economic stability. These bankers are inclined to use their excess dollars to buy U. S. gold if they think the dollar's value is likely to be diminished by any general rise in prices.

Even more important was the Cold War. For Kennedy and his advisers, the foundation of America's total Cold War effort was a stable economy, and to achieve this a stable price level was essential. Although the President felt that a healthy business community was also essential to America's Cold War effort, he did not feel that higher profits were necessary at that moment. What was essential was a stable economy. And there was no doubt that the President felt industry was sympathetic to his objectives. "There was no question about the reason for the Government, the steel industry and the steelworkers sitting down to work this out," said one highly placed Administration official. "All the conversations, all the discussions were aimed at making it possible to keep steel prices down. It was a joint effort."

Obviously, in announcing its price rise when it did, U. S. Steel could not have picked a time better suited to anger the White House and cast, in the words of *Fortune,* "in the only possible manner that would draw four-column headlines in *The New York Times . . .*" Most people who followed the steel crisis of that April—from President Kennedy to the average business executive both in and out of the steel industry—have agreed that U. S. Steel's timing was extremely poor, to put it mildly.

The President was as concerned with the *way* in which Blough had handled the situation as he was with the increase itself. Blough's sudden announcement of the price rise—after the unions had been successfully restrained—was what brought the real fury from the White House. And despite Blough's repeated efforts to explain that he had made no commitment, even Joseph Block of Inland has conceded that there was at least an "implication" during the wage talks that a moderate wage advance would not necessitate a price increase. Union officials have said quite frankly that if they had had any idea that a price increase was coming they would have "raised their sights."

The Administration was not unaware of Blough's repeated statements concerning prices, but under the circumstances, these statements were looked upon as what one member of the Administration called "collective bargaining statements" —the kind of statements both sides are expected to make during a negotiation in order to preserve, for the record, their position on a given issue, even though they may act contrary to that position. Administration officials argue that their contention that everyone "understood" the price line would be held was supported by the shock which ran through the business and editorial world when U. S. Steel made its announcement. One union official said that on the following Wednesday morning one of the steel executives with whom he was still winding up the contract negotiations said of U. S. Steel's sudden move: "Just how stupid can you get? It's unbelievable!" As for Blough's argument that he had made it clear that a price rise was in the cards, an Administration official says that the fact that "the President, everyone in the Administration, almost every businessman and editorial writer in the country, were caught completely by surprise would suggest that it was hardly a clarion call."

Although the President viewed a price rise as a threat to his entire economic program, he did appreciate the problems facing the steel industry. If Blough had come to him—so the President maintains—during the wage talks and pleaded his case, the President would have made the effort to work something out. But Blough did not. And regardless of what his actual reasons were for doing it in the way he did, it appeared to the White House as either one of two things: (1) a challenge to the Administration on the broad issue of government intervention in labor-management disputes; or (2) as a personal affront to Democratic President John F. Kennedy designed to demonstrate in the most dramatic manner possible that American industry can be as tough as the much publicized toughness of the New Frontiersmen.

No matter what Blough's reasons were, the President accepted the challenge.

CHAPTER 3

Wednesday Morning, April 11:
The President Unleashes the
"Awesome Power"

> I can't imagine any wage restraint now by unions when
> industry exercises none. Unions will thumb their noses at it . . .
> —*Union official, commenting on the steel price increase*

At 8:45 Wednesday morning the President met with members
of his Administration at a regular pre-press conference breakfast of scrambled eggs and coffee. The group included Vice-
President Lyndon Johnson, Secretary of State Dean Rusk,
Ted Sorensen, White House Aide Myer Feldman, Dr. Heller,
Secretary Goldberg and Andy Hatcher. These sessions usually
break up around 9:30 A.M., but this one lasted an hour
longer—and the entire discussion centered around the steel
price increase. The President had calmed down to some extent since the previous evening's explosion, but he was still
sticking to Tuesday night's decision not to take the increase
without a fight. "Kennedy can be a hater," said one White
House official, describing the President's mood on Wednesday, "and right now I don't think there's much doubt that
he hates U. S. Steel."

Such was the White House atmosphere the morning of the
Administration's first full day of war with Big Steel.

The Wednesday meeting opened with Heller and Goldberg (who, incidentally, said he felt his resignation would be
necessary if the price increase was not rescinded) presenting
material which the steel task force had organized during
the night. Goldberg also handed the President a short
statement which had been prepared by Duane Evans,
Commissioner of the Department of Labor's Bureau of
Labor Statistics. It was entitled "Change in Unit Employment Costs in the Steel Industry, 1958 to 1961," and it presented figures showing that employment costs per unit of
steel output were virtually the same in 1961 as they were in
1958. (See Appendix B.) The President read it quickly.

A discussion followed on the question of what the ultimate
objective of the Administration's counterattack should be.

Led by Dr. Heller, the White House group had gradually
come to the conclusion that the main thrust should be directed at convincing a handful of the principal steel producers to hold the price line. In the steel market, Heller
argued that the high price steel sellers would have to come
down if enough of the others did not raise their prices.
Friendly sources in the industry had told one White House
aide that if producers of about 16 percent of the nation's steel
maintained a lower price, they soon would be doing about
25 percent of the business. And in a market as competitive as
steel, the other companies could not afford to lose this business to the lower price firms and would eventually have to
back down.

It was decided that Sorensen would draft the President's
statement for the afternoon's press conference, using the material which had been assembled during the night. At the
same time a work-from-within, divide-and-conquer attack was
decided upon—actually it was already under way. Since the
previous evening anyone in the Administration who knew
anyone in the upper echelons of the steel industry had been
urged to call him up and explain the President's point of view.

This telethon was to pick up momentum during the next forty-eight hours until virtually every prominent person in the business world—especially in the steel industry—who knew anyone in the Administration had received a call from him.

After the meeting broke up, the President placed a phone call to Luther Hodges. He wanted to discuss the price rise as well as Hodges' role in the counterattack. Hodges had just left for Capitol Hill to testify before a House maritime sub-committee, but his secretary reached him in his limousine and told him to call the President, which he did as soon as he reached the committee's offices. It was agreed that as soon as he finished his testimony Hodges would spend the rest of the day on the phone calling top businessmen around the country. The President also phoned Secretary Dillon in Florida. They talked at great length about the Treasury's revised schedule on tax writeoffs, but after much discussion decided that the plan which the Treasury had already worked out would not be altered.

On Wall Street that morning, U. S. Steel shares opened at 70¾—up 2¾ from the previous day. But the gain did not stick; by evening it was down to 70½. Despite the obvious enthusiasm of some industrialists and financiers for the price increase, the truth is that the immediate reaction to U. S. Steel's sudden move was mixed. There were of course many who agreed with the bankers who said that U. S. Steel "has every right to raise prices," and that the abdication of this right would be a concession to government control. But there were others—many others—who were not so sure: some felt that the price increase would not hold, that leading companies would have to cut costs later; others deplored the timing; some commented that it was bad politically and economically, and others said that although it was economically justified it was politically insane; others felt the higher prices would provide only temporary stimulus in an industry facing rising costs; some were worried about the edge a price boost would give to foreign competition. Most Wall Street analysts stuck to their conviction that steel stocks were still relatively unattractive. Although they agreed that the rise would bring higher profits this year, the long-run implications were, in their view, still cloudy.

The professionals along Wall Street were easily the most surprised people in the country. "I was shocked," said Kenneth Ward, of Hayden, Stone & Company. "The steel people could not have picked a worse time," said William Kurtz, senior analyst of Paine, Webber, Jackson & Curtis. "They need the money because they are victims of circumstances, but it's poor public relations. We were forecasting a price increase, but not at this time and not by this method." It was left to the chief economist for a New York bank to make the most succinct remark of the day: "U. S. Steel," he said, "opened Pandora's box of difficulties for the economy."

Elsewhere in the business community, reaction was as mixed and confused as it was on Wall Street. But one thing was certain: the price increase had come as a stunning surprise—for several reasons. Most businessmen thought that even if a steel rise did come, it would not come until after July 1 when the new wage increases took effect. Also, the wage settlement had quickly eliminated strike-hedge buying and the demand was now slack and not expected to show an increase until fall. Finally, almost no one expected an across-the-board increase, because even the old prices were weak on some steel products. The speculation had been that if a price increase did come—and most businessmen really doubted it —it would be a selective one (*i.e.*, just on some products) and about half the size of the one announced by U. S. Steel.

All morning, businessmen were being called to the phone by reporters and asked to give their views, and the truth is, businessmen weren't exactly sure how to react. Many of them felt, with the Wall Street experts, that this was not the time for a price rise, and most of them seemed to think it would make it difficult for their own businesses and their own pricing. But also they felt strongly that any business should have a right to set its own prices without the Government looking over its shoulder. "Steel is a major element in our costs, so from a purely selfish viewpoint we don't welcome a raise in steel prices," said Frederic W. Howe of the Crompton & Knowles Packaging Corporation in Worcester, Massachusetts, articulating the businessman's dilemma. "But I think people should run their own businesses without being influenced by threats from Washington, and it's good to see the steel industry do just that."

Of course, there were some who were downright jubilant because this would give them a good reason for putting through price increases they wanted to make anyway due to less publicized increases in other costs. In fact, several businessmen indicated that they planned to follow up with price increases of their own larger than the boost in steel alone would justify. Said a Midwest auto producer: "The move affords an opportunity to pass along to customers rising costs of everything, including the kitchen sink."

But there were others who were not so happy. "We stand to lose maybe a hundred and fifty thousand dollars that will come out of our pockets in gross profits on just those steel orders we have on the books now," said John E. Beall, President of Beall Pipe & Tank corporation in Portland, Oregon. His problem was that Beall, a steel fabricator, could not raise prices on orders already booked for its products. The Pullman-Standard Car Manufacturing Company also was hit. "Railroads are already short of money," a spokesman said, "and we haven't had a large order for nearly two years; this will only put another crimp in any possible upturn in rail-car building."

The question of how much the price increase would affect business and whether it would start a wholesale rise in prices produced a major debate in the business and economic world which started Wednesday morning, lasted through the entire three days of the steel crisis, and actually never was settled. Economists have never been quite sure exactly how much effect steel has on the general price index, and the studies which have been made are not much help. Two of the more recent ones, for instance, come to opposite conclusions.

In 1959, Otto Eckstein and Garry Fromm of Harvard published a study of the impact of steel on the economy for the Joint Economic Committee of Congress. Eckstein and Fromm's report concluded that the impact of the increase of steel prices on other industrial prices was large; that if steel prices had behaved like other industrial prices, the rise in the total wholesale price index would have been 40 percent less since 1953. The rise in steel prices, said this report, is a critical part of the inflation in industrial goods prices in recent years.

On the other hand, after the steel strike of 1959, James P. Mitchell, then Secretary of Labor in the Eisenhower Administration, appointed a study group under the general direction of Professor E. Robert Livernash, of the Harvard School of Business Administraton, to prepare a report on inflation. Frank E. Norton, of the University of California at Los Angeles, was picked to study steel prices for the Livernash report, and he concluded that "the exploratory analysis undertaken in this study suggests that the independent influences of steel prices on inflation has been modest in the postwar period."

Would the 1962 increase have an immediate effect on prices in general? Businessmen were not sure. In a hasty poll taken Wednesday morning, the *Wall Street Journal* found that of 50 companies which used steel, 35 thought they would probably raise prices in the months ahead if the price of steel went up throughout the industry. "The raise in steel prices will undoubtedly cause a price increase for us," John Langlois, Executive Vice-President of Childers Manufacturing

Company of Houston, Texas—makers of prefabricated steel building components—told the *Journal*. The rise was estimated at from 3 to 4 percent. The Budd Company, manufacturers of auto bodies and component parts, also planned a price rise. Because of the timing, price rises in the auto industry were expected to be delayed, but the general feeling in Detroit was that the price rise in steel made an increase in the cost of automobiles inevitable for 1963. In the can industry it was expected that price boosts wouldn't come until July 1, because the industry sells on a three-months-in-advance contract basis, but a sounding suggested that there, too, a price rise was inevitable. "In the past," said Lawrence Wilkinson, an executive vice-president of Continental Can, "a rise or fall in the price of tin plate [can-making steel] has meant a corresponding rise or fall in the price of metal cans, since the cost of tin plate is roughly sixty percent of the cost of the can." Other big manufacturers of products containing a large proportion of steel—producers of nuts, bolts, screws and other fasteners, builders of ships, etc.—indicated that they were in the same spot. The Whirlpool Corporation was facing an $800,000 a year cost increase as a result of the steel price increase. "This increase throws our cost reduction program right out the window," Whirlpool's co-ordinator of purchasing said gloomily, but unfortunately Whirlpool was in the same bind facing many manufacturers: it was not at all sure that it could afford to pass the price rise along to customers.

Unlike the *Wall Street Journal, Business Week* found in its survey of businessmen that there was considerable doubt as to whether the steel price increase could be passed along, primarily because of the rough competition. "It's not a question of whether industries want to raise prices, but whether they can," said one executive quoted in *Business Week.*

If the first reports from the business community revealed confusion and indecision about the price rise, they also revealed something else not calculated to gladden either party in the titanic battle which was brewing: some steel users were already talking about turning to foreign steel if the price increase stuck. "We're certainly going to explore foreign steel tremendously," said one Detroit auto parts manufacturer whose company had never used anything but American-made steel. Steel import firms on the West Coast were predicting that the increase in the price of domestic steel would naturally increase their steel imports, and most of them said they did not think foreign steel producers planned to boost their prices, which were already running from 3 to 10 percent below U. S. prices. And with our steel imports already running well above our steel exports, these comments from the Coast only emphasized President Kennedy's fear that the increase would quickly aggravate an already critical balance-of-payments problem.

It was not very good news for the steel industry either, but foreign steel was not its only worry. As early as Wednesday morning, businessmen were already talking about steel substitutes—aluminum, plastics, and the many other new products which have made life a little harder in the old-line steel companies. "Buildings are put on a strict budget," said one executive in the construction industry, explaining the demand for new materials in the building trade. "If steel costs go up, the builder goes back to the architect and asks for changes."

Obviously, on the first morning of the great battle, the steel industry had a wavering business community behind it. Businessmen were torn between their philosophical desire to see big steel give the Government a comeuppance and their own competitive and price problems.

But if the business community had its doubts, organized labor did not—to no one's surprise. George Meany, President of the AFL–CIO, accused the industry of defying the Government by "wanton price gouging." He added that "the power of government and our entire society is being tested by the economic might of a corporate giant and a major industry." And David McDonald, speaking to a convention of the Pennsylvania Federation of Labor in Pittsburgh, denied that the increase in prices had been caused by an increase in labor costs. "The united steelworkers," he said, "have never negotiated an inflationary agreement and certainly the current agreement cannot in any sense be considered inflationary ... Our agreements do not go into effect until July first. This indicates that if a price increase goes into effect it is a price-wage spiral rather than a wage-price spiral."

Meanwhile, in Washington, the lid was now off the Pandora's box of difficulties. Mike Mansfield, Majority Leader of the Senate, called the price increase "unjustified"; Speaker of the House John W. McCormack said the company's action was "shocking, arrogant, irresponsible"; Senator Hubert Humphrey, the Democratic whip, called U. S. Steel's action "an effort to affront the President and an irritant to labor"; Senator George Smathers, Democrat from Florida, said, "I'm a friend of business, but this was a dumb thing to do."

And the criticism did not come solely from the Democratic side of the aisle. Senator Jacob K. Javits, the Republican Senator from New York, who had once said the Republican Party should be proud to be the party of business, told the Senate, "I deprecate and deplore" the price increase and that it is "very likely to put the steel industry in hot water with the people of the United States." However, Republicans for the most part were silent. U. S. Steel's action had taken them by surprise, and most of them seemed inclined to caution—to see which way the wind would blow before rushing out to defend the steel companies.

There were more than mere words in the air in the Congress. Senator Albert Gore, who only the week before had commended the steel industry for a "noninflationary" wage contract, now claimed a "breach of faith with the American people" and began readying several proposals for Senate consideration, including: (1) creation of a national consumers' advisory board to inform the public about the impact of price increases; (2) enactment of a Taft-Hartley type of injunctive cooling-off period so the Government could temporarily ban proposed price increases in "monopoly controlled basic industries"; (3) permanent Government regulation of such industries similar to the way in which public utilities are regulated; (4) tight tax treatment of stock options for corporate executives.

At the same time, Representative Emanuel Celler, Chairman of the House antitrust subcommittee, said his subcommittee would launch a broad investigation of industrywide price-fixing beginning May 2. Senator Kefauver also let it be known that his antitrust and monopoly subcommittee planned a similar investigation, but added that he was holding off an announcement lest it appear that his subcommittee was unduly rushing into a very serious investigation. Kefauver was said to be scheduling his investigation to take place in about two weeks—it would evolve around six basic points, all of which had been touched on at one time or another in past Kefauver investigations of the steel industry:

1. That the price of steel has gone up during each of the postwar recessions, even at times when demand had been low, as at the time of the present price rise. This, he said, suggested that artificial elements had influenced the market;

2. That increases in prices have been made by steel companies in both good times and bad, by the same amount and with all companies arriving at the same price level;

3. That smaller companies, often more efficient than U. S. Steel, have frequently had higher profit rates—but have still raised prices at the same time U. S. Steel did;

4. That even companies which produce more of certain

kinds of products than U. S. Steel have followed U. S. Steel prices on those products;

5. That companies have frequently had opportunities to make more money at a higher rate of profit by keeping prices low and stepping up production, but have failed to take advantage of these opportunities when they occurred;

6. That the absence of independent pricing suggests the nonexistence of a really workable competitive system in prices.

Down Pennsylvania Avenue the Executive Branch was still silent, with most of the Administration officials involved waiting for the President to fire the first shot at his afternoon press conference. However, rumors of Administration action were coming out of governmental agencies almost as fast as reporters could call their contacts in the Government: the Treasury Department would abandon its plan to liberalize the tax depreciation schedules; the Justice Department would launch an antitrust probe; the Federal Trade Commission would do likewise; the Defense Department would shift defense contracts to steel companies holding the price line, as would other government agencies making large purchases of steel. A *Wall Street Journal* Washington correspondent even reported that the Internal Revenue Service had been ordered to make an intensive check of U. S. Steel's stock option plan, which had existed for years to give incentive benefits to the corporation's executives. The same reporter also said that investigators in the IRS's intelligence division had begun an audit of tax reports of many other top steel executives. Although this latter power is a traditional weapon often used by a party in office to help achieve its objectives, its use in the steel crisis was firmly denied by the White House. It was also denied by the Treasury Department and the Internal Revenue Service.

*   *   *

As the morning wore on and long before a single company had followed U. S. Steel's lead, it was becoming increasingly obvious that the key company in the dispute would probably be Inland Steel. By almost any standard, Inland Steel is an unusual company. In the first place, as much as any business-man in recent times, Clarence Randall, one-time president and chairman of the board of Inland, who served in Wash-ington under both Democratic and Republican administra-tions, is the personification of the "industrial statesman." And Inland's present Board Chairman Joseph L. Block, who served with Randall, appears to have interited his mantle. A slender, soft-spoken man who stands only five foot two, Block often acts like a giant in a world of industrial giants. His father headed the group which founded Inland Steel in 1893, and young Joseph grew up in the industry. He is a student of American history and government and an advocate of public service by businessmen. During World War II he served for three years as a hardworking dollar-a-year member of the War Production Board. More recently, Block had been a member of President Kennedy's advisory committee on labor-management relations. Block's attitude about public service grows out of a deep conviction concerning the role of the businessman and the corporation in society. "A cor-poration can be a good citizen too," he once said. "What is good for the general public must be good for business." How-ever, other businessmen—especially in the steel industry—tended to look upon Block's concern for the national welfare in a somewhat different light: "I think Block caught Potomac fever," says one steel executive, commenting on Block's serv-ice on the government advisory committee. "That happens to a lot of businessmen who hang around Washington too long."

Speaking in November 1962 before the annual conference of the Controller's Institute of America, Block, who is a Republican, concluded with these remarks which effectively sum up his philosophy on the relationship between government and industry: "We hear some of our colleagues repeatedly assert that government, in a free society, has no place whatsoever in economic affairs. But such a viewpoint is contrary to historic fact, and totally unrealistic . . . Government must point the way, for only government is the representative of all the people, and the voices of all segments of the economy must be heard. . . .[1]

In the eyes of his fellow steel executives, such policies may be considered the result of his Potomac fever, but if so there has been little evidence that Inland's stockholders have any complaints. Although Inland is ranked eighth among the nation's steel companies, it is number one in its ability to make profits. One explanation for this is the fact that it is located in East Chicago, Indiana, in the center of the area which consumes one-third of the nation's steel. About 80 percent of Inland's shipments go to firms within a 300-mile radius of the plant. "They are sitting on a gold mine," said one competitor, with more than a touch of sour grapes, "and frankly they would have to be stupid not to do well." However, that Inland Steel's management is not stupid is well known, and according to most experts, its ability to make profits is based on considerably more than a favorable geographic location.

One other reason for Inland's steady progress in the viciously competitive industry is its long-range concern for sales—a not surprising fact when you consider that Block and the company's President John F. Smith, Jr. came up through the sales department. "The whole blamed outfit is

---

[1] That such thoughts were more than mere words to Block was demonstrated back in 1952 during the Korean war when the steel industry was offered a price increase by the Office of Price Stabilization. Inland decided not to apply for the increase, with Block making the following explanation: "Another spiral of inflation," he said, "can only be prevented by making no change in either wages or prices. There has been no wage advance, consequently we are not advancing our prices."

run by salespeople," grumbles one Pittsburgh steel executive who maintains that his own firm puts the emphasis where it ought to be—on production and production costs.

But as far as Inland is concerned, sales and salesmanship are considered among the most important aspects of its business. "For years," says one steel buyer quoted in the *Wall Street Journal*, "most steel companies let it be known they were doing us a favor in selling to us, but Inland salesmen were always anxious to serve us no matter how small the order. We aren't forgetting that now, when there's overcapacity and all the producers are looking for our business."

The Inland sales department makes the final decision on whether or not to interrupt production schedules in order to fill a special order, and even the company's production chief concedes that the ability to please customers "more than compensates" for the trouble and expense involved.

In short, Inland is rapidly gaining a reputation as the most progressive company in an industry too often accused of remaining steadfastly wedded to outmoded business practices. It has adopted most of the progressive policies of the typical twentieth-century American corporation, and the company and its management are in touch with the times and with their customers. It is common knowledge in the steel-buying community that if you have a problem with Inland, you don't have to beat around the bush; any one of Inland's top managers can be reached by picking up the phone.

On April 11, 1962, Inland officials received a great many phone calls—not just from steel-consuming customers. Anyone in the Kennedy Administration who knew anyone at Inland was encouraged to put through a call. Joseph Block, a personal friend of Arthur Goldberg's, was vacationing in Japan, and was difficult to reach by telephone, but for the rest of his executives the calls began early in the day.

At 7:45 A.M., Philip D. Block, Jr., Vice-Chairman of Inland, was called to the phone at his Chicago apartment. The caller was Edward P. Gudeman, Undersecretary of Commerce. Gudeman had known P. D. Block for more than thirty years; they had been schoolmates together at the Harvard School for Boys on Chicago's South Side. "I didn't ask P. D. what Inland might do," said Gudeman several days later. "I didn't want them to feel that the Administration was putting them on the spot. I just wanted him to know how we felt and to ask his consideration."

Other calls put through to Inland on Wednesday included one to President Smith by Henry H. Fowler, Undersecretary of the Treasury, and another from Secretary Goldberg to Leigh D. Block, Vice-President for Purchasing. Both Inland and government officials insist that there was no call from the White House or from any other government official to Joseph Block in Japan. In all the calls to Inland (as to other executives in the steel industry) there was no attempt to coax and there were no threats. The approach was to explain the Government's position and to let it go at that. In the case of executives whom New Frontiersmen felt were real friends of the Administration, they were asked to call their friends and in some cases issue statements. In Fowler's conversation with Smith, the emphasis was on the effect of the steel increase on exports and imports and the further pressure it would put on the balance of payments. Although no concrete assurances were asked or volunteered, Administration officials did learn in their calls to Inland that the company would hold the line for at least another day or two.

Inland was not the only target for the Administration's telephone barrage. Walter Heller had contacts in Armco Steel, sixth largest steel producer in the nation, and so did others. Through calls made to Armco, it was learned that this company was also holding off for the time being, although no public announcement, one way or the other, would be made. Other calls included several by Secretary

McNamara to a number of friends in the industry—including one to Edward J. Hanley, President of the Allegheny-Ludlum Steel Corporation. (Hanley said later that he advised Secretary McNamara that "if he waited, economics would take care of the situation," but added that he thought it was too late for his advice to have any influence; that the Administration had already decided on its course of action.) Another call was made by Undersecretary of the Treasury Robert V. Roosa to Henry Alexander, Chairman of the Morgan Guaranty Trust Company, which is represented on the board of U. S. Steel and widely considered a powerful voice in its decisions. An official at U. S. Steel itself—not Roger Blough—was called by Secretary Hodges; Secretary Dillon was also on the phone from Florida, calling friends in New York. Undersecretary of State George Ball also was dialing. Exactly how many calls the President made during Wednesday's telephone blitz—or for that matter during the entire seventy-two hours of the war with big steel—is not known; there were certainly several personal calls to friends in the industry, and one to Edgar Kaiser in California.

The telephoning also included a peppering of calls made by the Democratic National Committee to Democratic governors around the country. Committee spokesmen asked the governors to do two things: (1) make statements supporting the President; and (2) ask steel producers in their states to hold the price line. The committee itself issued no statements in its own name. "Politics," as such, were to be kept out of the conflict.

But the telephone calls and the Government action—actual, implied, threatened and rumored—were not enough to hold back the first wave of U. S. Steel's support. The President and his advisers had thought that the other steel companies would wait at least a day before following U. S. Steel's lead, and during that time the Administration fighters had hoped to have launched such a furious counterattack that the other companies would hesitate before taking action. But the move came sooner than expected. Shortly before noon on Wednesday, Bethlehem Steel, in a brief two-sentence statement, announced that it also would raise steel prices $6 a ton—less than twenty-four hours after Bethelehem President Martin had told reporters that it would refrain from raising prices.

CHAPTER 4

Wednesday Afternoon, April 11: A Bitter "Tongue-lashing"

> We're not in business to make steel, we're not in business to build ships, we're not in business to erect buildings. We're in business to make money.
> —*Frank Brugler, Controller of Bethlehem Steel Corporation*

At noon the President flew out to the airport in his helicopter to meet the Shah of Iran and his party. As he stepped from the helicopter he was handed the bulletin reporting Bethlehem's decision to raise prices. The news rocked him somewhat, although he did not show it. But he was fully aware that many of the other steel companies would attempt to follow U. S. Steel and Bethlehem before the full impact of his counterattack would be felt. He was right: As *Business Week* said, commenting on Bethlehem's decision: "After that it looked like a race against time for other producers to get themselves on record before Kennedy's press conference at 3:30 P.M. Most of them made it." By the time the welcoming ceremonies for the Shah were completed and the President had escorted the party to Blair House and returned to the White House, several other companies had followed Bethlehem: Republic, the Wheeling Steel Corporation, Youngstown Sheet and Tube Company, and Jones & Laughlin. Six of the big twelve steel companies had now raised their prices.

However, the fight was far from over. Despite the rush to follow U. S. Steel and Bethlehem, when the President went on television a sizable portion of the industry was still holding out. Leonard C. Rose, for instance, President of Colorado Fuel and Iron Corporation, the nation's tenth largest steel producer, said: "We are presently studying the situation but have had no opportunity yet to firm up our plans. We are certainly considering the plight of our stockholders and feel that some action should be taken with respect to our steel prices." Other companies still studying the situation included Armco, Kaiser Aluminum, McLouth and Inland. These were five of the big twelve, and their significance lay in the fact that they produced about 14 percent of the nation's steel—which was close enough to the Administration's goal of persuading companies representing 16 percent of the nation's steel facilities to give considerable encouragement to the Administration's counterattack.

Meanwhile the President was preparing for his televised press conference—and as several million televiewers were soon to see, he was still boiling mad. Rumors had been going around that Kennedy had actually known about the price increase for several days; that he was too smart to be trapped in such a way; and that the Administration would actually welcome the inflation which would result from the increase. One rumor even hinted that the White House and the Justice Department had planned it this way—that they had set a trap for the steel companies, which would enable them to proceed with the antitrust and price-fixing charges they had been quietly preparing for a year.

But the President's obvious fury soon silenced such talk. In addition to the "deep, deep affront" which the President, in the words of one of his aides, felt he had received, there was now the blatant and open challenge to the Government's antitrust laws, as a result of the other major steel producers' rush to raise their prices to exactly the same level set by U. S. Steel. Very seldom had the nation been given such a dramatic example of the so-called "administered prices" being administered. For a year the President had been holding back the more liberal Democrats in his Administration and in Congress, many of whom had waited restlessly for eight years for a chance to do something about pricing in the steel industry. Now it appeared that it would be impossible to hold back the liberals from an all-out war against big business, something which Kennedy wanted desperately to avoid. And the explosive situation had been brought on by the very businessmen he had tried the hardest to protect; the anger he was soon to display to the nation was not hard to understand. Of course, when the boss of any organization is mad, his staff is often madder, and the White House staff was no exception. Some of the President's aides were even comparing what Blough had done to what the Russians had done on nuclear testing the previous summer—that is, to sit at the negotiating table trying to get everything you can, knowing all along you have no intention of keeping your side of an unwritten and unsaid, but perfectly understood, bargain.

Ted Sorensen, as angry as anyone, had been working on the President's opening statement all day, but it was not finished until 3:22 P.M., just eight minutes before the President was to go on the air. President Kennedy was grim as he prepared to leave the White House for the four-minute ride over to the State Department, where the press conferences are held. He had the statement in his hand as he left, and worked on it in the car on the way over. He was still asking questions: When had the last contract been signed? When did the contracts go into effect? When had Blough put out the public statement about the price increase? Sorensen and Andrew Hatcher rode with him in the car, answering his questions and watching him pencil in his own last-minute changes in the statement. The final product, in the words of one White House aide, had "the real Kennedy touch."

The moment the President emerged from the elevator which took him to the basement level of the State Department, it was obvious that he was getting ready to unload both barrels. The usual twinkle was gone from his eyes, and the flickering smile to friendly correspondents was missing. He clenched his teeth, set his jaw, and paced across the rug, with Assistant White House press secretary Jay Gildner and Hatcher hurrying along behind. His rolled-up statement was clutched in his left hand. When he reached the platform, he smoothed out his papers on the walnut rostrum before him, then stiffened both arms and gripped the sides of the rostrum. "Good afternoon, I have several announcements to make," he said grimly. Then he began one of the most blistering attacks ever directed by an American President against an American individual or organization:

> . . . The simultaneous and identical actions of United States Steel [he continued] and other leading steel corporations increasing steel prices by some six dollars a ton constitute a wholly unjustifiable and irresponsible defiance of the public interest.
>
> In this serious hour in our nation's history when we are confronted with grave crises in Berlin and Southeast Asia, when we are devoting our energies to economic recovery and stability, when we are asking reservists to leave their homes and families months on end and servicemen to risk their lives—and four were killed in the last two days in Vietnam—and asking union members to hold down their wage requests, at a time when restraint and sacrifice are being asked of every citizen, the American people will find it hard, as I do, to accept a situation in which a tiny handful of steel executives whose pursuit of private power and profit exceeds their sense of public responsibility, can show such utter contempt for the interest of one hundred and eighty-five million Americans . . .

When the President reached this point in his statement—
the end of the first page—he lifted the page with his left hand,
turned it over and put the page down in a deliberate gesture
of anger. He glanced up, drew his lips thin, and began to
thump the rostrum with his right forefinger. Then he
doubled his fist. "His right hand seemed to take off by itself,"
commented TRB in *The New Republic*.

The President continued:

If this rise in the cost of steel is imitated by the rest of the
industry, instead of rescinded, it would increase the cost of
homes, autos, appliances and most other items for every
American family. It would increase the cost of machinery and
tools to every American businessman and farmer. It would
seriously handicap our efforts to prevent an inflationary
spiral from eating up the pensions of our older citizens and
our new gains in purchasing power. It would add, Defense
Secretary Robert S. McNamara informed me this morning,
an estimated one billion dollars to the cost of our defenses at
a time when every dollar is needed for national security and
other purposes.

It will make it more difficult for American goods to compete
in foreign markets, more difficult to withstand competition
from foreign imports, and thus more difficult to improve our
balance-of-payment position and stem the flow of gold. And it
is necessary to stem it for our national security if we're going
to pay for our security commitments abroad.

And it would surely handicap our efforts to induce other
industries and unions to adopt responsible price and wage
policies.

The facts of the matter are that there is no justification for
an increase in steel prices.

The recent settlement between the industry and the union,
which does not even take place until July first, was widely
acknowledged to be noninflationary, and the whole purpose
and effect of this Administration's role—which both parties
understood—was to achieve an agreement which would make
unnecessary any increases in prices.

Steel output per man is rising so fast that labor costs per ton of steel can actually be expected to decline in the next twelve months. And, in fact, the Acting Commissioner of the Bureau of Labor Statistics informed me this morning that, and I quote, "Employment costs per unit of steel output in 1961 were essentially the same as they were in 1958." The cost of major raw materials—steel scrap and coal—has also been declining.

And for an industry which has been generally operating at less than two-thirds of capacity, its profit rate has been normal and can be expected to rise sharply this year in view of the reduction in idle capacity. Their lot has been easier than that of a hundred thousand steelworkers thrown out of work in the last three years.

The industry's cash dividends have exceeded six hundred million dollars in each of the last five years; and earnings in the first quarter of this year were estimated in the February twenty-eighth *Wall Street Journal* to be among the highest in history.

In short, at a time when they could be exploring how more efficiency and better prices could be obtained, reducing prices in this industry in recognition of lower costs, their unusually good labor contract, their foreign competition and their increase in production and profits which are coming this year, a few gigantic corporations have decided to increase prices in ruthless disregard of their public responsibility.

The steelworkers' union can be proud that it abided by its responsibilities in this agreement. And this Government also has responsibilities which we intend to meet.

The Department of Justice and the Federal Trade Commission are examining the significance of this action in a free competitive economy.

The Department of Defense and other agencies are reviewing its impact on their policies of procurement.

And I am informed that steps are under way by those members of the Congress who plan appropriate inquiries into how these price decisions are so quickly made and reached and what legislative safeguards may be needed to protect the public interest.

Price and wage decisions in this country, except for a very limited restriction in the case of monopolies and national emergency strikes, are and ought to be freely and privately made. But the American people have a right to expect, in return for that freedom, a higher sense of business responsibility for the welfare of their country than has been shown in the last two days.

Some time ago I asked each American to consider what he would do for his country, and I asked the steel companies. In the last twenty-four hours we had their answer.

When the President finished this statement, he simply frowned. Immediately the hands went up and a correspondent yelled: "Mr. President!"

"Just one moment," the President responded coldly. "I've one other statement here." He then proceeded to read a long announcement regarding the possibility of returning to private life the national guard units which had been called to active duty during the Berlin crisis.

When he finished this statement, he pointed to a reporter with his hand raised, who asked: "Mr. President, the unusually strong language you used in discussing the steel situation would indicate that you might be considering some pretty strong action. Are you thinking in terms of requesting or reviving the need for wage-price controls?"

"I think that my statement states what the situation is today," the President replied. "This is a free country."

In all the conversations [he continued] which were held by members of this Administration and myself with the leaders of the steel union and the companies, it was always very obvious that they could proceed with freedom to do what they thought was best within the limitations of law.

But I did very clearly emphasize on every occasion that my only interest was in trying to secure an agreement which would not provide an increase in prices, because I thought that price stability in steel would have the most far-reaching consequences for industrial and economic stability and for our position abroad, and price instability would have the most far-reaching consequences in making our lot much more difficult.

When the agreement was signed—and the agreement was a moderate one and within the range of productivity increases—as I've said, actually, there'll be reduction in cost per unit during the year—I thought, I was hopeful we'd achieved our goal.

Now the actions that will be taken will be—are being now considered by the Administration. The Department of Justice is particularly anxious, in view of the very speedy action in other companies, who have entirely different economic problems facing them than did United States Steel—the speed with which they moved the—it seems to me to require examination of our present laws and whether they're being obeyed by the Federal Trade Commission and the Department of Justice.

And I am very interested in the respective investigations that will be conducted in the House and Senate, and whether we shall need additional legislation, which I would come to very reluctantly.

But I must say the last twenty-four hours indicate that those with great power are not always concerned about the national interest.

Another question pertaining to the steel crisis followed: "In your conversation with Mr. Blough yesterday," asked a reporter, "did you make a direct request that this price increase be either deferred or rescinded?"

"I was informed about the price increase," the President replied abruptly, "after the announcement had gone out to the papers. I told Mr. Blough of my very keen disappointment and what I thought would be the most unfortunate effects of it." He continued:

And, of course, we were hopeful that other companies who, as I've said, have a different situation in regard to profits and all the rest than U. S. Steel—they're all—have a somewhat different economic situation—I was hopeful, particularly in view of the statement I saw in the paper by the president of Bethlehem, in which he stated—though now he says he was misquoted—that there should be no price increase—and we are investigating that statement—I was hopeful that the others would not follow the example, that therefore the pressures of the competitive market place would bring United States Steel back to their original prices—but the parade began.

But it came to me after the decision was made. There was no prior consultation or information given to the Administration.

The next question was from a woman correspondent who asked whether, with spring being here, it perhaps was not time to permit the wives of servicemen to join them overseas—that everyone knew that they would get into much less trouble and do a much better job if the wives and their children were with them. This brought a good laugh from the correspondents, but the President remained grim. When he replied, he could not refrain from contrasting the sacrifice made by the servicemen and their wives to the "last twenty-four hours."

There was a question about whether the President had been notified when the Strategic Air Command had recieved a false alarm last fall. The President replied that the incident had been "overstated." Then a reporter asked: "Mr. President, if I could get back to steel for a minute. You mentioned an investigation into the suddenness of the decision to increase prices. Did you—is the position of the Administration that it believed it had the assurance of the steel industry at the time of the recent labor agreement that it would not increase prices?"

We did not ask either side to give us any assurance [the President said], because there is a very proper limitation to the power of the Government in this free economy.

All we did in our meetings was to emphasize how important

it was that the—there be price stability, and we stressed that our whole purpose in attempting to persuade the union to begin to bargain early and to make an agreement which would not affect prices, of course, was for the purpose of maintaining price stability.

That was the thread that ran through every discussion which I had, or Secretary Goldberg.

We never at any time asked for a commitment in regard to the terms—precise terms—of the agreement from either Mr. McDonald or those of Mr. Blough, representing the steel company, because, in our opinion, that is—would be passing over the line of propriety.

But I don't think that there was any question that our great interest in attempting to secure the kind of settlement that was finally secured was to maintain price stability, which we regard as very essential at this particular time.

That agreement provided for price stability up to yesterday.

Two questions later, another reporter asked: "In your statement on the steel industry, sir, you mention a number of instances which would indicate that the cost of living will go up for many people if this price increase were to remain effective. In your opinion does that give the steelworkers the right to try to obtain some kind of a price—or a wage increase to catch up?"

"No. Rather interestingly, the last contract was signed on Saturday with Great Lakes, so that the steel union is bound for a year. And of course I'm sure would have felt—going much further if the matter had worked out as we had all hoped. But they've made their agreement and I'm sure they're going to stick with it. It does not provide for the sort of action you suggest."

When he finished, the President pointed to Edward P. Morgan, a correspondent for the American Broadcasting Company.

Mr. Morgan said: "Still on steel, Senator Gore advocated today legislation to regulate steel prices somewhat in the manner that public utility prices are regulated, and his argument seemed to be that the steel industry had sacrificed some of the privileges of the free market because it wasn't really setting its prices on a—on a supply and demand but what he called 'administered prices.' Your statement earlier and your remarks since indicate a general agreement with that kind of approach. Is that correct?"

"No, Mr. Morgan," replied the President, "I don't think that I'd stated that. I'd have to look at—and see what Senator Gore had suggested and I'm not familiar with it. What I said was, we should examine what can be done to try to minimize the impact on the public interest of these decisions, but though we had of course always hoped that those involved would recognize that, I would say that what must disturb Senator Gore and Congressman Celler and others—Senator Kefauver—will be the suddenness by which every company in the last few hours, one by one, as the morning went by, came in with their almost, if not identical, almost identical price increases, which isn't really the way we expect the competitive private enterprise system to always work."

Another question, and then back to steel. "In connection with the steel situation," asked a reporter, "is there not an action that could be taken by the executive branch in connection with direct procurement of steel under the administration of the Agency for International Aid—I mean the aid agency. For example, I think the Government buys about one million tons of steel. Now, could not the Government decide that only steel—steel should be purchased only at the price, say of yesterday rather than today?"

"That matter was considered, as a matter of fact," replied the President, "in a conversation between the Secretary of Defense and myself last evening. At that time we were not aware that nearly the entire industry was about to come in, and therefore the amount of choice we have is somewhat limited. Too, on this thing, in the case of identical bids, which the Government is sometimes confronted with, they decide to choose the smaller business unit rather than the larger. I'm hopeful that there will be those who will not participate in this parade and will meet the principle of the private enterprise competitive system in which everyone tries to sell at the lowest price commensurate with the—their interests. And I'm hopeful that there'll be some who will decide that they shouldn't go in the wake of U. S. Steel. But we'll have to wait and see on that, because they're coming in very fast."

This was followed by two more questions on steel:

Question: Mr. President, two years ago, after the settlement, I believe steel prices were not raised. Do you think there was an element of political discrimination in the behavior of the industry this year?

The President: I would not—and if there was, it doesn't really—if it was—if that was the purpose, that is comparatively unimportant to the damage that—the country's the one that suffers. I—

Question: Mr. President—

The President: If they do it to spite me, it really isn't so important.

Question: To carry a previous question just one step further, as a result of the emphasis that you placed on holding the price line, did any word or impression come to you from the negotiations that there would be no price increase under the type of agreement that was signed?

The President: I will say that in our conversations that we asked for no commitments in regard to the details of the agreement or in regard to any policies of the union or the company. Our central thrust was that price stability was necessary and that the way to do it was to have a responsible agreement, which we got. Now, at no time did anyone suggest that if such an agreement was gained that it would be still necessary to put up prices. That word did not come until last night.

The final steel question came when a reporter asked: "Mr. President, the steel industry is one of a half-dozen which has been expecting a tax benefit this summer through revision of the depreciation schedules. Does this price hike affect the Administration's attitude?"

"Well," the President replied briefly, "it affects our budget. Secretary Dillon and I discussed this morning, of course, all this. The matter is being very carefully looked into now."

Three questions later, Merriman Smith of the Associated Press closed the conference with his traditional "Thank you, Mr. President." The President left the rostrum and went into a little anteroom outside the large auditorium. He flopped into a chair and sat silently for about a minute, no one speaking. Then Hatcher and Sorensen congratulated him, but he said nothing. He was not at all happy about what he had had to do. Later as he watched a taped version of the press conference on a White House television set and heard his own stern words coming back at him, he turned to one of his aides and said: "I can tell you what the New York *Herald Tribune* editorial will say tomorrow." He was right.

Seen in person, the President's anger was even more apparent than it appeared on television or in the transcript of the press conference. He hardly ever looked at anyone in the audience, just at everybody—or right through them. At one point, pointing to a questioner, he even growled: "Yeah?"— a term he had never used before in a press conference. And the President's wrath was felt around the nation. Later a *Fortune* editorial would charge that his press conference statement was couched in "the rhetoric of the garrison state," and the following morning, writing in the *Christian Science Monitor,* Richard L. Strout described the President as speaking in a cold anger that had apparently been building up all day and as giving the steelmen a "tongue-lashing" almost unparalleled in modern times.

*   *   *

In a paneled room in front of a television set nineteen floors above Manhattan's Trinity Church, a dozen or more top executives of U. S. Steel took their tongue-lashing in stony silence. Afterward, *Newsweek* correspondent Hobart Rowan asked Roger Blough: "What weight would you say you gave to the Administration's reiteration of the need for price stability?"

Blough replied: "Against the background of thinking in terms of costs—which is the background I think in—the Government's position was one of the factors that was weighed very heavily, along with all the others we have to contend with."

Rowan then questioned whether "the Government went too far in asserting the national interest," and Blough replied: "I'm not critical of people who make suggestions . . . but the President apparently feels that we acted contrary to the public interest. Well, I feel that a lack of proper cost-price relationship is one of the most damaging things to the public interest."

Of one thing U. S. Steel officials were certain: the company would have to reply to the President's press conference attack. A decision was made that Roger Blough would hold a televised press conference the following afternoon.

Among the rank and file of the unions, the reaction to the President's blast at the steel companies was immediate; at the 100-inch plate mill at U. S. Steel's Homestead plant in Pittsburgh, it was all they talked about on the 4 P.M. to midnight shift. Anthony Amantea, a veteran of twenty years in the plant, said: "We got a dirty deal. We signed a contract with a few measly fringe benefits and no increase and then they jack prices up six dollars a ton. We pretty much supported the union—most of the fellows did—when they didn't demand an increase for us. We were trying to stop inflation and we were pretty satisfied with the steel settlement." At U. S. Steel's Clairton works, twenty-eight-year-old Mike Mihalov commented to a New York *Post* reporter: "The way they raised the price six dollars a ton, they'll be able to pay for the benefits they gave us in about two months and the rest is just more profit for them."

Meanwhile, the moves by the Executive Branch of the Government mentioned by the President were already under way. The Justice Department had indicated the day before the possibility of an antitrust suit, and it was especially interested in the statement by Bethlehem's Edmund Martin, which had come over the White House AP wire the previous afternoon. If this statement was true, it might be used to support the charge that U. S. Steel, because of its great size, exercised an undue influence over the rest of the industry. The statement took added significance Wednesday, after Bethlehem Steel announced that it would raise its prices. Sometime around 6 P.M. Wednesday, Attorney General Robert Kennedy ordered the Federal Bureau of Investigation to find out exactly what Martin had said. He also instructed his Department to press ahead on gathering information in support of Justice Department antitrust action with all possible speed, which meant that a dozen or so top Justice Department attorneys worked until late Wednesday night preparing for the Department's next move in the steel case.

Oddly enough, Archibald Cox, the Solicitor General, was still blissfully aloof from the steel crisis on Wednesday evening. He had been given no assignment, and late that afternoon he had taken off by plane for Tucson, Arizona, where he was scheduled to make two speeches to the Arizona Bar on Thursday. However, on arriving at his hotel in Tucson shortly after 10 P.M.—after midnight, Washington time—he was given a message to call the President immediately.

There were also signs of activity in the Treasury Department late Wednesday afternoon. Despite the telephone agreement between the President and Dillon not to alter the Department's new liberalized depreciation schedules, hints from the Department were suggesting that these schedules would be given a second look. The word was also being passed that the Defense Department and other agencies responsible for placing purchase orders with the steel industry were planning to review their procurement policies.

At the same time, Federal Trade Commission Chairman Paul Rand Dixon, announced that his agency had begun an informal inquiry which could lead to penalties up to $5,000 a day for violation of its consent order of June 15, 1951. This decree bound the industry to refrain from collusive price-fixing or maintaining identical delivered prices and contained a general prohibition under which the steel companies were enjoined from jointly "adopting, establishing, fixing or maintaining prices or any element thereof at which steel products shall be quoted or sold, including, but not limited to, base prices."

Members of Congress had often raised their voices in the past when steel companies had raised prices, demanding that this consent decree be enforced, but until now the FTC and the Justice Department had been reluctant to move because of the difficulty in proving collusion. The legal staffs of both agencies had consistently argued that "parallel pricing" by itself was not evidence of collusion. However, a fresh look at this position was now being promised by Mr. Dixon. At a Wednesday evening press conference he said that he was not quite certain what direction the commission's investigation would take until it had been established just how many of the steel companies had followed the lead of U. S. Steel. But he stressed the point that the FTC had ample powers for handling the investigation. "We have all the powers enjoyed by Congress itself," he reminded reporters, "including investigations openly or confidentially, subpoenas, and private or public hearings."

It was a busy day for the Administration, but the battle

was just beginning. A full-scale council of war was scheduled for 8:30 A.M. the following morning, to be attended by all the major figures in the Government's now openly declared war against big steel. The President was furious, the "awesome power" of the Federal Government had been unleashed, and the steel industry knew that it was locked in its most deadly struggle in a decade. By the end of the day on Wednesday, it looked dark for the steel industry, but as *Business Week* commented: "It didn't look like a losing fight—only like a tussle that would be won only at the cost of a severe whipping."

The day closed in the White House with the President's aides nervously monitoring the incoming telegrams in response to the President's press conference. They were not encouraged by the first wire, which read: MR. PRESIDENT WHY ARE YOU PICKING ON THE STEEL INDUSTRY?

That evening the President and the First Lady entertained at a state dinner for the Shah of Iran and the Empress. In a toast to his guest, President Kennedy—appearing almost as a man without a care in the world—said that he and the Shah shared a common "burden." Each of them had made a visit to Paris and each of them might as well have stayed at home, for the Parisians only had eyes for their wives. The party watched Jerome Robbins' *Ballet USA,* which the First Lady has seen so many times that she could probably do some of the numbers herself. The party and the press also watched the First Lady, and as one enthusiastic society reporter wrote, "pencils were literally sailing off the page as journalistic note-takers attempted to record Mrs. Kennedy's pink-and-white prettiness and the diamonds pinned into her high-puff hairdo." Queen Farah also kept the "note-takers" busy. "It was a matter," said one, "of groping for adjectives superlative enough to describe her gown and her jewels—the most blindingly impressive ever beheld on any visiting crowned head."

It was an appropriate backdrop for the President, who was

continually called to the phone, where he set in motion a series of dramatic, behind-the-scene diplomatic maneuvers which were to give the steel crisis an added flavor of excitement; the kind of intrigue the Washington press corps loves so well.

Actually, the "secret diplomacy" in the steel crisis began as early as Tuesday night when a New York businessman named Hal Korda put through a call to his friend Charles Bartlett—a Washington correspondent for the Chattanooga *Times* and a personal friend of the President's.[1] Korda, head of the Korda Leasing Company, knows most of the men in the upper echelons of U. S. Steel, and was the man who first introduced John F. Kennedy to Roger Blough. Korda and Bartlett discussed the steel crisis Tuesday night, and they both agreed that trouble was ahead and that it might be a good idea to try to keep communications open between the steel community and the White House. On Wednesday, Korda went down to U. S. Steel headquarters to test the climate. He found its officials standing firm on their position, but that they had been somewhat surprised at the reaction in Washington. However, not even Korda quite anticipated the extent of the President's reaction at his Wednesday afternoon press conference, and after the press conference, he decided it was time to move more quickly. He called Bartlett again Wednesday evening.

The effort here was to try to get both sides together for a talk, and according to Korda, it was not very easy. Blough's position was that he did not want to appear to be cowering under the Administration's wrath, whereas the President and Goldberg were also reluctant to make the first move, on the grounds that they were the ones who had been affronted; that, under the circumstances, there was a limit as to how far the White House should go in trying to reach a reconciliation—

[1] It was Bartlett, along with *Saturday Evening Post* Editor Stewart Alsop, who was responsible for the article which set off the sudden flap in December 1962 over Adlai Stevenson's role in the Cuban crisis.

especially since all reports indicated that U. S. Steel was still standing firm on its increase. However, in a series of calls Wednesday night between Korda, Bartlett, a high Administration official and eventually the President, it was finally agreed that Goldberg would contact Blough Thursday morning in an effort to bring the two sides together again, at least to the extent of exploring possible ways of healing the breach.

The party at the White House was over about midnight and just as the President was preparing to retire, the call from Archibald Cox in Tucson, came through. Cox had been Chairman of the Wage Stabilization Board during the Korean war and is something of a specialist in labor law. He is also a long-time friend and adviser of the President and had often worked with young Senator Kennedy on speeches and statements concerning labor strikes and steel prices. Hence Cox was probably the President's oldest—in point of service—adviser on labor-management relations.

Now the President asked him what suggestions he might have for rolling back steel prices. Cox replied that he would give the matter serious thought. From past experience, he had decided that the antitrust laws alone could not cope with the steel problem; that special legislation was necessary. As a result, during most of Wednesday night and Thursday morning Cox thought about the problem and made voluminous notes concerning legislation which might be enacted to restrain the steel industry from acting contrary to the public interest. He made on Thursday his first two speeches and immediately returned to Washington to study the problem further.

Meanwhile in New York, Roger Blough was spending an almost sleepless night during which he wrote most of his Thursday afternoon reply to the President. "I decided on a temperate answer," Blough said later, "although it would have relieved a lot of tension and frustration if I had yielded to natural impulses, as others in industry did later. But that is not my way. I was sure that an angry answer would only deepen the rift between government and business which was already so apparent. A tempered answer, I felt, would be more useful to the United States and everyone, including industry."

CHAPTER 5

Thursday Morning, April 12:
The Gathering Storm

> The President conveyed his political popularity into political power. That's what popularity is for. It's like money in the bank. It's to be used.
> —*Senator Hubert Humphrey*

The Solicitor General of the United States was not the only member of the Government working on the steel case in the early hours of Thursday, April 12. Agents of the Federal Bureau of Investigation, responding a little overzealously to orders from the Attorney General, were also in action.

At about 3 A.M. the telephone rang in a two-story duplex in Philadelphia's Burholme Park section. It was the home of Lee Linder, a business reporter for the Associated Press. Linder had covered the Bethlehem Steel stockholders' meeting in Wilmington for the AP on Tuesday, and it was his story that Bethlehem's President Martin had been quoted as saying that he was opposed to a rise in the price of steel. It had been an ambiguous statement, made all the more confusing by the fact that on Wednesday a Bethlehem official had said that Martin had been misquoted.

When Linder answered the phone, a voice on the other end said: "This is the FBI, and we're coming right out. Attorney General Kennedy says we're to see you immediately."

"Who is it?" demanded Linder's sleepy wife.

"The FBI," replied Linder.

"They've got their nerve," his wife shot back. "Hang up on them."

Instead, Linder asked if this were an antitrust investigation, but received no answer. He then told the caller that he would telephone the FBI office himself immediately. He hung up and dialed the local office, reaching the same man he had just talked to. The man insisted that FBI agents were coming right out to see Linder.

Two of them arrived about an hour later. They showed their identification cards and Linder let them in. They settled down in the living room and proceeded to question Linder about the Tuesday meeting and particularly about President Martin's statement. Linder thought of offering coffee, but decided that he didn't want any and that the agents didn't deserve any. He later gave this summary of the interview: "I repeated what the AP had reported, that Martin had said there should not be any steel price rise, that in fact competition in the United States and from foreign sources should result in price reductions."

About 4 A.M. John Lawrence, Philadelphia Editor for the *Wall Street Journal,* was called by the same FBI agents. They wanted to come out to talk to him about Martin's statement, but he refused to let them come. "I told them I had nothing to say," said Lawrence, "so they gave up."

James T. Parks, Jr., business writer for the Wilmington *Journal,* arrived at his office about 6:30 A.M. and found two FBI agents waiting for him. Parks said they asked him about his story on the Bethlehem stockholders' meeting and advised him to keep his notes. Actually Parks had recorded pretty much the same remark quoted by Linder in his AP account—"There shouldn't be any price rise. We shouldn't do anything to increase our costs if we are to survive." However, because his story did not appear until after Bethlehem had announced its price rise, he had not used the quote.

Despite all the furor which the nocturnal visits of the FBI was to arouse, the newsmen involved—although understandably irritated by calls in the middle of the night—took the whole business with relative calm in the cold light of day. Later Linder said: "My wife said she thought the FBI should have apologized for disturbing us, but they didn't." The only comment from the FBI was: "When an FBI agent is called out on an assignment, he goes at once."

Parks, commenting later about the agents, said: "The two fellows were most polite. I was a little put out by this guy Martin saying he had been misquoted, but I understand after talking with Bethlehem Steel this morning that they did not deny the story."

Later Tuesday morning Bethlehem Steel issued an official statement closing the incident, at least as far as the corporation was concerned. It read:

> Neither Mr. Martin nor the company has issued any statement concerning remarks attributed to him at the annual stockholders' meeting on April 10. In response to an inquiry from Washington, made yesterday, a Bethlehem representative explained that Mr. Martin was quoted incorrectly as saying that "there should not be any price rise even after the new labor contract goes into effect on July First."
>
> Mr. Martin was, in fact, indefinite about the matter of prices. He indicated that the further increase in costs which will result from the new labor agreement is unfortunate at a time when we were trying to hold the price line.

At the White House, Thursday morning began with a full-fledged council of war. The first two White House meetings on steel had been more or less spontaneous: the one Tuesday evening just happened; the Wednesday morning one was actually a previously scheduled press conference briefing. But Thursday's was different. It was scheduled for 8:30 A.M. in the Cabinet Room, had been especially called to meet the steel crisis, and was attended only by the men who would be primarily responsible for organizing and following through on the Government's counterattack. Present were Ted Sorensen, who had been chosen to head up the government team; Robert Kennedy; Secretaries McNamara, Goldberg and Hodges; Undersecretary Henry Fowler (sitting in for Douglas Dillon, who was still in Florida); Paul Dixon, Walter Heller, and several of their aides. The President had not planned to attend the meeting because of other duties, but he did manage to drop by for a few minutes just as the meeting was getting under way.

Considering the furor over the Administration's reaction to the price increase, which was already breaking out in the business world and in the conservative communities around the country, it is well to pause a moment to look at this group directing the Government's fight. Despite the screeches soon to be heard from the nation's conservative element, it would be hard to find a genuine card-carrying "radical" among them.

First there were the two Kennedys—both millionaires in their own right and sons of a self-made businessman said to be worth at least $250 million. Although known as a "pragmatic liberal," the President had been denounced by the liberal Americans for Democratic Action for his economic policies, and some of his Cabinet and top-level appointments had caused considerable disappointment in the liberal wing of the Democratic Party. In addition, for months the President had been trying to woo the business community and had been bending over backward to convince it that he was not antibusiness. The result was that by the time the steel crisis erupted, the business community—although still slightly suspicious, as it would be of almost any Democrat—had begun to warm up a little, and occasionally some kind words had even been written about the President in publications considered very close to big business—*Time, Fortune, U. S. News,* etc.

At the same time, liberal Democrats had been displaying considerable restlessness over the President's economic program and were beginning to wonder when he would start to press for some of the big spending programs which they felt were necessary to "get the country moving again." Although the climate was soon to change, by the spring of '62 only the far right still looked on John F. Kennedy as a wild-eyed radical. The rest of the country felt that he was just as interested in preserving a sound economy as the next man—and maybe, because of the family fortune, a little bit more so.

As for his brother Robert, he had never displayed unusually liberal economic leanings and had achieved quite a reputation for his fight to clean up the labor unions while serving with the McClellan Committee. Although it was generally agreed that he had done an acceptable job as Attorney General, he had still not established much of a reputation as a trust buster or zealous enforcer of the antitrust laws. Not that he had ignored them, but his policy—possibly in line with his brother's efforts not to antagonize businessmen—seemed to be one of not going out of his way to make trouble for business.

Ted Sorensen, on the other hand, the President's Chief Counsel, would have to be labeled "liberal"—he had even written articles for *The New Republic* and *Progressive,* which automatically gave him a liberal status in the eyes of most conservatives, even those who had not read the articles. But by now Sorensen's thinking was so in tune with the President's that it was hard to tell where his left off and Kennedy's began—and vice versa. "They're inside each other's skin more than any other superior and subordinate I've ever seen," said one man who had been shot at politically by the Kennedy-Sorensen team during the 1960 campaign. "When Jack is wounded, Ted bleeds," another observer had said.

As a result of the unusually close bond between the President and his chief counsel, if Kennedy was now accurately described as a "pragmatic liberal," then so was Sorensen; and if the President was anxious not to be known as antibusiness, so was Sorensen. As an old friend had been quoted as saying in one of the many hasty biographies written about the New Frontiersman: "Ted is an intelligent, rational liberal; not the kind you have to lock the Treasury door against. He was brought up in a liberal new-idea atmosphere, and new ideas have lost their forbidden-fruit tang for him."

Arthur Goldberg, having for so long represented the labor unions as counsel for the AFL–CIO, would naturally be considered with some suspicion, especially now that he was in a position where he could reach the President's ear. But despite the fact that Goldberg had been the driving force behind nearly every major union gain in the past twelve years, he could hardly be called a "radical." *Fortune* had once bestowed on him the title "Labor's Man of the Year," and Senator Barry Goldwater had described him as "probably President Kennedy's outstanding choice as a Cabinet member." Goldberg was a labor man all right, but one of the things on which his labor reputation rested was his long and most successful fight to help drive the Communists out of the unions. Of his own liberal development in the Chicago labor movement, Goldberg says: "In my youth there were plenty of radicals around, but I was never even a socialist, nor was anyone in my family."

Most businessmen had forgotten that Goldberg had been a lawyer for the unions and not a union official; that he was not a professional labor leader who had come up through the ranks—the kind of man most labor leaders had hoped Kennedy would appoint as Secretary of Labor. It is an open secret that when Kennedy was considering his Cabinet, George Meany presented him with a list of six candidates approved by labor—all elected officials of the big unions. Goldberg was not on the list, and it is generally agreed that he never forgot this snub. It has also been an open secret that

Goldberg's performance as Secretary has not always been looked upon with enthusiasm by top labor leaders. A good many powerful figures in the labor movement have been just as annoyed at Goldberg's intervention in labor-management disputes as businessmen have been, and of course more so when he has had to come down hard on the labor unions, as he did in the steel wage negotiations. In Pittsburgh, just before the steel contract was initialed on March 31, 1961, one prominent labor official was heard to say: "I sure wish Kennedy had put Goldberg on the Supreme Court." And others —many inspired by his vigorous opposition to the shorter work week (one of labor's pet objectives)—were known to feel that "Arthur leaned over backward to show that he was not pro-labor."

One of the men at this meeting who might understandably give some concern to the business community was Walter Heller, a former professor at the University of Minnesota. Heller is a tall, slender professional type whose thick horn-rimmed glasses and tweedy look give him an air of the other-worldly college professor so often mistrusted by businessmen. He has a reputation as a New Dealer and is an expert on public finance and tax policy. He believes in pushing the economy toward a higher rate of economic growth, but is equally concerned about the uses to which the increased growth is put. With Kenneth Galbraith, he believes that increased economic activity should be devoted to improving society—with stepped-up educational, medical and welfare programs—rather than to a self-indulgent scramble for material goods. However, Heller is at best a "mild-eyed liberal" (a term coined by Charles Seib, author of a brief biography of Heller) who does not fit the liberal stereotype at all. He is not an ivory tower academician, his liberalism being much closer to the President's pragmatic variety.

There was also Henry Fowler, long-time liberal Democrat who during World War II had served as assistant general counsel of the Office of Production Management and the War Production Board. During the Korean war he had returned to government service as deputy administrator and administrator of the Defense Production Administration, and later as director of the Office of Defense Mobilization. In 1953 he had resumed private law practice, but as far as businessmen were concerned, Fowler's credentials as a government interventionist were well established. However, it must be remembered that Fowler was representing the Treasury Department, which was headed by Douglas Dillon, a lifelong Republican who had served in the Eisenhower Administration and who would have been Nixon's Secretary of State.

If Henry Fowler worried businessmen, Paul Rand Dixon really scared them. As counsel and staff director of Kefauver's Senate Antitrust and Monopoly Subcommittee from 1957 until 1961, Dixon was known as someone with a long-time interest in the antitrust laws, and it was presumed by businessmen that he had just been sitting and waiting for some excuse to turn loose his antitrust staffers and that this might be it. Still, as chairman of the FTC in an administration as tightly run by the President as John F. Kennedy's, Dixon would probably only go as far as the President directed him to; the real problem was how much of a green light the President would give him. "The statutory authority under which the FTC acts is very broad," Dixon had been quoted as saying when he took office. "We're not antibusiness; we're antitrust. We're antiabuse of economic power and antimonopoly when it's not regulated, antirestraining trade practices, antifalse and deceptive advertising practices. This needs to be said," he added. "Many people think some wild things are going on here, some actions being readied here that will be against the business interest. Far from it. We're trying to free up the business system. Since 1914 when this agency was created, one of its principal functions has been to see to it that business competition in America will stay free and unchained."

Also present at the meeting were two former businessmen, Robert McNamara and Luther Hodges.

When McNamara agreed to come to Washington as President Kennedy's Defense Secretary, he had just been appointed president of the Ford Motor Company, which is hardly a lair of radicals. Admittedly no admirer of old-school labor leaders, McNamara holds a strong business point of view, although an independent one. His personal appearance is deceptive. "You might mistake him for a mathematics professor in a small college," Stewart Alsop once wrote of him in the *Saturday Evening Post*. But behind this appearance is one of the sharpest minds in the Kennedy Cabinet. *Business Week* once described him as a "prize specimen of a remarkable breed in U. S. industry—the trained specialist in the science of business management who is also a generalist moving easily from one technical area to another."

Finally there was Luther Hodges, a former buisnessman who had "retired" eleven years before to run for Governor of North Carolina. He had worked in the textile control division of the OPA during the war, and had had his fill of dictated prices. Not only was Hodges known to favor a minimum of government interference in business, he had also gained a reputation as "antiunion" while Governor, because of a decision to call out the National Guard to maintain order in a textile strike. If Luther Hodges, as Secretary of Commerce, was a "radical," he was probobly the only one in the country who liked to boast that he drove a Thunderbird.

This, then, was the group of men who would soon be directing the Administration's fight with big steel. If the group as a whole had any label, it would have to have been that of the President's—"pragmatic liberal." And if, among Kennedy's closest advisers in the steel dispute, Goldberg, Heller, Dixon and Fowler were considered too liberal by the conservatives, then it could also be said that McNamara, Hodges and Dillon (who would soon be returning from Florida to

take an active part in the fight) were considered too conservative by the liberals.

As the meeting came to order the atmosphere was a little
grim but not depressive, and tempers seemed to be back to
normal. Most of the men had had a chance to read their
morning papers, and the first samplings of editorial and public reaction were encouraging. The *Wall Street Journal* and
the New York *Herald Tribune* were, of course, violently opposed to the position taken by the President. But it is significant that even these two avid spokesmen for business were
cautious in endorsing the wisdom of a price rise in steel at
this time. "Now for our own part," said the *Wall Street Journal,* "we have no way of knowing whether this steel price
increase was a good decision or a bad one for the company . . ."

The *Herald Tribune* was even more disturbed: "The price
rises are regrettable, to put it mildly. Steel's forbearance from
price increases last fall . . . aroused hope for price stability.
And that hope was strongly reinforced with conclusion of the
new contract . . . United States Steel's action shattered that
hope . . ."

There were, however, more than just doubts felt by two of
the nation's leading liberal newspapers which lined up
squarely behind the President. *The New York Times* agreed
with the President that U. S. Steel's action was an "irresponsible defiance of the nation's interests," and the Washington
Post's editorial was headed MR. BLOUGH'S GREAT MISTAKE.
Of the morning columnists most widely read in Washington,
only David Lawrence, to no one's surprise, sided with the
steel companies. Mr. Lawrence called Kennedy's statement "a
severe blow against the sound system of private capitalism in
America" and said that the President had made the "worst
blunder" of his political career. Even Arthur Krock said that
the steel industry's position was "vulnerable" and that it had
invited the President's attack. James Reston wrote a long

and sympathetic column in which, after comparing the steel crisis to the Bay of Pigs disaster, he tried to explain not only the President's anger but his long efforts to make both labor and management more conscious of the public interest. Walter Lippmann, the dean of Washington oracles, virtually lowered the boom on the steel industry, said to be guilty of a "rude" decision made without "anyone speaking for the consumers and for the national interest," although he did attempt to point out that the issue at the "root of the whole affair" was America's declining industrial supremacy, about which something had to be done.

The meeting had just begun when the President entered, clutching a handful of telegrams. Everyone rose, as is the custom, and he was hardly seated in his black leather chair before he let out a mild gripe about James Reston's comparing the steel crisis to the Cuban disaster of the previous spring. He didn't want that idea to get around, and he told the men attending the meeting so. Then the President pushed his handful of telegrams across the huge Cabinet Room conference table. "We're way ahead," he said, commenting that the telegrams were running 2½ to 1 in favor of the White House action.

He began to give orders. First he wanted to make sure that public opinion was kept favorable. He instructed the key Cabinet men to hold press conferences within the next couple of days and to emphasize what the steel price increase meant to their departments, to the nation and to the people. It was decided that McNamara would hold a press conference on Friday and that Dillon would hold one on Saturday.

U. S. Steel had announced that Roger Blough would hold a press conference at 3:30 that afternoon, and the question of how best to answer Blough was discussed. It was finally agreed that the Administration would submit a rebuttal to Blough and as quickly as possible. The man elected to give it was Luther Hodges, who had a previously scheduled luncheon engagement in Philadelphia. It was decided that Hodges would go to New York immediately after his luncheon and hold a press conference at 5 P.M.

The President made it plain that he wanted all his Cabinet members on record as being opposed to the price rise, and that he wanted every man, woman and child in the country to know what the rise meant to the individual American. He also made other assignments: A fact book was to be issued as soon as possible, containing the Administration's arguments against the need for a price increase; a special report from the Bureau of Labor Statistics was to be prepared. The pressure was also to be kept on the remaining members of the steel industry who had not raised prices; they were to be painted as shining examples of business virtue.

The President did not remain at the meeting for more than fifteen minutes; he had to attend another meeting with the Shah of Iran. When he left, Sorensen took over. The details of the Government's counterattack were discussed. It was agreed that the Justice Department would be the principal offensive force for the Government. The Federal Trade Commission was instructed to leave most of the action to the Justice Department, which was felt to be in a better position to act and to have had a little more experience in carrying through the kind of attack planned. Two approaches to the Justice Department's investigation were decided upon: (1) to investigate collusion in price fixing; and (2) to study the extent to which U. S. Steel had become a monopoly endangering the national interest.

The question of using Defense Department procurements as a wedge against the price rise was also discussed. The Secretary of Defense felt there was a limit to how much shifting of defense orders could be done without endangering the defense program. It was McNamara's feeling that although some defense contracts might be shifted to companies holding the price line, the basic idea was not practical; boycotting the big steel producers would be risky. Still, it was agreed that Defense officials were obliged to seek the lowest possible prices for materials purchased for the national defense with the taxpayers' dollars.

Another idea discussed was a tariff reduction which would encourage foreign steel imports, the idea being that lower tariffs and increased steel imports would force the big producers here to rescind the price increase. However, it was generally agreed that this was a vindictive approach and that the influx of great amounts of foreign steel would also hurt the steelworkers who had, after all, acted in good faith during the wage negotiations. This idea was completely abandoned. The idea of emergency wage and price controls never came up.

It was agreed that legislative investigations on the Hill should be encouraged, but it was felt that there would be little chance of the investigations doing much short-term good. They might produce a law which would prevent such an incident happening again in the future, but this would be a long-run gain and not much help in the present crisis.

The meeting finally broke up around 9:30. The mood was generally optimistic, but not one of overconfidence. Although the line had broken and a parade had followed, there was still hope that if enough pressure was brought to bear, the companies which had not raised prices could be persuaded to hold the line. If this was done, it was felt that the rest would break, although at least one important figure at the meeting felt that the steel companies would stand together. The men scattered to their offices, where they set about carrying out their assignments—including a continuation of the telephone blitz to contacts in the steel industry.

One important call to the business community that Thursday morning was made by Arthur Goldberg to Roger Blough. It had been suggested by the President and arranged the night before on the Korda-Bartlett "line." The conversation was strained and awkward with neither side knowing exactly what to say. It ended in an impasse, but later in the morning, at the suggestion of steel officials, a meeting was arranged by the President to take place that afternoon in Washington between Robert Tyson and Secretary Goldberg.

As the morning wore on, Andy Hatcher made public the tabulation of the first 500 telegrams which had been received at the White House—they were running, as the President had said, 2½ to 1 in his favor. It was also becoming apparent that the editorial reaction around the country was firming up on the side of the Administration. Of 68 newspapers and columnists monitored, 40 sided with the President, 16 with the steel companies, and 12 took a neutral position. Again it is significant that even among those papers which supported U. S. Steel's act there was considerable skepticism as to the wisdom and timing of the move. However, U. S. Steel did have its hard core of defenders such as columnist David Lawrence, who kept up his own running battle with the Administration not only during the entire steel crisis but long into the aftermath period.

On the other hand, the papers and columnists supporting the President were equally vocal and less inclined to hedge on their position. And they seemed to carry a consistent theme to the effect that the action of the steel companies was deliberate and that it presented the President with a challenge he could not ignore. "The sudden confrontation of Big Steel against Big Government," said the *Christian Science Monitor*'s Acting Business Editor George H. Favre in a relatively neutral editorial, "can scarcely be described as anything less dramatic than a throwing down of the gauntlet. And this fist of iron is entirely bare of velvet . . . Big Steel has chosen to deliberately antagonize the President. It has issued a challenge which the industry's leaders must have fully expected he could not and would not ignore, unless they are guilty of gross underestimation of the Kennedy Government."

However, it was left to the St. Louis *Post-Dispatch* to cut, as it so often does, to the heart of the issue, coming as close as any editorial that day to explaining the volatile reaction of the Administration; "It looks very much as if the steel masters used the President and his Secretary of Labor, who happens to have been the steelworkers' own agent in the 1960 settlement, for the purpose of beating down wage demands prior to a price decision they had in mind all along."

Despite the storm clouds gathering in Washington and despite the evidence that public opinion was slowly swinging with the President, the big steel companies were not daunted. Two more announced a $6-a-ton price increase on Thursday —the National Steel Company (which made 7 of the big twelve in the parade) and the Pittsburgh Steel Company. Thomas E. Millsop, Chairman of the Board of National, said: "There can be no doubt that the several increases in costs since the last price increase in August of 1958 abundantly justify even greater price adjustments than are now being made."

Pittsburgh's statement took a slightly different direction. "For several years," it read, "in order to meet competitive market conditions we have been forced to sell our products at price levels which, by any standard, would have to be considered inadequate."

Another company—the Alan Wood Steel Company—said it was still studying the situation. However, from the company president's statement it was obvious which way the pricing wind at the Alan Wood was blowing. "We feel price adjustments are overdue," said Harleston Wood. "As a relatively small producer, we have felt the profit squeeze increasingly throughout the last four years and are much concerned with the added costs of the current labor agreement."

If the gathering storm in Washington did not prevent additional steel companies from announcing price increases, it did have one effect: on Wall Street the stock market slumped to a new low for 1962, with steel leading the retreat. U. S. Steel, on 54,000 shares sold, was down 1⅛ at 67⅜. All during the morning and early afternoon Thursday, Wall Street was astir with rumors that Roger Blough was going to announce a retreat at his press conference, which contributed considerably to the unusually shaky market.

Meanwhile Blough himself was doing a little sounding. Thursday morning he called Secretary Dillon in Florida to get his reaction to the situation. Dillon argued that the timing of the price increase was extremely poor and that its effect on the industry would be bad.

This effect, as a result of the Government's response, was already proving harmful. By Thursday morning the Government was in action all along the front. At the Justice Department, a group of lawyers who had worked on the Government's case until 10 P.M. Wednesday were back at their desks early Thursday and kept at it all through the day. At the same time FBI agents were beginning to show up at the offices of steel producers with subpoenas requesting information and a look at the files. The eight companies that had received subpoenas were: Armco, Inland, U. S. Steel, Bethlehem, Republic, Jones & Laughlin, Youngstown Sheet & Tube, and Wheeling Steel. All of them except Armco and Inland had announced price increases.

From the Treasury Department there were still hints that another look would have to be given to Bulletin F—which would contain the revised procedures for tax write-offs and depreciation schedules. This was necessary, Treasury officials maintained, because of the prospect of increased Pentagon spending of a least $1 billion as a result of steel price increase. The problem now, they hinted, was whether the Treasury could afford the tax losses which would result from the liberalized depreciation allowance schedules and tax write-offs. The allowances would cost the Government an estimated $25 million. At the same time, if Congress passed the Administration bill giving investment tax credits to companies that modernized their equipment, it would cost the Government another $100 to $125 million. Even friends of the tax legislation agreed Congress would probably hesitate to pass this legislation now.

At the Pentagon it was being said that the Buy America Act's preference for domestic companies contains several exceptions that might be used if it was decided to buy more foreign steel.

For instance, one section of the Act removes restrictions when it is determined that the cost of the domestic product "would be unreasonable or that its acquistion would be inconsistent with public interest." The word was also out that the Pentagon would make an announcement Friday concerning steel, and the speculation was that two alternatives were being considered: (1) to persuade companies which had not raised prices to hold the line by promising them a larger share of defense orders; (2) to urge defense contractors to use more foreign steel. There were, however, obvious limitations on this second alternative, because of the fact that any large-scale purchasing of foreign steel would only aggravate the balance-of-payments problem.

At noon Secretary Hodges was just arriving at the Drexel Institute in Philadelphia, where he was to address a luncheon group before going on to New York. In his speech he denounced price-fixing and unethical business conduct which undermines confidence in the free enterprise system. Immediately after lunch, he left for New York, where he would give the Administration's answer to Roger Blough's afternoon press conference.

CHAPTER 6

Thursday Afternoon, April 12: Roger Blough in the Teeth of the Storm

Let us pause briefly to observe that a "free" society is not a synonym for a "free and easy" society. A more apt description would be a "free, responsible, and responsive society"—one in which individuals, bonded together as a nation, are at once possessed of freedom of choice, a personal sense of respect for the rights of their fellows, and an abhorrence of compulsion in mutual affairs—a society in which individuals are responsive to the changing boundaries of thought, of culture, and of conscience.

—Opening words from a series of lectures, "Free Man and the Corporation," given by Roger Blough before the Columbia University Graduate School of Business in 1959

One disquieting development for the steel industry was the fact that so few people in positions of power had rushed forward to defend U. S. Steel. The Republicans, to whom big business normally turns for support, had been unusually silent on the question of the price rise, and when a Republican voice did speak out it usually managed to avoid the basic issues. For instance, Representative William E. Miller of New York, Chairman of the Republican National Committee, at a news conference Thursday afternoon issued a statement denouncing Attorney General Kennedy for sending FBI agents out in the middle of the night to question private citizens. "This is reminiscent of the days of Hitler when the German people lived in fear of the knock on the door in the middle of the night," Miller said. Congress should act, he demanded, "to see that the irresponsibility of the Attorney General's office is not used to promote totalitarianism in America . . ."

Although the business community no doubt appreciated Miller's blast and very likely shared his views, the fact that his statement completely avoided the issue of the price rise itself was handwriting on the wall. And there had been more handwriting earlier in the day when the Senate and House Republican leaders—Senator Everett M. Dirksen and Representative Charles Halleck—held their weekly news conference. They cautiously suggested that the Kennedy Administration was "looking in the wrong place for the basic cause of inflation." Said Dirksen: "The Kennedy Administration not only is setting records as the biggest spending administration in peacetime history, but has been red ink ever since it took office. Apparently everybody is supposed to make sacrifices except the New Frontier spenders." Recalling that the President had sent twenty-four messages to Congress already that year, Mr. Halleck said: "We would like to suggest a twenty-fifth presidential message. It would call for a cut-back in non-defense spending. It would not only help stem the threat of inflation but would be applauded by all Americans who are filling out their income tax returns for April Fifteenth."

Most reporters covering the "Ev and Charlie show" went back to their typewriters and wrote that Republican leadership was bending over backward to keep from being drawn into the fight. "This is an economic, not a political, issue"— a quote by Mr. Halleck appearing in almost every account of the press conference—could mean only one thing: as of Thursday, the Republican Congressional leadership sensed that the voters were siding with the President against the steel companies, and had decided that the wise thing to do was either remain silent or take a stand against the Kennedy tactics, which most Republicans had already done anyway.

One Republican voice to speak out on the basic issue was that of Senator Roman L. Hruska of Nebraska, who said: "I don't think any elected official has a monopoly on letting this nation progress. Even private citizens have concern about this—a good deal of concern." These were the kind of words the steel industry wanted to hear, but Senator Hruska stood virtually alone. Republicans seemed to have lost their tongues. "The whole matter should be studied," Representative Thomas Curtis, of Missouri, said cautiously. "Until we have the facts, I suggest we lay off politics." And in Michigan, George Romney felt that the President's indignation was understandable. "Time after time when the public interest is threatened," Romney said, "the Government has felt it necessary to negotiate between monolithic employers and monolithic unions. We will not escape these predicaments which sap our strength in the world struggle until we deal with the root of the evil—excessive concentration of power."

The way most Republicans—especially those running for office in 1962—felt was more accurately summed up the next day by syndicated columnist William S. White, known to Washington as a conservative Democrat. "If Big Steel thinks the Republicans like its policy," wrote White, "let Big Steel privately ask any major Republican officeholder. If Big Steel wants the Republicans to carry the congressional elections in November, let Big Steel ask Republicans today how they see their chances in the wake of a price increase . . . This correspondent can tip Big Steel off, for a fact, that it is about as popular today in the Republican Party as would be an outbreak of measles."

However, by Thursday afternoon Big Steel did not need to be tipped off. From two Republicans running for public office in November, Roger Blough received an eyebrow-lifting telegram: Representative William W. Scranton and James van Zandt, candidates for the gubernatorial and Senate nominations in the Republican primaries in Pennsylvania, wired

U. S. Steel that "the price increase at this time is wrong—wrong for Pennsylvania, wrong for America, wrong for the free world. The increase surely will set off another round of inflation. It will hurt the people most who can least afford to be hurt."

By Thursday afternoon, when Roger Blough was preparing to meet the press and the nation, it was becoming more and more evident—even to the steel community—that the country was being aroused against big steel. On the floor of the Senate that day, Senator Dirksen had said that a great company like U. S. Steel "is entitled to have its day in the court of public opinion." U. S. Steel was having its day all right, but it was not turning out exactly as it had hoped; there must have been more than one U. S. Steel executive who thought, Thank God, we don't have too many days like this—in the court of public opinion or anywhere else. As the national anger began to mount—aroused in part by the President's televised news conference and in part by the reaction of the press—steel executives could only read these words of Columnist William S. White and grudgingly admit their accuracy: "The great community of American business in general is in no way to blame for Big Steel's decision. But it would be wise to make that point very clear. Big Steel has elected to stand alone; let it so stand, very plainly before the public gaze."

Big Steel was preparing to stand alone before the public gaze, and the man it had chosen for this critical assignment was Roger Blough. "By midmorning Thursday," said *Business Week* of the decision to make Blough the spokesman, "steelmen were intrigued with the news that Blough would reply to the President in a televised press conference. From the standpoint of a polished performance, quite a few of them would have preferred any of several other men. But in steel, the chairman of the corporation has got to be the industry spokesman—at least as inflexibly as the sun must rise in the east."

If the steel industry was run by a set of cold, inflexible rules, then it was primarily because the rules were made by a group of men often considered just as cold and inflexible. And in many ways Roger Blough is considered the prototype of today's big steel executive. Unlike most of the leaders in the generation preceding him, Roger Blough did not come up through the rough and tumble of the steel mills. He is a Yale graduate lawyer who first came to the attention of U. S. Steel's former president, Benjamin Fairless, when Blough led a team of twenty lawyers defending U. S. Steel against the monopoly charges of a congressional investigating committee. This was in 1939, and Blough was thirty-five years old and a lawyer with the Wall Street firm of White and Case. Blough impressed Ben Fairless, who commented that Blough was "thorough, tenacious, and had the ability to dig below the surface." Three years later Fairless brought Blough aboard as general solicitor for U. S. Steel. Blough soon knew the company inside and out and for ten years he served in Pittsburgh, helping to organize the far-flung corporation into a system of divisions centering around a strong central authority. In 1952, Fairless created the special post of vice-chairman of the board and Blough moved to New York to fill it. He became, in Fairless' words, "my right bower," and three years later when Fairless retired, Blough moved into the top spot. The company maintains that Blough was hand-picked by Fairless, but rumors still persist that Blough was brought from Pittsburgh with the help of Wall Street interests who had had a long-standing feud with Fairless.

At any rate, since 1955, U. S. Steel has been headed by one of the most controversial men in the industry. Blough has an army of admirers such as Sidney Weinberg, senior partner of Goldman, Sachs & Company, who says, "He's my idea of a real Supreme Court judge"; and Irving Olds, former U. S.

Steel chairman, who says that "Blough was one of those fellows who turn up no more than once in ten years."

But there are others who feel that Blough is more difficut to fathom. "He's a man you don't get to know much," says David McDonald, head of the United Steelworkers. "He stays in an ivory tower." Another union chief has been quoted as saying: "He's a cold fish and I sometimes think he's just unable to make a decision." A high government official who gives Blough top marks for his work in restoring the effectiveness of the business advisory council after its tiff with the Administration, says, "He certainly can be charming, but he turns it on and off." The most oft-quoted remark about Blough is that more than anything else he seems like a "warm, likable IBM machine."

Regardless of his merits as a corporation head, it was generally agreed that Blough was not the man to take on President Kennedy in a debate about steel prices—a fact which was perhaps substantiated Thursday afternoon at the U. S. Steel press conference.

Before Blough went on the air, he received a telephone call. Earlier in the day, Robert Roosa, Undersecretary of the Treasury, and Dixon Donnelley, one of Secretary Dillon's aides, were speculating as to whom they might call in the business community who might be able to get through to Roger Blough. They first hit on Bernard Baruch, but when Roosa put through a call to Baruch it was learned that he was out of town. They then decided to call Alfred Hayes, head of the Federal Reserve Bank of New York, and Henry Alexander of the Morgan Guaranty Trust, a member of the board of U. S. Steel. Roosa outlined the President's position and urged these men to see what they could do to make Blough reconsider. At least one of them did get through to Blough before his press conference, and it is felt by at least one of the participants in the dispute that this last-minute call had some effect on Blough, possibly even restraining his comments on the air—although Blough maintains that his decision to be restrained had been made on the previous evening.

The press conference itself was held in the small ground-floor auditorium at U. S. Steel headquarters and it was reported in the press with considerable contempt by several newspapermen. "It's just like a Hollywood première," one wire-service reporter muttered, trying to make his way through the maze of television cables and wires in the long narrow room.

More than a hundred press and radio-TV reporters were packed into the small room and the confusion was made worse by the fact that U. S. Steel officials had insisted that all bags be searched—New York police, they said, had ordered it because of the fear that someone might be carrying a bomb.

President Kennedy was having a busy afternoon at the White House. He had lunched with the Shah of Iran until almost 3, and other business kept him busy until 4. At 4:15, General Lucius Clay arrived for a conference, but the President did not seem disturbed at having to miss the broadcast. When someone asked him if he wanted to listen to Blough, he snapped back, "I don't need to listen to him." But virtually everyone else at the White House did. In the pressroom, reporters clustered together around the battered old TV set in the corner; Ted Sorensen watched Blough from his office, and Hatcher from his. And just to make certain that the White House would have the complete record, the Army Signal Corps taped the complete radio version.

In New York, Secretary Hodges arrived at the University Club at 3:40 P.M., ten minutes after Blough had gone on the air. While Hodges shaved and changed his shirt, his assistant William Ruder tried to take notes on the radio broadcast (there was no television set in the room), but was not very successful: the Manhattan static was so bad as to make listening virtually impossible. At the same time, another task force from the Commerce Department was also in operation; this one in the Department's field office on the 61st floor of the Empire State Building. A row of stenographers was organized in front of a radio and instructed to take one question and answer apiece and transcribe them immediately. At 3:30 the stenographers braced themselves, pencils poised —but their radio also gave forth a steady squawking. Fortunately, a third Commerce Department task force attended the conference in person, so at least one set of notes was available to Hodges.

Blough opened his show with an unemotional reading of a 1,500-word reply to the President. Combined with the answers to the reporters' questions which followed, it stands as the best public explanation U. S. Steel offered in defense of its sudden price rise:

> When the President of the United States speaks as he did yesterday [Blough began] regarding our Corporation and its cost-price problems, I am sure a response is indicated and desirable.
>
> Let me say respectfully that we have no wish to add to acrimony or to misunderstanding. We do not question the sincerity of anyone who disagrees with the action we have taken. Neither do we believe that anyone can properly assume that we are less deeply concerned with the welfare, the strength, and the vitality of this nation than are those who have criticized our action.
>
> As employees and stockholders, we along with thousands of other employees and stockholders, both union and nonunion —must discharge faithfully our responsibilities to United States Steel; but as citizens we must also discharge fully our responsibilities to the nation. The action we have taken is designed to meet both of those responsibilities.
>
> One of the nation's most valuable and indispensable physical assets is its productive machinery and equipment, because its strength depends upon that. I among others share the responsibility of keeping a portion of that plant, machinery and

equipment in good working order. To do that our company, like every other employer, must be profitable. The profits which any company has left over after paying its employees, its other expenses, the tax collector, and its stockholders for the use of their resources, are the main source of the plants and equipment that provide the work that thousands of workers now have. Had it not been for those profits in the past, the millions with jobs in many varieties of business would not have those jobs.

But that machinery and equipment must be kept up to date or no sales will be made, no work provided, no taxes available and our international competitive position, our balance of payments, our gold reserves and our national growth will seriously suffer.

None of us is unaware of the serious national problems and no one is unsympathetic to those in the executive branch of government attempting to conduct the affairs of the nation nationally and internationally. But certainly more rapid equipment modernization is one of the nation's basic problems as outlined by Secretary of the Treasury Douglas Dillon.

Speaking before the American Bankers Association last October, he said: "More rapid equipment modernization by industry is vital to the success of our efforts to remain competitive in world markets and to achieve the rate of growth needed to assure us prosperity and reasonably full employment. I think it highly significant that all the industrial countries of Western Europe—except Belgium and the United Kingdom—are now devoting twice as much of their Gross National Product to purchases of industrial equipment as are we in the United States. And Belgium and the United Kingdom—the two European countries whose economic growth has lagged in comparison with the rest of Western Europe—are devoting half again as much of their GNP to the purchase of equipment as are we."

What this all means is that as a nation we keep ahead in the race among nations through machinery and equipment, through good productive facilities, through jobs that are vitally linked to the industrial stream. Surely our workmen are as good as any in the world, but they must have the tools with which to compete. In other words, we compete as a company, as an industry and as a nation with better costs and better ways of production.

Proper pricing is certainly part of that picture and that is what is involved here, however it may be portrayed. For each individual company in our competitive society has a responsibility to the public as well as to its employees and its stockholders to do the things that are necessary pricewise, however unpopular that may be at times, to keep in the competitive race.

Now, may I say several things with respect to any misunderstandings that have been talked about?

First, the President said, when questioned regarding any understanding not to increase prices, "We did not ask either side to give us any assurance, because there is a very proper limitation to the power of the Government in this free economy." Both aspects of this statement are quite right. No assurances were asked and none were given regarding price action, so far as I am concerned or any other individual connected with our corporation. Furthermore, at least in my opinion, it would not have been proper for us, under those circumstances, to have had any understandings with anyone regarding price.

Second, I have said a number of times over the past months that the cost-price relationship in our company needed to be remedied. As recently as February sixteenth, while the labor negotiations were going on, I referred, in an interview, to the steadily rising costs which we had experienced and I said, "And you're asking me how long that can continue to increase and how long it can be borne without some kind of a remedy? I would give you the answer that it is not reasonable to think of it as continuing. In other words, even now there should be a remedy. If any additional cost occurs, the necessity for the remedy becomes even greater." This very real problem has been discussed in recent months with a number of individuals in Washington, and I am at a loss to know why anyone concerned with the situation would be unaware of the serious deterioration in the cost-price relationship.

In this connection, President Kennedy, in his letter of last September sixth addressed to executives of the steel companies, said: "I recognize, too, that the steel industry, by absorbing increases in employment costs since 1958, has demonstrated a will to hold the price-wage spiral in steel." I am sure that anyone reading the reply that I made on September thirteenth to that letter could not infer any commitment of any kind to do other than to act in the light of all competitive factors.

Third, it is useful to repeat here that hourly employment costs have increased since 1958 by a total of about twelve percent and that other costs have risen too. The net cost situation, taking into account employment and other costs, has risen about six percent since 1958. All this is without regard to the new labor contract. When costs keep moving upward and prices remain substantially unchanged for four years, the need for some improvement in the cost-price relationship should be apparent.

Fourth, in view of the cost increases that have occurred, the thought that it costs no more to make steel today than it did in 1958 is quite difficult to accept. For U. S. Steel costs since 1958 have gone up far more than the announced price increases of yesterday.

Fifth, higher costs at the same selling price obviously mean lower profits. Our own profits of five-point-seven percent on sales in 1961 were the lowest since 1952.

Sixth, the increase of three-tenths of a cent per pound in the price of steel adds almost negligibly to the cost of the steel which goes into the familiar, everyday products that we use. Here, for example, is the amount by which this price change would increase the cost of steel for the following items:

Automobiles	
Standard size	$10.64
Intermediate size	8.33
Compact size	6.83
Toaster	.03
Washing machine—wringer type	.35
Domestic gas range—4-burner	.70
Refrigerator—7.7 cu. ft.	.65
303-size food can	.0005

Seventh, it must be remembered that the process by which the human needs of people are met, and the process by which jobs are created, involve importantly the role of the investors. Only when people save and invest their money in tools of production can a new productive job be brought into existence; so our nation cannot afford to forget its obligation to these investors. Nor can we, in United States Steel—who are responsible to more than three hundred and twenty-five thousand stockholders—forget the many Americans who have a stake in our enterprise, directly or indirectly.

Over half of our shares are held by individuals in all walks of life; and no one of these individuals owns as much as two-tenths of one percent of the total stock. Most of the rest is held by pension funds, insurance companies, charitable and educational institutions, investment companies and trustees representing the direct or indirect ownership of large numbers of people in America.

I have touched upon a few matters here in the hope that those who are so seriously concerned with these things—and the public at large—will recognize that there was nothing irresponsible about the action we have taken. My hope is that this discussion of our responsibilities, as we see them, will lead to a greater understanding, and a more thoughtful appraisal, of the reasons for that action.

Blough finished his statement, paused for a moment organizing his papers, then said: "Now, gentlemen, I'm ready for your questions." The reporters' questions were sharp and biting, and the atmosphere crackled with hostility. It was obvious that, as far as the attending reporters were concerned, Mr. Blough and U. S. Steel were on trial and it was up to Blough to provide the defense. He did the best he could, but his performance was certainly no match for the one given by the President the previous day.

A complete transcript of the press conference follows:

Question: Mr. Blough, you say that no commitment was asked or given during the wage negotiations, regarding a price increase. And yet, at your joint news conference with Mr. Mc-Donald, he, speaking first, mentioned the noninflationary nature of the agreement, and the newspapers, radio and television played that as the biggest feature of the agreement.

I am wondering if you can tell us why there was no denial at that time or in this week that is past, on your part, that an agreement that an increase was intended.

Blough: Well, Mr. Cronkite, I do not think that Mr. Mc-Donald was talking about the agreement that had just been concluded; that he was referring in any way, shape, or form to the price of steel.

There wasn't any occasion, therefore, to make any denial. You might have a slight difference of opinion with Mr. Mc-Donald, as to whether a two-and-a-half percent cost increase, which is required by the new agreement, is inflationary or noninflationary. That gets you into quite a discussion.

In our opinion, the output per man hour of steel that we have experienced since 1940 is about one-point-seven percent, which is considerably below the two-and-a-half percent required by the contract.

Question: In the face of the competition that steel is facing, not only from foreign competition, but from other commodities in this country, commodities which are competing with you on price, how can you justify to the stockholders the increase in price in steel at this time?

Blough: I thought that my statement pretty well explained that.

Question: That explains the increase in profits, sir, that you seek to achieve. But do you not run a risk of a distinct loss in volume?

Blough: In my statement I said you become noncompetitive. Your costs are higher if you have insufficient prices to provide the machinery and equipment that is necessary to remain competitive.

Our problem with respect to foreign competition is certainly a very serious one. There is no question that the plants and equipment abroad are, in many cases, the equal of ours and that we are having quite a difficult time from the standpoint of foreign competition. There is no question about that.

But if you do not provide the new plant and equipment that is necessary to keep up with that foreign competition, you are going to fall behind in the race much further than you have. Now, I pointed out in my statement that Mr. Dillon said that, in many of those nations they were providing two times the amount of their Gross National Product that we are providing in this nation to provide the plant and equipment that is necessary to compete.

That is the serious problem that our nation faces, and that is the reason you have got to have sufficient prices to provide some profit which can, in turn, be plowed back into that machinery and equipment.

Question: Mr. Blough, you say in your statement that no assurances were asked by the Federal Government, and none was given by U. S. Steel, regarding price action. How, then, do you account for the intense reaction by President Kennedy to your price increase?

Blough: I quoted from President Kennedy's statement, in response to a question in which he said that he hadn't asked for any assurance from us. I think that is a sufficient support for my statement.

Question: You, here today, as I understand it, are defying the President of the United States in his request yesterday. What are your views in general on the White House role in the steel labor negotiations, and the price dispute? Do you think the President has been acting in the public interest?

Blough: Well, now, first let me correct your preamble to your question. I am not here today in any sense defying anyone. I would like to make that perfectly clear. I am here today explaining the cost-price situation in which we found ourselves and why we took the price action.

With respect to the action of the White House in connection with labor matters, I would say that I think that is a matter that can better be handled by the White House than by me. I have no criticism. I do believe that when the air clears a little bit, I think we will all realize that this type of, shall I say—assistance?—has some limitations.

Question: Have you been served with a subpoena to appear before a U. S. Grand Jury investigating matters relating to steel?

Blough: My understanding is that the company has been served with a subpoena to produce some papers, but I haven't personally been served with any subpoena to appear before the Grand Jury.

Question: If some price rise was a necessity, why weren't the Government and the union made aware of this need?

Blough: Well, I tried to make perfectly clear in my opening statement that I personally have been talking about this sort of thing for a long time. I wonder if you will recall that last September there appeared to be a thought on the part of some people that some company in the steel industry might increase its prices.

You recall what happened there. Letters were exchanged between the President and the steel companies, with respect to that matter. Without indicating the effect of the exchange of the letters, it would seem to me that that might serve as additional evidence that there was a serious cost squeeze so far as the steel companies were concerned.

Question: When did the company's executive committee, sir, approve the price increase; and was the actual decision made before the signing of the labor agreement with Mr. McDonald?

Blough: The decision to have a price change?

Reply: Yes, sir.

Blough: It was authorized by the executive committee Tuesday of this week—Tuesday afternoon.

Question: In view of your own statement about the urgent need to modernize in the face of foreign competition and the possibility that steel production will drop this summer, would you accept a public commission study of the merits of your cost-squeeze case, to report back by September first, we'll say?

Blough: Well, if I understand your question, you are asking whether we would accept some sort of an independent study as to the merits of our situation?

Reply: Yes, sir.

Blough: Well, I don't know under what circumstances that study would be made. There have been a number of considerations of that kind in the past. I really believe that it is quite important, in the kind of a society that we have, that individual companies in as highly competitive an industry as we have—and in every industry for that matter—should make their own price decisions.

Question: Mr. Blough, all the major industries, the textile industry, for example, have been the first to receive depreciation tax relief. And of course it has a great rate of obsolescence, and that may be explained. Could you tell us whether this decision would affect the textile industry adversely, and would you give us some estimates of what a heavy piece of capital equipment, like a loom, might cost?

Blough: Well, I am sorry, I am not very well versed on the textile industry. I know of nothing in connection with this steel matter that would, in any way, affect the textile industry.

Question: Can you foresee any changes in the tax laws or any changes in depreciation allowances that would permit you to reconsider the price rise?

Blough: Well, all I can say is that this problem that is related to pricing is a continuous thing. All the factors that are involved in decision-making are taken into account time after time over many years.

Now, if there are changes in the tax laws that are beneficial from the standpoint of depreciation, which is certainly something that is needed, that would be, for sure, a factor that would be taken into account, of course.

Question: The President seems to have been quite upset at the way he was informed. Do you feel, in the light of what has happened since then, that perhaps you could have given him a little more advance notice than you actually did?

Blough: Well of course I am quite concerned with the President's concern. In the kind of an economy that we have, I am not quite sure that it is feasible for anyone to be going to the White House to consider a price increase, even as important a one as this. Now, I would like also to say that I am not sure it would have been the right thing to do under all the circumstances.

Question: The President said in his news conference yesterday, the six-dollar-per-ton cost rise may add a billion dollars to our defense budget. Will you comment on this, please?

Blough: Yes, I'd be glad to! I am not sure how this estimate is made up. I am sure that, so far as direct steel sales to the Defense Department is concerned, that the total tonnage, estimating it any way you wish, to all subcontractors and everybody else—even if 1962 is an extraordinarily large year for purchases by the Defense Department—it could not amount to more than, say, three or three and a half million tons.

Now, those are the direct and indirect purchases, and that, of course, would be, oh, something in the nature of twenty million dollars. And where the "billion dollars" comes from, I don't know, unless someone made a projection that this in some way would extend to other things.

I should point out, in connection with that, this price increase in steel isn't the only price increase that has occurred in the American economy. There have been quite a number, and there have been a number of price reductions, just the same as there have been price reductions in steel, so this question of movement of price is a very volatile thing.

Question: Are we to understand, sir, from your statement, that the only possible way a price increase could have been averted would have been through a new contract that substantially reduced your employment costs, and if so, did you mention this to Mr. McDonald during the negotiations?

Blough: I think Mr. McDonald stated that he did not discuss prices with us, and that's certainly the fact! And we should not be discussing prices with the union.

Question: Mr. Blough, in view of your stressing the need to modernize your plant and in view of the fact that United States Steel's capital expenditures dipped a hundred and fifty million from 1960 to 1961, what plans does United States Steel have for the purchase of capital equipment, and particularly of machine tools in the coming fiscal year?

Blough: I can answer that by saying that will depend entirely on our earnings. If our earnings are up, we will purchase more capital goods.

Question: And when will that decision be made, sir?

Blough: As the earnings improve!

Question: Mr. Blough, would you care to comment on the statement made earlier today in a wire-service dispatch which quotes a government attorney saying this action by United States Steel has overtones of violations of two sections of the Sherman Antitrust Law?

Blough: Well, I don't know what he is referring to, if he made that statement, and I would question the statement.

Question: Sir, the justification for the price increase you have just given us—do you feel that applies equally to the increases announced by the other steel companies?

Blough: The other steel companies will have to speak for themselves.

Question: Mr. Blough, in view of the comments made regarding foreign competition during the labor negotiations in which United States Steel made several major speeches regarding the element of foreign competition, could you explain it to those of us who don't understand these things very well just how you meet competition by raising your price?

Blough: You don't meet competition by having a facility produce a product that can't compete, costwise, with the imports. You've got to have a facility which can compete costwise. Your problem, as I have tried to explain before, is to have enough to buy the machinery and equipment to make the kind of products, to make the quantities of them that will enable us, costwise, to get the business which, in turn, provides the employment.

Question: Well, some of us have a problem here. United States Steel sells twenty-seven percent of the total steel products; it seems unlikely that you would take the risk of raising your prices without some confidence that competing firms would do the same thing, and we are wondering, was there an understanding to this effect among the steel companies, or United States Steel's competition—

Blough: I can understand this simply—no understanding of any kind!

Question: Some significance has been attached to the fact that the steel companies, in 1960, did not raise prices under a Republican administration. Could you comment on that?

Blough: Well, I think you gentlemen can readily see that I do not know anything about politics! [Laughter]

Question: Was the alternative of selective price increases over a long period of time ever considered in lieu of any across-the-board increase that you have gotten?

Blough [after having the question repeated]: The answer is yes.

Question: You said that the decision to increase prices was made Tuesday, and yet you had indicated, quite a long time previous to that, that this cost situation that you faced was severe, and I am wondering what was different on Tuesday that wasn't different—that wasn't the situation—say, a week before, that made you make this decision on Tuesday. Was it the labor settlement? What bearing did it have?

Blough: There were—there are always a number of factors. Bear in mind that we had additional employment costs increases last October first—in fact, some in September! Now, we had experience with that quarter, final quarter of last year, and we had further experience this year. This was a decision that was—that involved many, many factors. There is no single factor that's involved in it.

Question: Mr. Blough, is it correct—and if it is—is it correct that foreign competition in steel in this country amounts to only about one week's production of the American steel industry, and if so are you determined on this price issue to remain on a collision course until the Government is forced to take some action that will be detrimental to all business?

Blough: Well, first, let me explain the second part of your question. This is an effort on our part to improve our cost-price relationship. At the moment, it's—I have no knowledge whether it will continue, or whether it won't continue, because it will depend on what our competition does, primarily.

As to the foreign competition that you mention—the size of it—I made a little calculation some time ago. Bearing in mind that we are losing markets abroad, as well as having increased tonnage coming into this country, the total difference in, say 1961, over our foreign competition picture compared with, say five or six years before, would mean a difference of five or six million tons of ingots. Now that, as has been previously stated, would represent as much as forty thousand jobs, so this question of competition from abroad is a very serious one.

Question: Mr. Blough, you have said that you need increased profits in order to modernize your plants. Many corporations, however—including public utilities—when they want to expand their investment, issue new shares of stock rather than tax the consumer through higher prices. Why do you choose this route rather than seeking new equity capital in the corporation?

Blough: Well, let me say that we have been required to borrow, since 1958, about eight hundred million dollars. Now, whether we borrow the money from investors and pay it back, or sell stock to them and try to improve our facilities from the proceeds of that stock, is a question of management choice.

The point I make is that we have gone outside for a great deal of the money we have needed, and I must say that, if you borrow money, you've got to have the cost-price relationship that will give you enough profit upon which you pay the taxes, and after having paid the taxes, then you return the money that you borrowed—and we intend to do that.

Question: Mr. Blough, would the administration's pending proposal for accelerated depreciation on new plant expenditure —on new plants—help you in your situation, and if so to what extent?

Blough: Well, there are a number of features in the proposed tax bill, as you know, and if the bill should become law and if that particular feature is in the law, then—to the degree that we'd be able to take advantage of it—it would be helpful. But there are a number of ifs connected with any tax bill, including the amount that the new tax bill would cost us which, in turn, might offset to a degree, or to a large degree, any benefit that you would get from the particular provision that you spoke of.

Question: Mr. Blough, you said in your statement that your letter of September thirteenth—anyone reading your letter of the thirteenth—quote, "could not infer any commitment of any kind to do other than to act in the light of all competitive factors." Could you tell us how the competitive situation for such steel products as structural steel or tin plate or concrete re-bars or wire and cable, which are suffering intense competition and which have had price weaknesses has changed since September thirteenth so as to require any price increase?

Blough: Well, since September thirteenth I think the entire economy has improved. And when the economy improves, the demand for steel increases, and one of the ways that the economy improves is when plant and equipment and all the other things that you talk about are purchased by people that have enough funds to purchase them. That's what helps build up economy. Now, in my view, the economy is in an improved condition today, compared to last September.

Question: Mr. Blough, some representative from the Government said your actions had been taken by a, quote, "wholly irresponsible handful of people"—handful of steel executives. Would you reply to this?

Blough: I tried to explain, I thought, that our action was taken responsibly.

Question: Mr. Blough—one thing, Mr. Blough! There is still talk nevertheless, sir, in Washington, that the increase—coming as it did right on the heels of the labor pact—was timed to check expanded government influence in collective bargaining; in other words, that you acted politically as well as economically. Could you comment on that?

Blough: Well, I tried to explain, before, that I knew nothing about politics, and I have given you all the reasons why we had to change our—

Question: There was no political motivation, sir?

Blough: I don't know what more I can say about that!

Reply: Thank you, sir.

Blough: I am sure that the answer to your question is, there is no possible, conceivable political motivation that I would know about. I don't believe that I would even know how to operate in that area.

Question: Some expectation has been expressed that foreign competition and the substitution of other materials might force a revision in this price schedule. Has your executive committee made any estimate of the extent to which foreign competition and the substitution of other materials might cut into the gains that you anticipate from this price increase?

Blough: It was one of the considerations that we took into account.

Question: And have you determined—

Blough: And, you understand, there is nothing sure about being in business! The competitive situation, today, is a different one than it was yesterday or tomorrow. The type of analysis that you are required to make all the time is a fundamental one. Under all the circumstances as we saw them, we thought this was the advisable thing to attempt to do.

Question: Have you resolved what you think the net gain will be in a year's time?

Blough: I haven't any findings to give you.

Question: Mr. Blough, as of the time of the start of this press conference, Armco and Inland Steel—the two major producers —as well as the larger specialty producers Ludlum and Crucible, have not yet raised prices. If they don't go along, how long can you stick to your price increase before you rescind? Or would it affect you?

Blough: It would definitely affect us, and I don't know how long we could maintain our position.

Question: Would it be a matter of days?

Blough: I wouldn't want to state a specific number of days.

Question: But if they don't follow within a reasonably short period of time, you would expect to have to rescind, at least on some products, then?

Blough: It would make it very difficult for us!

Reply: Thank you!

Question: There have been a lot of people who fear this move by United States Steel may lead to further government regulation of all industry in the United States. Have you taken this into consideration when you made your price rise?

Blough: I saw no reason to think that any change in the price of steel would lead to government regulation. I still see no reason for that to happen.

Reply: There are those who may disagree, sir!

Question: Mr. Blough, for the last—more than a year—the inflationary psychology which has gripped most of the economy has been pretty well dampened down. There is considerable fear, now being expressed, that your increase in the price of steel will touch off a new rise, a new wave of inflationary psychology. How seriously did you take this national problem into consideration in making your decision?

Blough: Well, we considered everything connected with the price change, and I doubt very much whether what you say will happen, and I'd like to explain why. Our problem in this country is not the problem with respect to prices; our problem is with respect to costs. If you can take care of the costs in this country, you will have no problem taking care of the prices. The prices will take care of themselves.

Question: Mr. Blough, what was the labor cost of a ton of steel in 1958, and what is it in 1962?

Blough: Well, some tons of steel take a certain number of man hours, and other tons of steel take other man hours, and if you are talking ingots, it's one thing, and in any event I don't know that I have a specific figure to give you. But I am sure of one thing—that the employment costs which, at the end of 1961 were four dollars and ten cents an hour—now, that's the average employment cost for the industry, about four dollars and ten cents an hour—

Question: Per hour?

Blough: . . . on a per-hour basis was—

Question: What is the cost per ton?

Blough: It was up. I would say forty cents over what it was in 1958.

Reply: On the hours!

Question: You dispute the President's figures on unit costs and on profit. I wonder if you have any theory as to how he could have gotten hold of figures that, in your opinion, are so far off base?

Blough: No, I don't have any theory.

Question: In that connection, if I could follow up—since there is a dispute between the President's economists and yourself over the costs of a ton of steel, would you then agree to open up to a congressional committee or some other public body, the data on which you arrive at your estimates, so that the public may make some judgment on this matter?

Blough: First of all, the discussion about the cost of a ton of steel means very little. If you look at the return which the industry has made year by year, or U. S. Steel has made year by year, you will see that, taking into account all the costs on all the tons of steel, the result has been going downhill. Now that ought to be a satisfactory answer.

Reply: It isn't, sir. I'm sorry.

Question: What reaction have you received from the metal-working industry throughout the country to your price hike? Have you received any immediate reactions from the big two auto manufacturers, and the little three?

Blough: I personally have had no contact with the auto manufacturers, and I don't know what their reaction is. As to others, I am sure there are many who think that the price change was all right. There would be some people who would feel otherwise. That happens every time.

Question: Would you give us the details of this subpoena that was served on U. S. Steel, and whether or not U. S. Steel would welcome an investigation by the antitrust subcommittee of the Congress and by the antitrust division of the Justice Department?

Blough: Well, I don't have the details of the subpoena. In fact, I don't think I have seen it. But so far as welcoming investigations, I don't believe it is going to make much difference whether we welcome the investigations or not.

Question: The first three months of the year are over. Could you give us any idea of what U. S. Steel's profits will look like for the first quarter, from here on, as compared to last year? And to what extent is that profit picture related to the action taken on prices?

Blough: Well, as I think you know, we only discuss our profits for the quarter at the quarterly meeting. But I can tell you that our profits for the first quarter are far from satisfactory.

Question: Mr. Blough, you indicated that you didn't inform the President at an earlier date for certain circumstances. Will you please indicate what those circumstances were?

Blough: I am not sure that I follow your question, sir. Would you repeat it?

Question: The question before was: Why wasn't the President acquainted with the situation of the price rise in an earlier period of time? And you said you didn't, because of some circumstances. I wondered if you would indicate some of those circumstances.

Blough: I think you must have misunderestood me.

Question: Then I will repeat the question: Why wasn't the President informed of this at an earlier date?

Blough: The President was informed of the price rise in what I hoped was as courteous a manner as could be devised under all the circumstances.

Question: Were you surprised at the reaction of the President, Mr. Blough?

Blough: I think the answer to that should be that I was.

Question: Can we pursue this a bit further? [The] U. S. Steel Corporation, I think, prides itself on good public relations. Was any consideration given, prior to the announcement of the steel price increase, as to how to best cushion the effect on the public and on the Government?

Blough: Mr. Worthington, as you recall, put a release out that stated the reasons for the price change, and I would like to commend to you all that you read that release. It contains a lot of valuable and interesting information, and I believe that some of the problems that we have had, with respect to the price change, would not have occurred if people had taken the time to read that release.

Question: The President's Council of Economic Advisers' analysis shows that, while U. S. Steel profits have dropped the last four years, the profits of the other seven major steel companies have remained about the same. How do you explain that?

Blough: Well, I am not familiar with the analysis. I would like to say one other thing. We have been going about, almost an hour, and although I would be very happy to see you gentlemen on other occasions—and I hope that invitation doesn't get me into too many conferences with you—I would like at this point, if you are willing, to terminate the questions.

Reply: One other question, Mr. Blough—

Blough: I would like to finish, thank you.

The reporters were still clamoring for more questions, but Blough persisted in cutting off the interview. It was all over. Big Steel had presented its case, and there was nothing to do but sit back and await the reaction.

When it came it was not very good. Mary McGrory, for instance, writing in the Washington *Star,* described Blough's performance as "colorless," adding that "Mr. Blough conveyed the impression that he was a country boy far from home." *Time* called it "too late, and too little." Murray Kempton, writing in the liberal New York *Post,* commented that "nothing in Blough's performance . . . would indicate that he is guileful enough to contrive the confusion that passed through the industry on Wednesday while U. S. Steel's competitors were deciding that the way to save competition was to raise their prices too. . . ." However, the hardest criticism of all to swallow came from a friendly quarter: "Having seen Blough's hour-long inquisition," said *Business Week,* "Pittsburgh quite frankly was critical. It hadn't expected Blough to match Kennedy as a performer, but it had expected the best possible case for the industry—and quite a few men simply don't believe they got it."

To make it worse, Blough had provided the first public hint that Big Steel might crack. His statement that U. S. Steel would definitely be affected if Inland and others did not go along on the price rise, was duly noted by everyone: to Blough's supporters, it was morale-shaking evidence that Big Steel was weakening; to his competitors, it was a sign that the price rise was not going to stick; and to Administration officials in Washington, it was the first public evidence that a victory was possible. Of course, in fairness to Blough it should be said that the remark was very possibly a deliberate one; the dropping of the ladder from which, if necessary, U. S. Steel could eventually climb down from the limb.

Actually, the question of Inland and Armco and others which had not announced a price increase was beginning to worry the leaders. By Thursday night, the holdouts should have joined the parade, and Roger Blough and U. S. Steel officials knew it. However, what very few people outside the inner sanctum of Inland Steel knew was that sometime during the day on Thursday, Philip Block and two other Inland officials had reached a decision not to raise prices. They had called Joseph Block in Japan to discuss the matter with him, and all hands agreed on holding the line.

At this point an interesting mix-up occurred which was to contribute to the drama of the following day. After Inland officials in Chicago had agreed over the telephone with Joseph Block that there would be no price increase, there was a discussion as to whether or not to hold a meeting of the board of directors to confirm the decision. Joseph Block said that it was not usual to hold a board meeting to discuss price matters, but that he would leave it up to the men at the home office. However, when he hung up he was under the general impression that no board meeting would be held and that

Inland's decision would be announced immediately. But in Chicago, Inland officials decided they would hold the board meeting Friday morning and delay making the announcement until after the meeting.

At 5 P.M., a half hour after Blough's conference ended, Secretary Hodges held his press conference in the Empire State Building. There was an added significance to Hodges' appearance. It should be recalled that when President Truman siezed the steel mills in 1952, his Secretary of Commerce, Charles S. Sawyer, did not agree with the decision and did everything possible to obstruct the President's move. Although Kennedy's 1962 battle with the steel industry cannot be compared to Truman's seizure of the steel mills (which was eventually declared unconstitutional), it is significant that Kennedy had the complete support of his Cabinet—including his "spokesman" for business at Cabinet meetings, the Secretary of Commerce.

Hodges began by reading a brief statement in which he said he was shocked at the action of the steel companies and explained again the President's reasons for opposing the price increase. (See Appendix C.) During the questioning, Hodges insisted that during the wage negotiations a promise had been implied by the steel companies not to raise prices. "I believe the President felt that the price line would be held if wages did not rise," said Hodges, adding that he was sure the public also had that impression. To illustrate, he said: "I will tell you a personal experience. Night before last, Mrs. Hodges heard me talking on the telephone during the night and she asked me the next morning what was going on. I told her I had been conferring on the announced rise in steel prices. She exclaimed: 'But they said they wouldn't!' "

"I believe the reaction of most people was that," said Hodges.

He also discussed the inflationary spiral and the tax credits which new legislation would give the steel industries—$35 million to U. S. Steel alone, plus an additional $10 million from the liberalized depreciation allowances. Hodges said that "any firm or industry is free to set prices as it sees fit," but added that "it is free to make mistakes, and I believe the steel industry's mistake is a tragic one. It's action is a disservice to the country and to the business community as a whole." As a former businessman, Hodges said, "I am confident that the business community as a whole is disturbed by this development." The price increase, he said, was ordered by a "handful of men who said in effect that U. S. Steel comes first, the United States of America second." Hodges also dropped a thinly veiled threat that the steel company's action could lead to a change in the economic philosophy and program of the Kennedy Administration.

Although Hodges' press conference was to be the Administration's answer to Blough, for the most part it was ignored by the press. Much of what he said was completely lost in the rush to report Roger Blough's show, and only a few papers carried more than a quote or two of Hodges'.

Meanwhile that afternoon, wheels were turning within wheels as Robert Tyson and Arthur Goldberg kept their scheduled meeting. Tyson, Hal Korda and some U. S. Steel officers had flown down to Washington early in the afternoon, and rather than meet in public, sought privacy in a Washington hotel, miraculously managing to avoid any contact with the press. However, the meeting itself was a long-drawn-out and fruitless session during which Tyson and Goldberg more or less went over the same ground covered in the public debate between the President and Blough. Goldberg did present several courses of action designed to ease the tension, but all of them were rejected by Tyson. By the time the meeting ended—somewhere between 5 and 6 P.M.—it was evident that both sides had reached a serious impasse.

*   *   *

For most Administration officials involved in the steel case, the day was coming to a close, but in the Pennsylvania Avenue offices of the Justice Department the lights were still burning. Earlier that afternoon Paul Dixon had held a press conference in which he said that the FTC was standing by to "give every cooperation we can to the Justice Department." The word was around, however, that the Justice Department and not the FTC would be primarily responsible for pressing the Government's antitrust case, and at 7 P.M. Attorney General Kennedy made it official. He announced that he had "authorized a Grand Jury investigation into the steel price increases . . . in New York City." He also said that the Justice Department was studying U. S. Steel to determine whether the corporation "so dominates the industry that it controls prices and should be broken up."

Just before issuing his statement, Robert Kennedy shed further light on his investigations in some remarks to a group of visiting Fulbright professors. "There are two questions we are interested in," he said. "One is whether the steel companies got together and agreed to raise prices. If they did, that would be a violation of the law, and they would be subject to criminal penalties. The second question is, if one company, namely U. S. Steel, so dominates the industry that it controls prices and should be broken up."

In a celebrated case, the electrical equipment industry had already been found guilty of price-fixing, but perhaps the pattern was different in the steel industry. Perhaps the power of U. S. Steel was so great that there was no need for industry leaders to get together; it was simply a matter of follow the leader. In which case, so Justice Department lawyers argued, U. S. Steel was becoming too big for the national welfare. "U. S. Steel has powers equally as broad as some of the utilities, perhaps greater," a top Justice Department official told a Washington correspondent. "They should be regulated or broken up." As for breaking up U. S. Steel: "It's a tough law-suit," said this official, "but I believe it can be done."

Such was the thinking at the Justice Department in the heat of the crisis. And considering the closeness of the President to the Attorney General, it must be assumed that the President concurred in the ultimate objectives of the Justice Department investigations. And also considering the well-known tenacity of the Attorney General—displayed first in his crusade against Jimmy Hoffa, and later in his enforcement of the civil rights laws—it must be assumed that once the Government was committed to the investigation, it would be pursued with the usual Kennedy "vigah."

While the Justice Department was pushing ahead on its investigation, a far-reaching proposal for regulating prices in major industries was being prepared by Walter Reuther, President of the United Auto Workers. That night Reuther mailed to the White House a letter, the contents of which were made public earlier in the evening. Reuther proposed the establishment of a price board which would hold hearings before such price increases as U. S. Steel had announced could be made. Under his plan, price leaders in all major industries would be required to give advance notice of proposed increases and to produce all pertinent facts at a public hearing which must be held before such increases could become effective. Reuther said that labor unions, under his plan, would also be required to defend their collective bargaining demands in the same public hearings if a corporation held that the demands of the union would require a price increase. In his letter Reuther also condemned the U. S. Steel price increase. "I am confident, Mr. President," he wrote, "that you have the full support of the American people behind your effort to defend the attack on price stability—the economic Pearl Harbor—perpetrated by the United States Steel Corporation."

By the time Robert Kennedy was meeting with the Fulbright professors at the Justice Department, the President was getting ready for another dinner with the Shah of Iran and his wife—this one to be held at the Iranian Embassy. While he was dressing, he was interrupted by the telephone several times—once to receive a report on the impasse reached that afternoon by Tyson and Goldberg. However, the President still felt that something might be gained by further talks, and at this point the President decided it might be a good idea to try someone other than Goldberg.

The man the President decided on was Clark Clifford, a Washington corporation lawyer who had once been President Truman's Chief Counsel. The President put through a hurried call to Clifford, and then went to the dinner, arriving at the Iranian Embassy with the First Lady around 8:15.

Clark Clifford was just sitting down to his dinner when the telephone call came from the President. Kennedy outlined the problem and pointed out the importance of holding the price line. He said that the cornerstone of his Cold War policy was a stable economy; that the cornerstone of a stable economy was a stable price level; and that the cornerstone of a stable price level was the price of steel. He also told Clifford about the Tyson-Goldberg meeting and asked Clifford whether he would be agreeable to talking with Tyson. Goldberg, said the President, was known to the steel companies primarily as an adversary, and he thought it might be wise to get someone who was known to the steel companies in a different light—someone who might develop a rapport.

Actually, Clifford was an excellent choice. He is a tall, handsome man whose personality and general bearing help him to be a very persuasive negotiator; at the same time, he is known as one who can be extremely firm without offending the person he is trying to persuade. Clifford was well known to both business and labor leaders, and was trusted and respected by both. As a White House adviser in 1946, it was he who had recommended to Truman that the Government

should threaten to draft railroad strikers into the Army unless they went back to work. Later, when John F. Lewis led
the coal miners into a strike in which the miners demanded
54 hours of pay for a 40-hour week, it was Clifford who urged
Truman to fight Lewis to the finish, arguing that if the
Government gave in one inch that it would touch off a wave
of strikes all over the nation. Although these acts put him
in good standing with the business community and alienated
some labor leaders, Clifford showed that he was not antilabor
by his strong fight, the following year, against the Taft-
Hartley law. His later associations with Senator Symington
during the Senator's unsuccessful bid for the Democratic
Presidential nomination had drawn him even closer to the
labor movement. However, his corporation law practice,
which he resumed in 1950, had also brought him into close
contact with the business and financial communities.

Clifford said that he would be happy to do what he could,
and the President said he would call back in a few minutes,
after he had talked with Tyson's group again. In about five
minutes a White House aide called Clifford and said that
Tyson would like very much to talk and that he was ready
now. It was then about 8 P.M.

Still anxious to avoid any publicity, Tyson's group said
it would prefer to meet on its private plane, which was parked
at the National Airport. Clifford agreed, and after hastily
finishing dinner, he drove out to the airport where he was
met in the Butler Aviation Building by Hal Korda. Korda
took Clifford out to U. S. Steel's plane, and he met Robert
Tyson for the first time. After a few brief amenities, Tyson
and Clifford settled down for a long talk which Clifford
estimates to have lasted about two and a half hours. Clifford
presented himself to Tyson as a friend of both sides, but made
it clear that he was in complete agreement with the President.
He said his purpose was to see if a tragic mistake could be
rectified, but he felt the mistake had been made by U. S.

Steel. For fourteen months, he said, the President and Mr. Goldberg had tried to create a healthy climate in the steel industry. They had worked to create an atmosphere of cooperation and mutual trust in the hope of promoting the national interest, but U. S. Steel's act had shattered all that. In addition, said Clifford, the President felt that there had been a dozen or more occasions in the months preceding the price rise when the company's leaders could easily have told him that, despite everything, the steel industry still might have to raise prices. Clifford said that the President felt he had been double-crossed.

Tyson then presented steel's side of the picture, arguing essentially in support of Roger Blough's position that there had been no commitment to hold prices down. Finally Tyson got around to saying that "we have made an irrevocable decision." At this point Clifford said that although he had enjoyed the meeting very much, he could hardly see any point in prolonging it. He said quite frankly that he had come out to try to persuade Tyson that U. S. Steel had made a wrong decision—for the company, for the economy and for the nation—but that if steel's decision was irrevocable, there was very little else to be said. Tyson did say that maybe something short of revoking prices could be worked out, and they discussed briefly the idea of a fact-finding committee which might be set up to study the President's charge that the steel industry did not need a price rise at this time. At the very end of the meeting Clifford told Tyson that if he thought his presence in this matter would be helpful, he would be ready to continue the conversations at any time, but added that it must be on the basis that no position is irrevocable—either on steel's side or the Government's. Tyson agreed with this, and it was further understood that if there were any future conversations that Arthur Goldberg would also participate.

Clifford drove back to his home and put through a call to the President. It was then after 11 P.M. He reported on the talks, and they both agreed that the picture looked rather dismal. Clifford described the note on which the conversation had closed and said, "I will be exceedingly interested in their next move. If they make no move to see us, then it means we have just been spinning our wheels—but if they show signs that they want to talk, that will be very significant, because I said there was no point in further discussions if either side's position was irrevocable."

Tyson flew back to New York and went directly to the Park Avenue apartment of one of U. S. Steel's officials. Most of the top brass of U. S. Steel were present, and the meeting quickly developed into an intense discussion of the situation and the day's developments. If there was any single turning point in the steel crisis, it probably came at this meeting. By now, U. S. Steel was fully aware of the President's anger and convinced that the Administration meant business. Although it had been somewhat surprised at the extent of his reaction, there had still been a reluctance to believe that it was anything more than a little added sound and fury for the benefit of a political audience. Now these officials knew better. Even more important, however, was the fact that Inland had not announced a price rise, and by this time the U. S. Steel group suspected that Inland would probably not go along. They also knew that if Inland did not go along, Bethlehem would rescind its increase and the line could not be held.

The discussion lasted until around 2 A.M., and by the time it broke up it was evident that Big Steel's girders were wavering. Inland's failure to move and the storm gathering in Washington were beginning to rock the foundations of a mighty industrial empire.

CHAPTER 7

Friday, April 13: Big Steel Caves In

> If we had raised our prices and Inland's stayed put, Inland would have moved so deep into our territory we'd have to put a moat around our plant in Middletown [Ohio] to keep them out.
> —*Logan T. Johnson, President of Armco Steel Company*

The first thing Friday morning—about 8:30 A.M., according to Clifford—the President called him and said: "Clark, that ray of hope you were looking for may be coming through the clouds. I've just talked to Roger Blough and he says it might be valuable if the conversations continued."

Both men felt that this was extremely encouraging. Since it had been agreed that Arthur Goldberg would be included in the next round of discussions, it was decided that Clifford would await a call from Goldberg as to the exact arrangements. A little while later Goldberg called Clifford and said they would fly to New York that morning to continue the talks and that he had made arrangements for an Air Force plane to take them. Clifford was to go to his office and await a call from Goldberg.

Meanwhile, in the midst of keeping his secret diplomacy going, the President also had his hands full restraining some of his own lieutenants from doing anything which might destroy the conciliatory mood he was trying to create. For instance, all during the steel crisis the National Broadcasting Company had been trying to arrange for Walter Heller and

Robert Tyson to appear on the *Today* show. Tyson, it must be said, was not very anxious to participate, but Heller, feeling that the Administration's case was irrefutable, was ready to go, and a "debate" had actually been scheduled for Thursday morning. However, the President felt that once the two men were brought together, no matter how much restraint was shown on both sides, it could not help but harden the attitude of both parties. So Thursday morning's program was canceled on the grounds that Heller was too busy.

NBC continued the pressure, trying now for a Friday appearance, and even went so far as to use the old trick of trying to get one participant (Tyson) down to the studio by telling him that the other participant (Heller, who was home in bed) was already on his way; then calling the other participant (Heller) and telling him that the other participant (Tyson) was already there. This was foiled by Tyson's waiting in a drugstore across from the studio while an aide reconnoitered, followed by a hasty series of phone calls on the communications "line" which had been established between New York and Washington. Thus a possible widening of the breech was avoided, and just as well, because Thursday afternoon's talks between Goldberg and Tyson had ended in a complete impasse, with both sides showing signs of stiffening. Further hot blood—especially in a public debate—might well have been a serious obstacle to Kennedy's behind-the-scenes diplomacy.

As *Business Week* put it: "On Friday, life in the price-boosting properties suddenly became tough as a week in jail." And it was indeed "Friday the 13th" as far as the steel companies were concerned.

The first news to jolt the price-boosting properties was a report from Kyoto, Japan, that Joseph L. Block had decided not to raise Inland prices. The word had gotten around as a result of an exclusive interview with Block by Keyes Beech, an overseas correspondent for the Chicago *Daily News*. Beech, who was also in Japan, had called Block late Friday afternoon about another matter. During the conversation Beech asked about the price situation, and Block—thinking that the decision had already been announced by his Chicago offices—said that Inland did not plan to raise prices. Beech asked if he had permission to wire his paper, and Block said certainly, but pointed out that it was late Thursday night in Chicago and that the decision had been announced that day.

Beech sent the story in anyway, and as a result, when Inland's board members met first thing Friday morning to discuss the price increase, they all had copies of the *Daily News* announcing Joseph Block's desicion not to raise prices! "Even though steel profits are not adequate," Block was quoted by Beech as saying, "we do not feel that an advance in steel prices at this time would be in the national interest." Block had added: "You don't negotiate steel prices with the labor unions, but in this case it must be pointed out that the union was asking the lowest wage increase in postwar years."

The story was widely circulated in the more than seventy-one newspapers that carry the *Daily News'* foreign service. Incidentally, Beech got quite a round of applause from his subscriber papers. "Beech gave us a jump on all the fast-breaking steel developments Friday," said New York *Post* Executive Editor Paul Sann. "It could well be that the story out of Tokyo turned the whole price trend around." This, of course, was somewhat exaggerated, but the story certainly jolted the business community. The word from Japan, which spread through government circles and the steel community with brush-fire speed, was the first indication that a major company was going to hold the price line. "This is a real bombshell," said one executive. Another steel official, quoted in *Business Week,* said: "If Inland didn't move, we were all dead."

Later that morning Inland headquarters in Chicago made it official. The decision had been ratified by the company's board, and an announcement was made that Inland definitely would not increase prices at this time "in full recognition of the national interest and competitve factors. It is untimely to make any adjustment upward."

Word of Inland's announcement first reached the President on the White House steps as he was saying good-bye to the Shah of Iran. When he was told the news, he said simply, "Good! Good! Very good!"

With Inland's position now official, all eyes—and ears—in the industry were turned toward Middletown, Ohio, home of Armco Steel, the nation's sixth ranking producer. If Armco—which had still not joined the parade and which had been strangely silent—held the line, things could get sticky indeed. (Pittsburgh recalled that it was Armco which had led the rebellion against U. S. Steel in 1958, when for the first time in nearly a decade U. S. Steel had not led the price increase upward. After waiting for a month for U. S. Steel to act, Armco had simply raised prices itself—a move which the rest of the industry ultimately followed, including U. S. Steel.) For about five hours Friday, Armco President Logan T. Johnson was under pressure from all sides before events taking place elsewhere in the industry finally took the spotlight off him.

The Kaiser Steel company had also failed to follow the leader. Out on the West Coast, Edgar Kaiser had been as silent as Armco; if Armco was unpredictable, well—Kaiser Steel was a veritable maverick. Pittsburgh did not have to be reminded that it was Kaiser Steel which had broken the steel industry's solid front against the United Steel workers in 1959 by signing a separate agreement with them before the major steel companies had come to terms. It was obvious that Friday was going to be a day of hedging statements and evasive comments while businessmen nervously waited to see what the steel industry would do and the steel producers waited to see what the big boys would do. On Wall Street everything was confusion. During the week, stock prices had plunged to their lowest level since mid-July 1961; sales were sluggish and everyone was tense. Rumors were everywhere. The most persistent one was that Roger Blough would resign. "Blough's going would have a kind of logic to it," one Wall Street pundit was quoted as saying. "It would symbolize a final peace with government, a final clearing of the air." U. S. Steel's headquarters, however, officially denied the rumor. One ranking executive said that Blough was "only fifty-eight years old and has seven good years to go," suggesting that no one is ever asked to leave U. S. Steel until his retirement age.

When word of Inland's decision not to raise prices reached the Street, Inland's stock jumped two points while all other steel companies remained off. "I could kiss Joe Block," said one Wall Streeter in his enthusiasm over the first break in the tension. But the prevailing note was still one of caution as the market waited to see what other companies would do. The market experts were not getting much to go on. The heads of at least two major steel companies decided to drop out of sight. One answered, "No comment" when asked what his company intended to do about its prices; the other said he had no comment "on anything." At about mid-day Leonard C. Rose came out cautiously with the statement that while his company (the Colorado Fuel & Iron Corporation) had to consider a price increase in light of rising production costs, it was "studying each of our products to determine the feasibility of specific price changes in the light of market conditions." This suggested that *if* CF&I moved upward with its prices, it would be on a selectively rather than on an across-the-board basis, as U. S. Steel had done.

A. S. Glossbrenner, President of Youngstown, told an Associated Press reporter in Pittsburgh that "only time will tell" whether Inland's decision would lead his company to cancel its price increase. And in New York, R. S. Reynolds, Jr., President of the Reynolds Metal Company, primarily an aluminum producer, took special pains to explain his statement made in Richmond, Virginia, on Wednesday. "I made the observation," he said, "that industry cannot continue to have rising costs without increasing prices. This was intended as a statement of general principle applicable to the aluminum industry. By no means should it be interpreted as passing judgment on the justification of a price increase in the steel industry." It looked as if U. S. Steel's support, even in friendly quarters, was beginning to fall away.

Although the early morning word from Joseph Block in Japan had sent a shock wave through the steel community, it was business as usual at the White House—and the business Friday morning was to continue the war against big steel, regardless of what Inland did. At 10:15 A.M. a meeting held in Ted Sorensen's office was attended by Solicitor General Cox and representatives of the Treasury, Commerce, and Labor departments; the Budget Bureau and the Council of Economic Advisers. The primary purpose of the meeting was to discuss the three kinds of legislation that Cox and the rest of the group felt should be considered. The three approaches were: (1) *ad hoc* legislation limited to the current steel situation; (2) permanent legislation imposing some types of restraint on wages and prices in the steel industry alone; and (3) permanent legislation for steel and other basic industries, setting up "fact-finding" procedures. Final decision as to what kind of legislation would be submitted—and whether *any* legislation would be submitted—was put off until a meeting soon to follow, which would be attended by the President.

While Sorensen, Cox and the other Administration officials were meeting, Secretary McNamara was also in action. At 10 A.M. the Pentagon had released its long-awaited statement on procurement, announcing that "where possible, procurement of steel for defense production will be shifted to those companies which have not increased prices." It also made reference to the balance-of-payments crisis which, McNamara emphasized, would be made even more critical by the steel price increase. (For full text of statement see Appendix D.)

At 11:45, McNamara held a press conference in the office of Arthur Sylvester, Assistant Secretary of Defense for Information. It was a crowded session, and although usually the Secretary's morning briefings are for background only, this one was on the record. After apologizing for the crowded conditions, McNamara read the 10 o'clock statement, noting a few changes which had been made. (The statement printed in the Appendix has the changes incorporated.) When he finished, he said: "I unfortunately have to leave here in seven minutes, but I will be happy to answer such questions as you must have."

The first question was: "What percentage of steel could you buy from companies which so far—" which the Secretary cut off before it was completed, and anticipating its essence, replied that he could not answer the question directly but that the matter was being studied. McNamara was then asked—in reference to his statement that we could not maintain our forces overseas if our trade balance did not improve: "How, in the interest of national security, can we help but maintain our forces overseas?"

McNamara replied: "This is a problem. We cannot maintain forces overseas unless the flow of gold, or the adverse balance of payments which leads to a flow of gold, is changed. That adverse balance cannot be corrected without an increase in our exports or the net trade balance, the difference between exports and imports. We cannot expect a favorable movement in our trade balance if our prices rise and particularly if they rise faster than the price of foreign competitors."

The reporters continued with a question obviously designed to elicit a statement by the Secretary of Defense, suggesting that U. S. Steel's price rise might indirectly result in bringing home Americans from overseas: "Mr. Secretary, do you have any estimate of how many people you would have to pull back from overseas?"

McNamara said: "No, I have no estimate. I will say quite frankly that I hope we won't have to pull back people from overseas, but we cannot run an adverse trade balance of the type that we have in the past two or three years indefinitely. It is perfectly clear that this would be impossible. The military operations abroad are contributing substantially to that adverse balance of payments; a net or rather a gross foreign exchange outlay of about three billion dollars is associated with our present overseas deployment. It is that overseas force deployment, and its associated cost of three billion, that cannot be maintained unless our balance improves."

The next questioner asked whether the Secretary felt, as a former head of a large corporation which purchased great quantities of steel, that the action by U. S. Steel was unwarranted or unjustified.

McNamara did not hedge on that one. "I stated," he replied, "that I consider in my judgment the price increase was an unjustified development, and I state that based on both my experience here and my experience in industry."

He then declined to answer three questions pertaining to the Defense Department's purchase of steel, after which a reporter asked him about a subject which had been receiving considerable comment in the press and with which many financial commentators had taken issue—his estimate that the steel price increase would cost the government $1 billion. "Can you say, sir," a reporter asked, "how you arrived at that estimate of a billion dollars?"

McNamara replied: "Yes, I will be happy to discuss it with you. I don't know that we have time now. It is based on the fanning out of the price increase throughout the remaining portion of the economy. This has been the experience in the past—I hope it will not be the experience in this instance. If the fanning-out process takes place, we can expect roughly a three-and-a-half percent increase on the bulk of our costs. The primary items not affected would be the personnel costs, the military personnel, and civilian personnel assigned to the Department."

Next question: "Even considering the gold outflow problem, are there any circumstances under which the Defense Department would consider the purchases of steel abroad at an advantageous price?" McNamara replied that that problem had not been faced, but added that the Administration did not wish to contribute to the unemployment problems already troubling our nation.

The last question was whether there was any plan to stretch out weapons' procurement to offset the rise in cost.

McNamara said: "No, there is no such plan, but it is a good question and one we will eventually have to consider, because we are operating within fixed appropriations. If our costs rise, we have two alternatives—to the Congress requesting supplemental appropriations, or . . . stretching out production as you have suggested."

The Secretary then added: "I regret having to leave you now. I know I am leaving a large number of unanswered questions, but the schedule for today is a little crowded, unfortunately." This brought a chuckle from reporters.

The reason for McNamara's hasty departure was that he had to attend a White House follow-up conference to Thursday morning's council of war. He hurried to the White House and arrived just about the time Sorensen's meeting with Cox and the others was breaking up. Sorensen immediately went into the second meeting, which was attended by most of the same group present at Thursday morning's session—including the President. Conspicuously absent, however, was Arthur Goldberg, off on his mission of diplomacy with Clark Clifford.

The President opened the meeting by saying that "it is very important that we not take any action that could be interpreted as being vindictive"—a reaction, possibly, to the cries of anguish already being heard in the business community.

The meeting was primarily a follow-up of Thursday's. Each Cabinet official reported his progress thus far and commented on the latest developments, especially on the soundings from the telephone campaign. There was a faint note of optimism in the air because of Inland's decision and because the Administration was by now pretty certain that Armco would not raise prices. During the meeting, word came from the West Coast that Edgar Kaiser had also announced that his company would not raise prices. This meant that companies producing close to 16 percent of the nation's steel had now officially held the price line.

However, the President's task force still felt that U. S. Steel and the other large producers were not ready to give in, and preparations were made for a long struggle. Lists of directors of the companies holding the price line were distributed, and each man was asked to call anyone on the list he knew. On this note the meeting broke up. The President was soon to leave for Norfolk for his long-scheduled review of the Atlantic Fleet; the rest of the men went back to their telephones.

The importance of these calls cannot be underestimated. They were not something each official did in his spare time or when he could get around to it. They were an organized, strategic, integral part of the Administration's campaign, with everyone who knew anyone in any position of responsibility in the business world calling him to emphasize the President's position and to find out which way the wind was blowing. Just who made what calls and how many were put through during those three days is virtually impossible to say. "Not even the President himself could retrace all the contacts that have been made in the past seventy-two hours," said one Administration official late Friday. Defense Secretary McNamara, for instance, spent virtually full time personally calling friends and contacts from his business days. Through these calls, the

Government men were able not only to emphasize repeatedly how angry the President was and how much importance he attached to price stability, but were also able to assess the business community's reaction to the sudden and surprising price rise. For instance, the dialers discovered that important segments of the business community were far more opposed to the increase than they had been willing to say publicly. Similarly, a director of one steel company told an Administration caller that U. S. Steel's move was "the worst thing that could have been done."

By Friday morning it was becoming more and more evident that public opinion had fairly well crystallized behind the President. The many and varied public-opinion indicators were beginning to give their readings, and there was overwhelming proof that the mood of the nation was decidedly against big steel. On Friday morning *The New York Times* published excerpts from the nation's editorial pages: 17 decidedly favored the President, while only 7 sided with the steel companies. Significantly, even the 9 papers which took a more or less neutral position seemed to feel that the wisdom of the steel companies' action was questionable, even though they might have had the right to do what they did.

Friday's editorial reaction continued to run in the President's favor. Of 17 newspapers and columnists surveyed for Friday, 11 favored the President; 5 sided with the steel companies; and 1 was neutral. As was to be expected, the most violent criticism of the President's reaction was to be found in the conservative Republican press.

The New York *Mirror,* for instance, concluded that "the President's economic advisers are attempting to subordinate the significance of profits, which means that an investor in an enterprise not only risks the dangers of faulty management, but also of Government policies, sound or unsound. Wise investors, who even today rarely net as much as they would get if they left their money in a savings bank, would, under such conditions, withdraw their funds from corporate enterprises, which not being able to meet the strain, would fall back on the Government for assistance. "The next step," predicted the *Mirror*, "could only be nationalization of industry, which would produce a police state similar to that of Nazi Germany, Fascist Italy or Soviet Russia."

Donald I. Rogers, financial columnist for the New York *Herald Tribune*, saw the President's reaction in a different light—as primarily the result of his uncontrolled Irish temper. "It's pretty easy for any but a blind man to tell a cart from a horse," wrote Rogers in his Friday morning column. "Mr. Kennedy's fury at the steel industry for its inflationary price increase is a reaction of a man who is so mad that he can't tell the difference. The steel price increase is the result of the inflation that has already occurred, and been masked in recent months, rather than the cause of any future inflation."

However, these voices were in the minority. More typical were the comments from *The New York Times* and the Washington *Post*, which concentrated their Friday editorials on Blough's Thursday press conference. "The reasons given by Roger M. Blough," commented the *Times*, ". . . for the steel price increase of $6 a ton fail to convince us of either the wisdom of the increase or of the industry's sense of responsibility in thus setting off what may well be a chain of inflationary price rises . . . The difficulty with the device the steel industry . . . has employed in pursuit of its objective is that raising prices will quite likely lower demand and aggravate competitive difficulties . . ." The *Post* hit Blough hard on his lack of candor with the President. "The chairman's statement," said its Friday editorial, "that there was no commitment to retain existing prices is no doubt true, but is essentially false. The Government, labor and the public, during the negotiations [between the steel industry and the united steelworkers] had drawn an inference that the *quid pro quo* for restraint by labor would be restraint by industry."

And of course in more liberal quarters the steel industry was the target for adjectives as harsh as the conservative community was firing at the President. "I didn't think the dinosaurs were back," wrote Max Lerner in the New York *Post*. "I thought they had died in the Hoover era, and that nothing so crudely maneuvered as U. S. Steel's price rise would be attempted in the 1960's . . . But I guess I was wrong."

By Friday even the *Wall Street Journal* had to concede that the climate of opinion was running with the President. "Perhaps in the supercharged air of the moment," said its editorial, "many Americans agree with the President's denunciation of business. But on further reflection," the *Journal* concluded optimistically, "it is possible they might find distasteful a rabid new government onslaught on the free economy."

Possibly, but as of Friday morning it did not look very probable—as the editors of the *Journal* should have been the first to concede. The results of their own soundings in the tricky waters of public opinion showed the man in the street to be even more aroused than the editorial writers who had sided with the President. In twenty cities where *Journal* reporters talked to people in supermarkets, on street corners and other places of congregation, they found that the great majority sided with the President; that more than 60 percent said specifically that the increase had not been called for at that time and would probably have a harmful effect on the nation's economy. "Kennedy is mad and so am I," said a Ford worker in Detroit. "Everybody agreed the new labor contract wouldn't increase prices, then the steel companies come along and take their gravy off the top. The Government shouldn't let them do it."

In Boston, a secretary said, "I don't think there was any justification for a price increase. They've always based increases on higher wages they gave to their employees, but this time the union went along and didn't demand higher wages, and still the companies raised prices."

In Philadelphia, a young telephone repairman had this reaction: "I think the union made a fair contract, and it didn't justify an increase in steel prices. I think we should do just what Kennedy says. The Government should investigate the steel company profits and see if they're justified. If they're not justified, the steel companies should be restricted to a fair profit but regulated like the utilities."

Of course, as the *Journal* pointed out, many people's reaction was dictated by his or her economic philosophy: "I'm a capitalist," commented a Philadelphia educator, "and I go along with the raise in prices." On the other hand, a machinist in Los Angeles said: "It just goes to show you, capitalism is no good. I'm not a Commie or anything, but we can't buy what's on the market now, and these big shots keep forcing prices up. JFK should put a stop to stuff like that. He should have authority to hold down these financiers."

The *Journal's* survey of the business community found a much more favorable climate for the steel companies. Two-thirds of the businessmen interviewed supported steel, but the same comment so often found in the pro-steel newspaper editorials was still heard: steel may be in the right, but its timing was wrong and the question of whether a price rise will help is still debatable. "In my personal opinion," said Paul J. Hemschoot, Secretary of Tung-Sol Electric, Inc., of Newark, "the steel companies had every right to do it. But it was poorly done, without thought of public relations. They should have conferred with the President and laid down their reasons. I don't mean they should have backed down if he objected, but they should have given him the opportunity to object."

Thus with the man in the street firmly lined up with the President, the majority of the nation's most influential newspapers critical of the steel companies' action, the business community only lukewarm in its support of the steel industry, and with companies representing 16 percent of the nation's steel-producing capacity holding the price line, it was inevitable that the pressure would begin to build up in the New York executive offices of U. S. Steel at 71 Broadway.

By noon Friday it was obvious that the steel community was as jittery as a fortress under seige, but what would be big steel's next move? Actually, the first members of the Administration's team to know the answer would be Arthur Goldberg and Clark Clifford, who had arrived shortly before noon to meet with U. S. Steel.

Instead of meeting at 71 Broadway, the group arranged a secret session at the Carlyle Hotel. All the participants managed to slip into the Carlyle unnoticed, and as a result, perhaps the most dramatic event of Friday took place in relative peace and quiet while reporters were descending on the major figures in the dispute all the way from New York to Japan.

When Goldberg and Clifford arrived at the Carlyle, the U. S. Steel group—consisting of Blough, Worthington and Tyson—was already there. The first order of business was a small lunch, during which very little business was discussed. After the trays were removed, the group got down to the subject at hand. In a later description of the U. S. Steel men at the meeting given by one of the conferees to a *Fortune* writer, Worthington was described as silent—"he didn't say a word all day long"—Tyson as "terribly worried," and Blough as "amiable and tenacious."

Goldberg opened the meeting with about a half-hour statement. This was followed by a series of "exceedingly unimpressive" (as one of those attending put it) arguments by Blough rationalizing the general price increase, followed, as a rule, by a Goldberg retort.

"Did we help you get a more favorable settlement?" Goldberg asked at one point.

Blough nodded an assent.

"Then what do you think we were in there for, Roger? There were eight to ten times during this period when all you had to say was 'Understand we are taking part in the negotiations, but understand that no one is going to interfere with our right to raise the price of steel!' Did you ever say that?" Goldberg asked.

Blough replied no, arguing again that he felt it was implicit that steel had the right to raise prices any time it chose.

So it went. For awhile, according to Clifford, the outlook was "abysmal." Boiled down, Clifford felt that the essence of the problem was simply that United States Steel—perhaps the nation's if not the world's most powerful corporation—had failed to weigh the consequences of its action. If this position was held, its own interests, as well as the interests of the nation, would inevitably suffer. The meeting could not exactly be described as hostile; Goldberg and Blough continued to call each other Roger and Arthur. It was, however, quite frank and businesslike, although Clifford stresses the fact that at no time did he state that if U. S. Steel rescinded its price increase the Government would call off all the action which had been initiated in the last two days. However, Clifford did stress that if the situation continued, it would very likely cause an upheaval in Government and the result might well be a series of investigations and counterinvestigations which would be most unpleasant for the steel companies and the nation. Clifford conceded that if the situation returned to what it had been prior to the price rise, it could not help but influence the climate in Washington. He also reminded Blough that John F. Kennedy might well be in office for several years and that it would be extremely difficult doing business in Washington after such a violent breach with the President.

It was obvious that the President had picked a tactful and convincing persuader as his emissary.

During the meeting, both Goldberg and Clifford, and then Blough, Tyson and Worthington, would retire to an adjoining bedroom where they would talk in private or place or receive telephone calls. There was little doubt that as the phone calls came in, Blough and his group were being fully apprised of the situation in the industry; that it was definitely known to them that Kaiser and Armco, as well as Inland, had all decided not to raise prices.

At the same time, another development in Washington added emphasis to the Defense Department's earlier statement about procurement. At about 2:30 Friday afternoon the Pentagon issued another statement, this one the copy of a "Memorandum on the Procurement of Steel for Defense Production to the Secretaries of Army, Navy, Air Force, and to the Director, Defense Supply Agency." It read as follows:

> The price increase on steel, just announced by a number of steel companies, can have a serious impact on the costs of our defense contracts. Defense Department funds have been carefully budgeted to procure the weapons and materials necessary to carry out assigned military missions. It is essential that every effort be made to conserve these funds through prudent purchasing to permit the maximum possible acquisition of programmed military requirements.
>
> In order to minimize the effect of the price increase on defense costs, instructions should be issued immediately to our procurement offices that werever possible steel will be purchased from those companies which have not increased prices. Contractors and their subcontractors purchasing steel for use on defense contracts should be given the same instructions. This policy will apply to existing contracts, provided that critical operational dates are not jeopardized, as well as to future contracts.

The implications of the increasing pressure from the Pentagon was not missed by U. S. Steel executives, or, incidentally, by officials of Bethlehem Steel out in Pittsburgh. Bethlehem, as it has been pointed out, had some coveted contracts with the Navy. Inland, however, maintains that the Pentagon's threat to shift contracts did not influence its decision. "We made our decision before McNamara made his," said President John F. Smith, Jr.

Gradually, as Blough and company took their telephone calls, the climate at the Carlyle Hotel began to change. Before long, the accusations, arguments and rationalizations about the past were replaced with conversation pertaining to the problem: What to do about the price situation now? Offers were tactfully made to U. S. Steel to help the corporation "save face," and finally Blough asked: "What excuse have we got?"

Three fact-saving possibilities were suggested: first, U. S. Steel might announce that a careful study and revaluation of the market had indicated that a price increase was not in the public interest, hence was being rescinded; second, U. S. Steel might say there had been a misunderstanding with the Administration and because the Administration obviously felt so strongly about the price rise, it would be tactful to rescind the price increase, thereby removing the source of conflict between government and the steel industry; third, U. S. Steel could say that some companies had not gone along with their price increase, and since it was not in the best interest of the corporation to engage in a price war, it was rescinding.

As the discussion of these alternatives progressed, it began to look as if Blough and his colleagues were leaning toward the third one—when Blough was called to the phone again. Soon Goldberg was also called to the phone in another room. Both had received the same message: at 3:25 that afternoon Arthur B. Homer, Chairman of the Board of Bethlehem Steel, announced that because of its desire to remain competitive, Bethlehem Steel had rescinded its price increase. Homer also said: "Although we still hold the opinion that a steel

price increase is needed, under the present conditions, to in-
sure reasonable earnings, to provide the funds necessary to
build more competitive facilities, and at least partly to offset
the past employment cost increases which have been absorbed
without price increases, we must remain competitive. For the
ultimate good and future welfare of our economy," Homer
concluded, "we must have lower costs to permit lower prices
for successful world competition and improved volume of
business and employment."

When the Carlyle conversations resumed, it was apparent
that U. S. Steel was ready to throw in the sponge. The only
question that now remained was how the corporation would
explain it. The talk continued until 5:10 P.M., and finally
Blough and his colleagues emerged from one of their bedroom huddles and said they had decided to rescind and that
the third alternative would probably be used as the explanation. The U. S. Steel representatives then left, saying that they
would issue a release in about half an hour. The steel crisis
was over.

Clifford and Goldberg remained at the Carlyle after the
others had left, to place a call to the President, who by this
time was in Norfolk. He had received the news of Bethlehem's decision on the plane flying down, and the fact that
Bethlehem was the first big company to move had taken the
President's party completely by surprise. The Administration's task force had made no special effort to persuade
Bethlehem to back down, and to this day there is considerable
speculation around Washington as to precisely what prompted
Bethlehem to lead the retreat. Perhaps, so the speculation
went, Bethlehem was concerned by the implications inherent
in President Martin's remarks and genuinely jolted by the
speed with which the antitrust effort was pushed. Also, it
was known that Bethlehem was concerned about Inland's
competition in midwestern markets and Kaiser's competition

on the West Coast, and that when those two companies did not go along on the price rise, Bethlehem had to back down. The explanation most often heard in the Presidential party was that Bethlehem had gotten wind that it was to be excluded from bidding on the construction of three naval vessels the following week and decided to take quick action.

The President took Clifford and Goldberg's call in the Atlantic Command Post at Norfolk. He was delighted to hear the news, to say the least, and said he felt that the steel companies had shown "great statesmanship" in rescinding the price increase.

Within a half hour after Blough and his colleagues left Goldberg and Clifford at the Carlyle, U. S. Steel issued this brief statement:

PITTSBURGH, PA., April 13—United States Steel Corporation today announced that it has rescinded the 3½-percent price increase made on Wednesday, April 11.

Commenting upon the price announcement, Leslie B. Worthington, President of the company, said: "The price decision was made in the light of the competitive developments today, and all other current circumstances including the removal of a serious obstacle to proper relations between government and business."

Only 27 hours after Roger Blough had faced a nationwide television audience, defending U. S. Steel's price rise, only 50 hours after the President's furious news conference denouncing Big Steel, and only 72 hours after he had made his celebrated call on President Kennedy, Roger Blough surrendered. Why? What was the explanation for the strange episode? A full discussion of the reasons behind the steel industry's abortive attempt to raise prices is saved for Chapter 12. However, when asked to explain the meaning of the reasons offered in Friday's brief surrender announcement, U. S. Steel spokesmen quite frankly said that the reference to a "serious obstacle" meant the all-out war unleashed by the White House, and that "competitive developments" meant the failure of several major producers to raise prices, plus the decision by Bethlehem to rescind its.

Ironically, at just about the time U.S. Steel was rescinding, the Pentagon was releasing still another statement in regard to Defense Procurement—this one pertaining specifically to U. S. Steel. The short release tells the story:

NAVY PLACES STEEL ORDER FOR THREE ADDITIONAL POLARIS SUBMARINES

The Secretary of Defense announced today that consistent with essential efforts to conserve funds available to the Department of Defense, a steel order for three Polaris submarines was placed today with the Lukens Steel Company, Coatsville, Pennsylvania, by the Chief of the Navy's Bureau of Ships.

The price was that prevailing at the company today, which is the same as the price prevailing on Friday, April 6, 1962.
The steel ordered has special high-strength properties. Lukens and U. S. Steel are the only producers of this material in the principal range of plate sizes.

Approximately 11,000 tons of steel are involved. Deliveries will begin in July and be completed in September.

Normally, U. S. Steel would have received about half this order, which was worth approximately $5 to $6 million. Now it was all to go to Lukens, which had held the price line. To rub a little more salt in the wound, the announcement of this shift had been advanced by about ten days. Later that night when an Administration official was asked what happens now, he said: "You might say this is just one dose of medicine U. S. Steel will have to swallow because of the way it's been acting."

On Wall Street, steel stocks took an immediate jump after Bethlehem's announcement. The rise in stock prices in the closing minutes was greater than the gain for the whole day, but it did not affect U. S. Steel. Its announcement of the retreat came too late to affect trading.

At the White House, it was reasonably quiet. The President had left for Norfolk in midafternoon. In the press office, Mrs. Barbara Gamarekian, one of Pierre Salinger's secretaries, was watching the Associated Press wire when the news came that U. S. Steel had rescinded. Quickly she tore off the story and ran to the office of Ted Sorensen, who happened to be talking on the phone with Andrew Hatcher, with the President in Norfolk.

"Well," Sorensen was saying, "I guess there isn't anything new."

Mrs. Gamarekian put the AP Bulletin on his desk.

"Wait a minute!" shouted Sorensen. Then he gave Hatcher the news.

The President was inspecting the nuclear submarine *Thomas A. Edison* when Hatcher reached him and gave him the news. He took it with barely a smile. A few minutes later, on board the cruiser *Northhampton,* he told a reporter: "I think the others will follow now. They can't afford not to."

The President was right. Within a matter of hours, the other steel companies which had followed U. S. Steel in raising prices were engaged in a rather disorderly retreat— or, as *Time* put it, a "precipitous rush to surrender." First came Jones & Laughlin, the nation's number four producer. It took J. & L. only two terse lines to surrender. Republic Steel, number three, went down with a little more eloquence. "We take this action," said Company President Thomas Patton, "to remain competitive even though it is our sincere belief that a price increase is needed at this time to offset to some extent the increased costs we have incurred since 1958."

Pittsburgh and National followed almost immediately. The last to throw in the sponge were Youngstown and the Wheeling Corporation. On the *Northhampton,* the President issued a brief statement: "The people of the United States are most gratified . . . In taking the action at this time [the steel companies] are serving the public interest . . ."

The feeling in Washington was one of quiet jubilation and restrained hurrah's. That afternoon Secretary Dillon had flown back from Florida with his press aide Dixon Donnelley. On the plane coming up they prepared a statement for release at the Secretary's Saturday morning press conference. It was described as very strong. When Dillon and his group arrived at the airport, they were met by Theodore Eliot, another of Dillon's aides, who smilingly reported that Bethlehem had bailed out. Dillon's party left immediately for the Treasury, and on arriving there the group was informed that U. S. Steel had just announced its decision to rescind. Dillon turned right around and went back to Florida. His "strong" statement schedule for release the following day was thrown into the wastebasket.

Also put in a bottom drawer, but no doubt held in reserve, was the draft legislation which had been discussed that morning in Ted Sorensen's office. By 6 P.M. Friday, officials working on the legislation had come up with a draft to be presented to the President for approval. Essentially it was a sort of Taft-Hartley Act for steel, calling for a 90-day rollback of the price increase, during which time a fact-finding board would consider its merits. However, a phone call from Sorensen halted work on the legislation, although it is important to stress that the draft had not been presented to the President for approval, hence there is no certainty that such a proposal would have been submitted to Congress.

Later that evening one Administration official commented that the real significance of the day's events was that the "guideposts" which the Administration had been trying to furnish for wage-price decisions would now be treated with new respect, whereas if the price rise had stuck, the economic council's efforts to provide guidelines might well have been scrapped. "This was the great turning point," one Administration official said Friday night. "The steel companies' price action assures that there will be stable prices for a long time to come."

It was generally conceded that the Administration had won a smashing victory—and perhaps it had. But in its hour of glory the atmosphere around the White House was anything but triumphant. It may have been a victory, but as one official involved in the struggle put it: "We're not crowing about it."

CHAPTER 8

The Economic Debate

. . . we have reluctantly concluded that a modest price adjustment can no longer be avoided in the light of the production-cost increases that have made it necessary.
—*From the statement by U. S. Steel announcing a price increase, April 10, 1962*

The facts of the matter are that there is no justification for an increase in steel prices.
—*President Kennedy at his press conference, April 11, 1962*

Despite the fact that the fireworks set off by the White House made it difficult to follow, there was a genuine and basic economic debate underlying the steel crisis, and this debate is still going on today. However, during the 72-hour confrontation between the steel industry and the Administration, the economics of the crisis seldom held the spotlight. Of course, both the President and Roger Blough touched on economic issues in their television appearances, but for the most part their real debate centered primarily around the issues of Presidential power, the national interest, and whether it had been understood that the steel industry would not raise prices if a "noninflationary" wage settlement was achieved. Two weeks after steel capitulated, Richard Mooney wrote a story based on the Administration's steel crisis "White Paper." When Mooney's story appeared on April 30, U. S.

Steel contacted Mooney and offered a rebuttal which appeared in the *Times* on May 28 under the headline U. S. STEEL DISPUTES GOVERNMENT. And that was the closest thing to a formal "economic debate" produced by the steel crisis.

Although the two parties engaged in the dispute did not directly debate the issues, the "debate" was carried on at length by outside parties—the press, economists, Congressmen, politicians, television commentators and the man in the street. And as was to be expected, the public debate often departed from the basic issues, at least as presented by U. S. Steel and the Administration. Despite the fact that the economic debate failed to capture the spotlight, a close examination of the basic arguments on each side reveals that U. S. Steel and the Administration viewed the state of the steel industry from fundamentally different points of view. (The economic aspects of this disagreement have already been touched upon in the foregoing chapters, and those readers interested only in the broader aspects of the steel crisis may omit this chapter, which is included primarily to outline as clearly as possible the economic debate between U. S. Steel and the Administration.)

The debate as such was initiated by President Worthington in his April 10 statement announcing U. S. Steel's decision to increase prices. (The statement is printed in Appendix A and should be read carefully by anyone wishing to follow the economic debate in detail.)

The Administration's first real response to U. S. Steel's Tuesday statement came the following afternoon in the President's opening statement at his press conference. (See Chapter 4.) In it the President summarized the Administration's countereconomic arguments which had been prepared to date. However, the complete "case" assembled by the Administration was not to be ready for several days. Although it has never been made public, the document is still in the files of the Council of Economic Advisers. "The material has been assembled," its introduction reads, "in case it may be of use to government officials still concerned with the steel question."

The "White Paper" makes the Administration's case in fourteen different points and following these points is as good a way as any to focus on the economic debate. Printed below are the Administration's arguments, taken from the "White Paper"; following each Administration point is the "rebuttal" by U. S. Steel, which came in several ways: at Blough's Thursday afternoon press conference; in the notes given to Richard Mooney; and in Blough's explanation of the steel company's action given at the U. S. Steel stockholders' meeting in May 1962.

THE DEBATE

The Administration

1. The Labor cost of a ton of steel for the industry as a whole has not risen since the last increase in the price of steel in 1958. Employment cost per-man-hour is up 12.8 percent, but at the same time output per-man-hour is up 12.6 percent, hence the employment cost per unit of output is up only .02 percent.

Labor productivity in steel depends not only on technical progress but also on the extent to which steel capacity is used. But from 1958 to 1961, there was only a small increase in the capacity used (from 60.6 percent in 1958 to 64.1 percent in 1961). Although it is difficult to extend the figure for 1962, it appears likely that the cost per ton of steel will not change appreciably during the years.

The Government further substantiated its case on labor costs in the November 1962 issue of the Department of Commerce's *Survey of Current Business*. In an article, "Corporate Profits and National Output," the Department maintains that, in general, labor costs in the period 1948 to 1962 had remained quite constant—about two-thirds of the total cost of the national output. The share of employee compensation in the 1962 gross national output was almost identical to that of 1948. In summary, the study found that the greatest factors contributing to increased corporate costs and the "profits squeeze" were capital replacement expenditures and taxes. Increased interest costs were only a minor factor, and labor costs remained constant.

U. S. Steel

1. The 12.8 percent increase for labor cost is a Bureau of Labor Statistics figure. United States Steel prefers to use the figure used by the American Iron and Steel Institute, which is 13.5 percent for wage earners of steel-producing operations of the industry.

More important, however, is the fact that shipments per man hour of *all* employees, based on ASIA statistics, improved only 7 percent over the same period. Thus labor costs have *increased*, in addition to the other costs incurred by the industry.

The Administration

2. Labor costs per ton of steel can be expected to decline under the terms of the recent settlement in the steel industry. Productivity advanced during the period 1958–61 at about 3½ percent a year in the steel industry. If it continues at this pace, it will outrun by a substantial margin the prospective increase in employment costs. This does not take into consideration the increases in output per-man-hour which may be expected as soon as economic recovery raises the utilization of steel capacity. CEA estimates, from post-war experience, that the output per-man-hour increased 4 percent for every 10 point increase in the use of capacity.

U. S. Steel

2. The figure of 3½ percent annual increase in productivity is a government calculation and is not supported by the in-

dustry; it was developed unilaterally without any meeting between government and industry economists. Shipments per-man-hour for the industry rose 7 percent from 1958 to 1961 and have grown at an average annual rate since 1940 of 1.7 percent. [This figure was influenced by the relatively low rate of shipments in 1960; a more representative, long term figure would be 2.0 percent.] It would not appear logical to project any gain in output per-man-hour over the rate of increase that has been sustained on a long-term basis, or about 1.7 percent per year. Further, only when the improvements in output per-man-hour are actually realized, can they be safely paid out.

A change in volume from one period to another will result in a change in output per-man-hour due to a certain fixed element of labor in steel making. However, this would not affect average annual improvement rates over a longer period of years.

Finally, projection of volume effects are hazardous; for example, steel industry's volume of shipments in 1961 was 8 percent over 1958, but the percent return on sales was down.

The Administration

3. Prices of major raw materials used in the manufacturing of steel have declined since 1958. Scrap prices are down 4 percent and there has been no significant change in iron ore. The price of coal is down 2.7 percent.

U. S. Steel

3. The steel industry has never made any effort to dispute the contention that the cost of raw materials has decreased since 1958.

The Administration

4. Steel industry profits have not been squeezed by rising per-ton costs of labor and materials. However, like the profits of most other industries, the steel companies have been adversely affected by the recession and an underutilization of capacity.

The cost-price relationship in the steel industry as a whole has not shifted appreciably since 1958. The steel price increase is designed to widen profits at relatively low rates of capacity utilization—not to "catch up." Actually, the industry has much more to gain from improved sales and a stepped-up rate of operation; much more to gain by prosperity. This is the real remedy for the "profit squeeze." But a price rise hinders the chances of full economic recovery. Industry has not operated at an annual rate of more than 67 percent of capacity since 1957. Its profits have suffered accordingly. This is not peculiar to the steel industry alone. If the steel industry were to increase its rate of operation to 90 percent of capacity without the price increase, its yield would be 13½ percent on capital invested; with the price increase, it would be 19 percent.

U. S. Steel

4. Steel industry shipments in 1961 were 66.1 million tons and that is what customers demanded. And costs, as has already been shown, increased. The use of the outmoded percent of capacity is misleading. People think of the high operating rate which followed World War II and Korea to satisfy a pent-up demand from the great depression and the war. They forget that over the long pull, steel, on the average, has used only about 75 percent of its capacity. There is no basis for assuming any sustained period of operating at 90 percent of capacity.

As for the percent return of capital, there are definite weaknesses in using this as a measure. Because of inflation, and particularly in an industry heavily invested in long-lived facilities, the return on investment can *appear* to be increasing even though in reality the company's profits are standing still or declining.

The Administration

5. The profit position of the major steel producers, other than U. S. Steel, did not significantly deteriorate in the period 1958–61.

The profit figures for the major steel companies are as follows:

COMPANY	PROFITS AFTER TAXES (In millions of dollars)	
	1958	1961
Armco	58	58
Bethlehem	138	122
Inland	48	55
Jones & Laughlin	23	32
National	36	33
Republic	62	57
Youngstown	22	23
TOTAL (7 companies)	387	380
U. S. STEEL	302	190

U. S. Steel

5. As for the argument that steel profits are not the only ones to have suffered but that the profit positions of the other major steel companies did not deteriorate significantly, it should be kept in mind that corporate profits may be at a dollar high, but they have not maintained their relative position. For example, in 1950 corporate profits were 8.6 percent of the net national product, but by 1961 profits were equal to only 4.9 percent of the net national product. If corporate profits had maintained their same relationship in 1961 as existed in 1950, corporate profits in 1961 would have been about $40 billion rather than the $23 billion they were. The tabulation below clearly demonstrates that corporate profits have not kept their relative position in the net national product:

	(In billions)		PERCENT OF CHANGE
	1950	1961	
Compensation of employees	$154.2	$302.9	96
Taxes on business	41.6	69.9	68
Proprietors' income & miscellaneous	46.9	80.0	70
Corporate profits	22.8	23.3	2
TOTAL NET NATIONAL PRODUCT	$265.5	$476.1	79

Labor has received a greater share of the net national product while corporate profits have declined. Further, the records show that this change is not unique for 1961 but rather has been a constant erosion of the relative position of corporate profits over a period of years.

The Administration's statement on profits—as confined to the steel industry specifically—is not accurate. As a percent on return of sales, profits have declined in each of the last four years. Volume during the first quarter of 1962 was probably as high as can be expected for any quarter this year. When the anticipated reduction in volume for the second and third quarters is considered, coupled with increased hourly employment costs effective July 1, 1962, it is very doubtful if profits in the steel industry will rise sharply this year. In fact, for the steel industry as a whole, it is more conceivable that profits could be squeezed even below the 1961 level. [According to U. S. Steel officials, the profit squeeze for 1962 was actually worse than estimated in May.]

The Administration

6. Price increases are neither a necessary nor a desirable means of obtaining funds for capital improvements.

Neither economic principle nor the actual experience of the steel companies affords a justification for the view that prices should be set at levels permitting 100 percent internal financing of investment capital. Capital improvements increase the value of the assets owned by stockholders; increasing prices to pay for them amounts to taxing steel users for the benefit of the stockholders. If an investment in modern facilities is profitable, it will, by definition, yield enough both to repay with interest any borrowing necessary to finance it and to earn a fair return for the stockholders.

Especially contradictory is U. S. Steel's argument that higher prices will improve competitive position. High prices can only make industry less competitive. Public statements by U. S. Steel officials do not even offer assurance that steel prices will be reduced as the cost-saving benefits of capital improvements are realized.

A policy of 100 percent internal financing would be a depressive influence on the economy. If all corporations did it, virtually the only outlet for the substantial savings of individuals would be residential construction.

The steel industry would save an estimated $110 million in taxes this year with the 8 percent tax credit proposal before Congress—U. S. Steel, $35 million.[1] The new depreciation regulations would give the industry another $24 million; U. S. Steel, $10 million.

The practical experience of the steel companies does not support their announced aversion to capital financing in the market. Steel companies' issues of new capital (virtually all bonds) have been $250 million or more every year except one since 1955. No public issue of any magnitude had more than $4\frac{1}{2}$ percent interest—only a little more than $\frac{1}{2}$ percent over the government rate. Almost no new stocks were issued. In short, the major steel companies could easily have obtained additional financing if they desired.

U. S. Steel

6. One economic fact which must never be forgotten is that when money is borrowed, profits must be adequate to pay the interest charges as well as to ultimately repay the principal. Thus, borrowing does not reduce the need for profits. Further, financing in the steel industry is not unique. For example, the following Source and Disposition of Funds statement for the period 1946–1961, inclusive, shows a very high degree of compatibility between companies comprising the steel industry and all corporations as reported by the U. S. Department of Commerce:

[1] The credit, as actually passed, amounted to 7 percent. (See Chap. 11.)

| | STEEL INDUSTRY | | ALL CORPORATIONS | |
	BILLIONS	% of TOTAL	BILLIONS	% of TOTAL
SOURCE				
Profits	$11.6	64%	$293.8	60%
Less dividends	6.1	34%	150.0	30%
Income reinvested	$ 5.5	30%	$143.8	30%
Depreciation	8.4	47	216.4	44
Long-term debt	2.5	14	88.9	18
Capital stock	1.6	9	40.5	8
Total Sources	$18.0	100%	$489.6	100%
DISPOSITION				
Plant and equipment	$14.7	82%	$373.9	76%
Working cap. & Misc.	3.3	18	115.7	24
TOTAL DISPOSITIONS	$18.0	100%	$489.6	100%

If tax laws relative to depreciation were adequate, the funds necessary to finance the replacement of facilities should be available through depreciation allowances. But due to the inadequacy in depreciation allowances, it is necessary to reinvest profits in the business merely to stay even.

Based on our data, it can readily be established that the investment credit in the Kennedy tax plan will not result in the savings estimated by the Administration. Its figures are grossly exaggerated. The tax credit plan covers certain specified types of assets, excluding such items as building and foreign investments. Further, such credits will not apply when the expenditure is made but rather when the asset is put into operation. In the case of steel industry investments, twenty-four to thirty months on the average will elapse between the date the project is begun and the date the expenditures would be eligible for credit. Accordingly, a credit of $35 million in 1962 would require qualifying expenditures of nearly $450 million on projects, all of which would need to be completed within the year 1962. Our total expenditure, including those which would not, as well as those which would, qualify in the first quarter of 1962 were about $55 million and we have no present plans for acceleration of this rate during 1962. Consequently, we believe that the maximum benefit U. S. Steel could receive from the proposed tax credit in 1962 would be no more than $5 to $6 million. [Actual "benefit" turned out to be closer to $8 million.]

It is also an interesting question as to just how one goes about spending $450 million annually when wear and exhaustion provisions are equal to only slightly over $200 million a year.

From what little we know of the Treasury Department's depreciation proposals, the benefit of $10 million appears very doubtful. But even if it were accurate, $10 million does not really begin to make up for the present inadequacy of depreciation allowances for tax purposes. The estimate that the tax offset—tightening up on expense accounts, foreign earnings and other items—would only cost industry $10 million annually appears substantially below the realistic figure.

The Administration

7. Raising steel prices is not the way to meet competition at home or abroad.

Prices of some competing products have actually fallen—at least 7½ percent since autumn of 1961.

Steel imports are up from less than $1 million in 1954 to more than $3 million in 1961. Also, the share of domestic production going into exports declined from 4.7 percent in 1954 to 3.2 percent in 1961. U. S. share of total world exports of iron and steel declined from 18 percent in 1954 to 11 percent in 1960. This situation was associated with a substantial rise in U. S. prices relative to foreign steel prices. Further price increases can be expected to turn more foreign customers away from American steel.

U. S. Steel

7. The steel industry cannot compete with foreign steel producers without proper pricing structure. The reason we are failing to compete with foreign producers is that much of our equipment has become obsolete and increased profits are needed to give us the money with which to modernize facilities. "You don't meet competition," said Blough at his press con-

ference, "by having a facility produce a product that can't compete, costwise, with the imports."

The Administration

8. A rise in steel prices can increase our balance-of-payments deficit.

The trade balance in iron and steel has gone down 5 million tons, or $774 million from 1954 to 1961. Between 1953 and 1961, American steel prices went up 24 percent compared with those of five foreign competitors (Belgium, Luxemburg, France, Germany, Japan, United Kingdom) taken together. In the past few years, American steel prices have been relatively stable while foreign prices have gone up 4 percent from a 1959 low. A price increase would erase this advantage. Recent reports from Europe indicate that foreign steel capacity is not fully utilized and that German steel producers are beginning to offer price concessions. Even more important, steel is a major raw material for many other export products. One-third of our exports are machine and automotive products.

U. S. PRICES RELATIVE TO FOREIGN PRICES: 1953=100

YEAR	U. S.	5 FOREIGN COMPETITORS NAMED ABOVE
1955	110	101
1956	119	113
1957	130	118
1958	135	109
1959	137	106
1960	137	109
1961	136	110

U. S. Steel

8. It is true that a rise in the price of steel may temporarily aggravate the balance-of-payments problem, but the situation cannot be corrected until the basic machinery in the steel industry has been modernized.

The Administration

9. The price increase in steel may endanger the outstanding record of over-all price stability in recent years.

The Wage-Price Index has been stable for four years. There has been no inflation in the recovery, which has helped exports. The economy is in the midst of an important test—whether price stability can be maintained during a sustained economic expansion which reduces unemployment and excess capacity to acceptable levels. So far, the economy has met this test very well.

The price increase will cost buyers of steel some $400 million. Unless this increase in cost is absorbed by steel fabricators and manufacturers of steel products, prices will rise.

U. S. Steel

9. The increase of three-tenths of a cent per pound in the price of steel adds almost negligibly to the cost of the steel which goes into the familiar, every-day products that we use. For instance, it will only increase the price of a compact-size car $6.83, a toaster 3 cents, and a 7.7 cubic foot refrigerator 65 cents.

The Administration

10. Steel price rise will increase Federal budget costs.

The Government spends $20 billion a year on hard goods and construction. Steel is a significant component of this expenditure. A one percent increase in the cost of hard goods costs the government $200 million a year. If the steel price increase is transmitted to other goods and a wage-price spiral is turned on, more costs will be incurred.

In his press conference statement, the President was more specific, stating that the 3½-percent price increase would cost the Government $1 billion a year. This estimate was based on a study made by a group assembled by Assistant Secretary of State Thomas D. Morris. The study was made in the fall of 1961 when a price rise was rumored. It showed that a 3½-percent increase in steel would cost the Government $500 million in defense spending alone, but after the price increase had fanned out through the entire economy, the eventual cost of *all* government purchases would be increased by another $500 million. During the steel crisis, Secretary McNamara, in a letter to President Kennedy, reiterated his belief that the price increase would cost the Government $1 billion.

U. S. Steel

10. Concerning the estimated $1 billion increase in government costs which would result from a price increase, when Blough was asked to comment on that at his Thursday afternoon press conference, he replied: "I am not sure how this statement is made up. I am sure that, so far as direct steel sales to the Defense Department is concerned, the total tonnage . . . even if 1962 is an extraordinary large year for purchases by the Defense Department, could not amount to more than say three or three and a half million tons.

"Now these are the direct and indirect purchases and that of course, would be something in the nature of twenty million dollars. And where the 'billion dollars' comes from, I don't know, unless someone made a projection that this in some way would extend to other things."

The Administration

11. Unemployment has been severe in the steel industry and an increase in the price of steel dampens the possibility of reducing the number of unemployed steel workers.

Employment in the basic steel industry was off 120,000, or 17 percent in the period 1957–1961. This was caused by the slow growth of output and significant productivity increases. From 1958 to 1961, unemployment in primary metals averaged 50 percent more than for all experienced workers. Production will rise with recovery, but the rise would be greater if prices remained constant.

U. S. Steel

11. Although this point never was answered specifically, it is obvious that U. S. Steel felt that an increase in the price of steel would probably not affect sales appreciably. As for em-

ployment, at his press conference, Blough said: "Your problem, as I have tried to explain, is to have enough [money] to buy the machinery and equipment to make the kind of products, to make the quantities of them that will enable us, costwise, to get the business which, in turn, provides the employment."

The Administration

12. Government's role in steel-labor negotiations has been to encourage a settlement which would neither require nor lead to an increase in steel prices.

At no time during the negotiations did the industry express to the Administration or to the union the view that the settlement under discussion would be inconsistent with price stability in steel.

U. S. Steel

12. Blough, of course, has insisted that at no time did U. S. Steel commit itself to hold prices down during the steel negotiations, and that, in fact, at least once while the negotiations were going on he made a statement in which he said the cost-price situation in the steel industry must be changed. As for informing the Administration that a price rise was coming, Blough commented at his press conference that "in the kind of an economy that we have, I am not quite sure that it is feasible for anyone to be going to the White House to consider a price increase, even as important a one as this."

The Administration

13. The steel-labor settlement was almost universally acclaimed as responsible and non-inflationary.

U. S. Steel

13. The 1962 contract increased labor costs by approximately 2½ percent. In contrast, since 1940 steel shipments per-man-hour worked has increased by only about 1.7 percent, and even this 1.7 percent is an over-statement of the true gain in productivity. Thus, the 1962 contract was inflationary. But more im-

portant, the current price increase was not in response to the steel wage settlement of 1962. There have been four wage increases since 1958, in addition to steadily mounting production costs. The "catch-up" price increase announced in April was substantially less than the cost increases which have occurred since 1958—without taking into consideration the additional costs from the new labor contract effective July 1, 1962.

The Administration

14. The timing of the price increase and the manner in which price leadership operates in the steel industry indicate that the increase was not the result of competitive forces.

In a competitive environment, the public interest is served by the independent price decisions of individual companies. Cost structures and the demand for steel interact to determine prices, and competition among firms in the industry protect the consumer from prices which get out of line with prevailing costs.

This action came at a time when the unit cost structure of industry had not changed for several years, following a wage settlement which promised a continuation of constant or declining unit costs, and when demand was still low compared to the steel companies' capacity. Under these conditions, competitive behavior would nullify an attempted price increase by any one company—even U. S. Steel.

U. S. Steel

14. The action was taken to enable the industry to become more competitive as soon as possible. At his press conference Thursday afternoon, Blough conceded that if Inland and Armco did not raise prices it would make it very difficult for U. S. Steel—which was an indirect comment on the competitive aspects of the steel price rise. [At the U. S. Steel stockholders' meeting on May 7, Blough made the further point that the fact that the price increase did not stick clearly demonstrated that steel industry pricing was intensely competitive.]

Thus we have the essentials of the economic debate. Which

party in the dispute was right on each point will be argued for some time by economists and other interested parties, and the determination of which side is "right" on each point is outside the scope of this book. "There is no simple answer to the basic issue," said one economist quoted in the Washington *Daily News* at the time of the crisis. This was, if anything, an understatement. The question of pricing in the steel industry alone is the subject of a full-length book—*Pricing Power and the Public Interest: A Study Based on Steel,* by Gardner Means—and it is recommended reading for anyone wishing to analyze further the economic issues inherent in the steel crisis.

But most important, when all is said and done, the steel crisis was not an economic controversy. Despite the fact that both sides supported their case with economic arguments and that there existed fundamental differences on economic questions, the steel controversy was the result of a power struggle in which—either by accident or design—U. S. Steel openly challenged the office of the Presidency, and the President chose to meet that challenge with the full powers of the office even at the risk of upsetting the peaceful relations he had worked so hard to achieve with the business community. He met the challenge and was successful in preventing a defeat for the office of the Presidency—but as we shall see, he paid a tremendous price for his "victory."

PART II

AFTERMATH

CHAPTER 9

The Immediate Reaction

Oh, didn't he do a good one!
—*Robert Frost, commenting on the President's action during the steel crisis*

In seventy-two whirlwind hours Roger Blough, big steel and the entire nation had learned how John F. Kennedy and his tight little staff viewed the powers of the office which they controlled. As Senator Kennedy, candidate Kennedy, President-Elect Kennedy and President Kennedy had said on numerous occasions, a strong President is one who does not hesitate to use the powers of his office to achieve objectives which he believes are in the national interest, and he—John F. Kennedy—had every intention of being a "strong" President. If this message had failed to reach Roger Blough and the executives of U. S. Steel by April 9, 1962, by April 13 they were fully aware that John F. Kennedy had meant what he said.

Although Roger Blough and other U. S. Steel officials may or may not have been impressed with the President's performance, in the immediate aftermath of the steel crisis, it was quite apparent that a good many people in Washington were. And although the word had gone out for no self-administered slaps on the back ("The President has set a tone of no gloating, no crowing," said one White House aide), there were those who found some postbattle crowing irresistible. Lem Billings, a friend of the President, said after the battle that there stood "Jack the Giant Killer, almost making you believe that he has the touch of the supernatural on his shoulder." One White House lieutenant said: "The President has come out of this stronger than if the affair had never happened . . . Everyone is going to be very reluctant to try to pull off what steel tried."

Such remarks were understandable in the immediate aftermath of a highly emotional struggle, but they were not to be heard for long. The Kennedy style of political operation is to marshal every bit of leverage at his command to swing a struggle his way, but once he achieves his objective, he does not gloat and he does not enjoy rubbing it in. In the Baltimore *Sun,* Thomas O'Neill wrote that Roger Blough emerged from the three-day battle with a "new understanding of the feeling of a canary caught in a concrete mixer—or a Kennedy opponent in a primary election," which are, if anything, understatements. But if Blough expected a long period of harassment from Washington and hostility from the White House, he was wrong.

In his talks with reporters and commentators immediately after the crisis, the President repeatedly emphasized that he was not at war with business and that he could not understand the "antibusiness" talk which even then was beginning to be heard. He pointed to the record and stressed that he had spent a whole year trying to encourage business, and to more than one reporter added, "and look what I got." The President felt that it would be difficult to find one thing he had done or said during his first year in office that could accurately be construed as antibusiness. He referred to his efforts to get a tax credit bill from Congress and the forthcoming revision of the depreciation schedules, both of which were "breaks" for the businessman which the previous Administration could have offered and did not. He also felt that his pressure on the steelworkers prior to the signing of the wage contract was proof enough that his efforts to control prices had not been directed at business alone. It irked him that in the rush to label him antibusiness, everyone had forgotten the fact that right in the middle of the steel crisis he had invoked the Taft-Hartley Act to settle the shipping strike. He stressed that he was sympathetic with U. S. Steel's problems, but also felt that he should get a little better response from business to his and the nation's problems.

Despite the slap in the face which the White House felt it had received from Blough and the steel industry, there was a genuine desire to keep the truce with the business community. Translating this thinking into the language of the nation's favorite Civil War, *Business Week* advised its readers that "like Grant at Appomattox [the President], is letting the vanquished forces keep their horses and sidearms."

As will be seen later, the business community was not going to accept an honorable surrender passively, and the possession of its horses and sidearms was to be small consolation for the humiliating and public defeat it had received at the hands of the President. "The Government and people of the United States have proved themselves more powerful than the men who run the American steel industry," was the Denver *Post*'s reaction, and although this should be obvious to every citizen from the time he reaches high school, it apparently came as a shock to the nation's top industrial leaders who had spent eight Eisenhower years enjoying the comfortable feeling that their power was at least equal, if not superior, to Washington's. Their reaction to defeat in the struggle between the Administration and big steel was to prove a deep and disturbing blow. Although the crisis was over, the real battle between the Administration and the business community was just beginning, though the depth of the business community's wound was not to reveal itself immediately. For the time being, at least, a truce appeared to be possible. There were of course many businessmen who agreed with the head of a leading machinery company quoted in

Business Week, who said, "A patch-up now is just window-dressing; the damage is irreparable." But in the immediate aftermath of the steel crisis it looked as if the business community as a whole was prepared to accept the President's obvious bid to bury the hatchet.

At least Roger Blough and U. S. Steel were. The Monday after big steel's capitulation, the White House phone rang and a voice said: "This is Roger Blough, the man you've been reading about." Blough seemed in rare good humor and wanted an appointment with the President, which he was given immediately. They met for forty-five minutes the following afternoon. Blough found the President a very gracious victor, and although Blough says he was willing to discuss it, the subject of the price controversy never came up; for the most part the discussion centered on business confidence. One definite decision to come out of the meeting was that a special committee of the business council, of which Blough was still chairman, would be set up to examine the balance-of-payments problem. The Blough-Kennedy talk ended on an amicable note, and as *Time* put it after the meeting, Blough "returned to the privacy of his Manhattan office overlooking New York Harbor. There, surrounded by charts and statements that explained U. S. Steel's economic position, he pondered how he had gone wrong."

While Blough pondered, the chain of events which he had set in motion continued to unfold. The first thing Monday morning, on the floor of the Senate, Humphrey and Gore announced proposals directed at the steel industry. Humphrey's idea was for a "top level, blue ribbon" presidential commission to conduct a sweeping inquiry into the practices and conditions of the steel industry. The commission was to be made up of prominent leaders from management and labor as well as economists, financiers and representatives of the general public. The objective would be a thorough analysis of the steel industry from the viewpoint of both the domestic and international situation. It would study conditions in steel plants, look into the needs for modernization, check into labor productivity, find out what the requirements were for expanding investments, and learn what could be done to make American steelmakers more competitive in world markets. It would report back to the President within a year, and during its work it would be authorized to use the facilities and personnel of any Federal agency, including law-enforcement departments. "Such an inquiry," Humphrey told the Senate, "should not be conducted in a partisan spirit or turned into a vendetta. It should be objective, fair and comprehensive. It should be removed from all possible party or partisan considerations. It should be an economic study and not a political exercise." Humphrey said that he had discussed the plan with White House aides, but had no idea whether the President favored it. He also promised to take it up at the weekly White House meeting of Congressional leaders scheduled for the following morning.

Senator Gore's proposal was a little less conciliatory. Right from the beginning, his announced intention was nothing less than the break-up of U. S. Steel, and the proposal he made Monday morning was for legislation making it easier for agencies waging antitrust warfare to get court orders dissolving existing monopolies. Gore accompanied his proposed legislation with a bitter attack on large corporations in general and U. S. Steel in particular. "The plain fact of the matter," he said, "is that United States Steel sets the price pattern for the whole steel industry"—a statement which did not completely ring true in light of the previous Friday's retreat by U. S. Steel. He did have a telling point, however, in his comment that the giant company was simply inefficient, with its prices set high enough to make a profit while more efficient companies such as Bethlehem Steel made better profits. He hastened to point out that U. S. Steel was not alone in suffering the evils of bigness and inefficiency. In his opinion, the real problem was that too many industries—and U. S. Steel was a classic example—were run by financiers or what he termed "money-market manipulators," instead of by managers who knew their business. Too many U. S. industries had become high-cost bureaucracies which were unable to provide proper management and adequate cost control because of their size, had floated too much debt without trying further public issues of common stock, had increased dividends rather than spend additional profits for needed plant expansion and modernization, and were using stock-option plans irregularly.

It was a sweeping indictment, and even if businessmen believed that the President wanted to bury the hatchet, it was obvious that at least some members of Congress were still in a warlike mood. The still hostile members, of course, included Senator Kefauver. On Monday afternoon Kefauver made public a list of twelve steel companies whose cost figures had been subpoenaed by his antitrust subcommittee. The data was to be supplied by May 14. The plan was to have it tabulated by the Comptroller General and presented to the Senate in averages of three companies, thereby keeping the cost information of any one company from being made public. "If the information had been in hand at the time of the price increase last week," said Kefauver, "an immediate appraisal of the propriety of the price increase could have been made."

On Tuesday morning Humphrey brought up his plan at the White House meeting, and although the Senator has described the President's reaction as "very friendly," others said the discussion was brief and that the idea was never given "serious" consideration. White House aides did say there was a "faint chance" that at some future date the President might appoint a special group to study the steel industry, but no immediate action was planned. There was, in fact, considerable speculation that Humphrey's proposal was actually a reflection of the Administration's "magnanimous" attitude; that the motive was to substitute an Administration study in place of what was expected to be a more vigorous probe by Kefauver's subcommittee. But if there was any truth to this speculation, the idea that it might prevent Kefauver from moving ahead was dashed Monday afternoon when he announced that he had served subpoenas on twelve major steel companies. On Tuesday, Kefauver announced that his hearings would begin in about six weeks.

It was unlikely that either Humphrey's or Gore's proposals would get very far in Congress without Administration support, and right now the White House seemed much more interested in letting the subject die. The President and his staff were aware that a great deal of explaining needed to be done, in the wake of the steel crisis, and as early as the following Saturday, work was begun on a conciliatory speech to be delivered before the U. S. Chamber of Commerce on April 30. At the same time, word was being passed by the White House that the President wanted peace with the business community. "I want business to do well," he said to one White House visitor. "If they don't, we don't." And on April 18, at his first press conference following the crisis, a relaxed and cordial President Kennedy made a public gesture of reconciliation.

I believe it will be appropriate to say a few words to follow up last week's events concerning steel prices [he said, after an opening statement on the disarmament treaty which the United States had just presented at Geneva]. First, let me make it clear [he continued, in striking contrast to his controlled fury of the previous Wednesday], that this Administration harbors no ill will against any individual, any industry, corporation, or segment of the American economy. Our goals of economic growth and price stability are dependent upon the success of both corporations, business and labor, and there can be no room on either side in this country at this time for any feelings of hostility or vindictiveness.

When a mistake has been retracted and the public interest

preserved, nothing is to be gained from further public recriminations.

Secondly, while our chief concern last week was to prevent an inflationary spiral, we were not then and are not now unmindful of the steel industry's needs for profits, modernization and investment capital. I believe, in fact, that this Administration, and the leaders of steel and other American industries, are in basic agreement on far more objectives than we are in disagreement.

We agree on the necessity of increased investment in modern plant and equipment. We agree on the necessity of improving our industry's ability to compete with the product of other nations. We agree on the necessity of achieving an economic recovery and growth that will make the fullest possible use of idle capacity. We agree on the necessity of preventing an inflationary spiral that will lead to harmful restrictions on credit and consumption, and we agree on the necessity of preserving the nation's confidence in free, private collective bargaining, and price decisions, holding the role of government to the minimum level needed to protect the public interest.

In the pursuit of these objectives, we have fostered a responsible wage policy aimed at holding increases within the confines of productivity gains. We have encouraged monetary policies aimed at making borrowed capital available at reasonable cost, preparing a new transportation policy aimed at providing increased freedom of competition at lower costs, proposed a new trade expansion bill to gain for our industries increased access to foreign markets, proposed an eight-percent income tax credit to reward investment in new equipment and machinery, and proceeded to modernize administratively Treasury Department guidelines on the depreciable lives of capital assets; and, finally, taking a host of other legislative and administrative actions to foster the kind of economic recovery which would improve both profits and incentives to invest.

I believe that the anticipated profits this year for industry in general, and steel in particular, indicate that these policies are meeting with some measure of success, and it is a fact that the last quarter of last year, and I think the first quarter of this year, will be the highest profits in the history of this country, and the highest number of people working, and the highest productivity. So that while there are serious economic problems facing us, nevertheless, I believe that progress is being made and can be made and must be made in the future.

Although the April 18 press conference was not as dominated by the steel crisis as that of the previous week, there were still a number of questions concerning the clash. For one thing, there had been wide press speculation that the Grand Jury investigation in New York would now be dropped, and one reporter asked the President whether this was true. The President replied that the Grand Jury would continue its investigation. He was also asked whether he agreed with conjecture that his victory over steel would help push his legislative program through Congress, to which he replied that he felt certain it would help get tax credit legislation through.

One reporter asked a very significant two-part question concerning future price increases and the President's attitude toward labor demands:

Question: Mr. President, two questions in the wake of last week's developments. First, assuming that a price increase in steel would eventually be necessary and justified, do you have any thoughts as to how this price increase would be reached? And, secondly, if some major labor union made excessive demands for wage increase, would you move as sharply against that union as you did last week against steel?

The President: Well, take the second part first. We worked very closely with the steel union in an attempt to persuade them that it was in their interest and the country's interest to meet the standards set by the Council of Economic Advisers, and it was done. That is why this matter came into particularly sharp focus last week.

Now, as far as the first part, I think that my original statement discussed our general views on it. This is a free economy.

These matters are reached by the process of competition and collective bargaining.

What we are attempting to do is to try to have them consider the public interest which, after all, is their interest, the problems involving price stability, national security, and all the rest. They are much interrelated.

This is particularly true in the basic industries. But the— our power is that—if the industry is competitive, prices are reached through the normal process of competition, and collective bargaining agreements are reached in a normal way. But we would like both labor and management to be very conscious of the public stake at this time, and that is what we are attempting to bring forth. We hope they will.

There had been considerable criticism of FBI agents waking reporters in the middle of the night to question them on something which could just as well have waited until the next day (see Chapter 5), and the President was asked whether he would comment on this. Although he had let it be known that he regretted the incident, and the Attorney General had said that he did not intend the FBI to act with such speed, the President treated the question as if its importance had become somewhat overblown.

Reporters have called up a good many people in the middle of the night themselves. [His first response was given with a smile.] . . . all we were attempting to do was to find out, so that we could decide about the Grand Jury meeting, whether the reports in regard to the quotations said one thing and then there was a statement that they were misquoted, and then the next day there was a clarification, and so we wanted the facts on this.

Now, both reporters were cooperative and I didn't realize they would be awakened at the time they were, and the decision was made early in the evening and I suppose making the connection, the FBI followed ahead. As I say, all of the reporters, except for the *Wall Street Journal*, were most cooperative. But the intention was not to disturb the reporters, and the intention was to get the information as quickly as possible so we could determine what action we would take before the Grand Jury. As always, the FBI carried out its responsibilities immediately.

The President was again asked whether he had been given assurances by the steel industry that there would be no price increase, and he again replied that no assurances had been asked or given. A last question pertained to what ideas the Administration might have to help industry modernize its equipment, which the President answered with a brief repetition of his opening statement.

It was obvious that the President was satisfied with having rolled back steel prices and that he was not inclined to press his victory any further. He wanted to let bygones be bygones and to convince businessmen that he had no intention of setting industrial prices. Furthermore, it soon became apparent that although the New York Grand Jury would continue to gather information, the Administration was not going to push too hard on the antitrust activities which had been started by the Justice Department and the Federal Trade Commission. And, although Senator Kefauver planned to continue his probe, Representative Celler soon let it be known that his proposed investigation would be dropped.

For one thing, despite the fact that the Administration was generally conceded to have won a decisive victory, it was becoming increasingly apparent in the days immediately following the struggle that the sudden unleashing of Presidential powers had rocked the nation and that even among Kennedy supporters there was some concern that he might have gone too far. Then, too, as time wore on, the depth of the hostility gradually building up—or being built up—in the business community was becoming more and more obvious. Considering the impact the steel crisis had on the nation and the open break with business which was soon to come, it is well to take a long look at the nation's immediate reaction. For the most part, it was intense and varied, with the President getting surprise support from some quarters and unexpected criticism from others. However, considering the consequence of the national reaction in measuring the public support the President might or might not have, it is important that an accurate assessment of the reaction be made. For the sake of convenience, the survey will be divided into four parts: (1) reaction in the press; (2) public reaction; (3) political reaction; and (4) reaction in the business community.

Press

The loudest and most agonizing reaction to the President's crushing victory over big steel came from the newspapers and columnists opposed to his action from the start. Led by a handful of opinion makers such as the *Wall Street Journal,* the New York *Herald Tribune* and syndicated columnist David Lawrence—all of whom have traditionally opposed any form of government interference in the affairs of business— a small segment of the press continued to remain in a state of shock for weeks. "We never saw anything like it," wailed the *Wall Street Journal.* "One of the country's companies announced it was going to try to get more money for its product and promptly all hell busted loose. Mr. Kennedy had his victory. The President himself said all the people of the United States should be gratified. Around him there was joy unrestrained at this proof positive of how naked political power, ruthlessly used, could smash any private citizen who got in its way. If we had not seen it with our eyes and heard it with our own ears, we would not have been able to believe that in America it actually happened." Lawrence was even more disturbed; day after day he railed against the Administration's action. "The only persons in the world who can truly derive satisfaction from President Kennedy's tragic performance," he wrote on his *U. S. News* editorial page, "are the advocates of state socialism—often a forerunner of Communism."

However, a handful of opinion makers do not make a trend. They may create enough noise to attract considerable attention, and by quoting selectively from them it is possible to suggest—as *Time* did in its "Press" section in the aftermath of the crisis—that a serious editorial revolt against the Kennedy Administration was brewing. On the other hand, by selective quoting from papers and columnists sharply critical of U. S. Steel, it would be just as easy to suggest that the nation's press was violent in its denunciation of big steel. Of course, neither was true, as even Roger Blough admitted. At the U. S. Steel stockholders' meeting held in May, Blough said that of the 741 newspaper editorials his public relations department had surveyed, 428—or 58 percent—had sided with the company's position. And even this fairly balanced reaction must be viewed in light of this comment made in an article in the *Columbia Journalism Review:* "Newspapers generally throw their editorial lot on the side of business in any conflict with labor or government or consumer," wrote Ben H. Bagdikian. "Any modern President who finds himself in conflict with the industrial or financial community can take it for granted that a vast majority of the press will be against him." Consequently, in one light it might be said that the press actually swung to the President, even though U. S. Steel's survey showed the balance to be slightly in favor of that company's action. (Blough said the nation's cartoonists did not line up as evenly. "They were two-to-one against us," he told his stockholders. "I guess they still think of me with a big cigar.")

However, any survey of press editorials covering 741 newspapers, by necessity must include a good many which took their opinion from the "canned" editorials sent out from the large national syndicates, and it is well known that such syndicates are extremely conservative. Also, a mere tabulation of editorials, putting them in one pile labeled FOR or another labeled AGAINST, does not tell the whole story. In one survey made of 74 of the nation's most important newspapers, columnists and financial writers, there was a slightly different story. Of these 74 opinion makers, the great majority either supported President Kennedy (37) or were neutral (2). Only 17 emphatically came out in favor of the steel companies' price rise, or against the President's efforts to force them to back down. However, even more significant, of the 17 papers which supported U. S. Steel, 7—or more than one third— were critical of the price rise. In addition, of the 20 neutral papers, 11 of them were also critical of it. Since all of the 37 papers supporting the President were critical of the price rise, this meant that of the 74 papers surveyed, 55 criticized the rise as either being unwise in view of the market, or very poorly timed in view of the recent "noninflationary" wage settlement. The explanations offered for the bad timing or misjudgment of the market ranged all the way from poor judgment to downright stupidity on U. S. Steel's part.

There is, however, still another side of the press reaction which does not show up in simple for-and-against tabulations. It should also be pointed out that of the 37 papers which supported the President, 9—or slightly more than one fourth— felt that he had gone too far in his use of the Presidential powers, were critical of the FBI's being called out in the middle of the night, or agreed with U. S. Steel that an increase in profits was essential. Similar positions were taken by 9 of the 20 neutral papers included in this survey. In other words, even among Kennedy supporters in the press, there were those who qualified their support to some extent, just as among U. S. Steel supporters there were those who felt the action had been unwise.

It would appear that the general editorial reaction of the U. S. press was a very balanced one, with some papers and columnists violently opposed to the Administration's action, some violently opposed to U. S. Steel's action, but most tending to side with the President either on the ground that a price rise just had not been in the cards then, or that U. S. Steel's timing had been so unfortunate as to justify the President's heated reaction. But running throughout the reaction was a genuine concern that perhaps the situation had not justified such an "awesome" display of Presidential power, even though the President might have been in the right.

Actually the press had a field day with the steel crisis, with just about every newspaper in the country seizing the occasion to deliver at least one strong editorial discussing the "awesome powers" of the Presidency. The most interesting comments of all came from Republican papers trying to see the brighter side of the incident, and by far the best example in this category appeared on the always pungent editorial page of the Chicago *Tribune*. The *Tribune* felt that Blough and company "had no more chance than, in their day, did the Light Brigade and the men of Pickett's Brigade." However, the *Tribune* did profess to admire the President's action: "This was not the Kennedy who couldn't make up his mind about the Cuban invasion [referring to the Bay of Pigs debacle] . . . and this was not the Kennedy who wavered on Berlin. This was a decisive Kennedy, an executive who knew what he wanted, and threw everything he had into the effort to gain his end . . . We do respect decisiveness in an executive and so do the people. We can only wish," added the *Tribune* sadly, "it had been displayed in a better cause."

But the great majority of newspapers, the wire services and the three major radio and television networks gave fairly straight and objective accounts of the controversy. Full weight was given to the position of both sides in the dispute, and although there might have been a temptation on the part of some pro-business news media to play down the President's position, this became difficult to do after Kennedy's own impassioned television presentation of the Administration's case.

Similarly, the two leading newsmagazines, *Time* and *Newsweek,* presented extremely objective accounts of the battle. *Time*'s coverage was especially significant, considering the reputation the magazine has for being both pro-business and anti-Democratic. The nature of the *Time* style of reporting, with its heavy use of action adjectives, is such that it is difficult for the magazine not to make one side of a dispute look heroic and the other villainous. If either side came out of *Time*'s version looking a little bigger than life, you would have to say it was the President. Although *Time* did finish its account with a few harsh words about his use of the "overwhelming might of the Federal Government," the general picture it painted of Kennedy was of a man of action who was not to be thwarted in pursuing what he thought to be the national interest. As for Roger Blough, *Time* said of his televised news conference that he did not "persuasively show how Big Steel could better meet increased competition here and abroad by raising prices."

For the most part, the magazines of opinion reacted about as expected, with liberal publications such as *The New Republic, The Reporter* and *The Nation* supporting the President, and conservative journals such as the *National Review* and *Barron's* critical of him.

Except for the Soviet bloc papers and the press of the more left-wing neutral countries, the foreign press reaction was almost invariably favorable to President Kennedy. This was especially true in Western Europe, where, according to Max Lerner, the struggle was viewed as "not just the steel barons against Kennedy but as symbol against symbol. It was the symbol of an economic oligarchy pitted against the symbol of the people as workers and consumers." The eventual Kennedy victory led to a measurable increase in his prestige in Europe and elsewhere and erased some of the doubt, as it did with the Chicago *Tribune,* concerning the President's decisiveness. The President's vigorous action to roll back prices was compared favorably with the struggles of past Presidents against economic interests. A French newspaper commented that "one could almost hear Theodore Roosevelt declaring war on the trusts," and Italian newspapers reached back to the New Deal to find a parallel, pointing out that U. S. monetary stability, the Administration's anti-inflation campaign and trade union peace were all threatened by what they described as the steel companies' *"coup de main."* After his victory, the President was described as having "won with flying colors, Irish tenacity, with enthusiasm and self-assurance stemming from the best New Deal tradition." The London *Economist* felt that the steel companies had done "their best [or worst] to bring back to Washington the antagonism between business and government that has always been associated with a Democrat in the White House." The Japanese press, after some initial enthusiasm at the possibility that Japanese steel exports might benefit from the price rise, was quite outspoken in its praise of the President's action.

As for the Russian press, even the careful reader of *Pravda* and *Izvestia* would have looked in vain for the full story of the steel crisis. The Soviet press reported it spottily, saying that the action of the steel companies reflected the Marxist-Leninist conception of a "capitalist" society in action and that the workers would be the ones to suffer most by the price increase. It stressed that the action emphasized the "cynical indifference" of the monopolies, which really run the United States, to the people's interest, and said that the President admitted that he could not interfere in the matter. Having crawled out on that propaganda limb, the Russians were then forced to shift direction when the steel companies retreated.

This was no problem, of course; it was just a matter of a few new press releases pointing out that pressure from Washington had forced the steel companies to retreat, but that the Administration's action was taken not because it had the people's interest at heart, but to save its own prestige. It was also intimated that one of the main reasons Washington acted was because the price rise would increase the cost of military equipment. The following translated statement from a Moscow radio broadcast sums up as well as anything the reaction of the Kremlin's propagandists:

> Washington's decision to lay siege to the steel barons was therefore in no way motivated by concern for the welfare of rank-and-file Americans, but by the wish to protect the interests of the most influential monopolist circles at the expense of a comparatively limited group of industrialists. Therein lies the truth which American propaganda is trying so hard to conceal or distort.

Public Reaction

Although public reaction is a little more difficult to pinpoint, early in the President's struggle with big steel it became quite clear that he very definitely had public opinion with him. Of course, each side reported that its mail supported its position. After the battle was over, the White House announced that it had received 2,000 telegrams and that they had run about 5 to 2 in favor of the President. Thousands of letters were also received, but no tabulation was made. On the other hand, Roger Blough told his stockholders that he had received about 3,600 letters and that 71 percent of them backed steel.

The majority of letters to the editors in the newspapers appeared to be in support of the President, and it should be recalled that the *Wall Street Journal*'s extensive survey showed the man in the street as siding with the President. The *Journal* conceded that the President appeared to have public opinion on his side, and after the battle was over, it quoted the Detroit autoworker who had said, "Kennedy is mad and so am I," and then devoted a long editorial to explaining why the man in the street should think twice before cheering the President's action.

There were other indications that the public had voted thumbs down on Big Steel's price increase. Officials at Inland, for instance, reported that hundreds of telegrams and telephone calls were received after the company had announced its intention to hold the price line and that they were almost unanimous in support of Inland's action. Officials said the messages came from the general public as well as from stockholders, other business firms and Inland's customers. Numerous columnists and other feelers of the national pulse also reported popular sentiment running with the President. Making his own private check of the Midwest's pulse, James Reston reported from Chicago immediately after big steel's retreat, that "one of the remarkable things about last week's uproar out here is the contrast between the statements of Roger Blough and the comments of casual passers-by in the streets of Chicago or even in the streets of Republican suburbs. Almost unanimously, the casual comments in the street favor the President, and, what is more surprising, a great many people demand to know why Kennedy didn't 'just take over and tell Blough what to do.'" Reston concluded, as did the majority of columnists and commentators, that U. S. Steel had been severely hurt with the public, a fact which was borne out by the reaction from Madison Avenue, where advertising men reported that the public relations industry was united in its astonishment at U. S. Steel's action.

In fact, as the dust began to settle on the steel crisis and steelmen began to take a less impassioned view of public reaction it became increasingly obvious to them that the steel industry in general and U. S. Steel in particular had suffered a severe public relations blow. Steelmakers viewed this so seriously that within three months they quietly hired the polling firm of Elmo Roper & Associates to make a survey of what people thought about them. The purpose was to give the industry the necessary information on which to base a big new public relations campaign. The sales pitch was to be: Steel is a progressive industry led by "experienced and forward-looking executives; everybody benefits if the steel industry is profitable." Although the pitch was decided on before Roper had finished its survey, the nature of the theme does give some idea of what steelmen imagined the public thought of them after the industry's run-in with the President. "We've made some bad public relations mistakes in the past," said a public relations official in a large steel company. "Now we are bringing the problem to the forefront as we never have before." Included in the six general themes to be featured in the new program was the idea that steel executives are "warm" and "human," which even the *Wall Street Journal* thought might be a little tricky to promote.

The Gallup Poll, which no one professes to trust but which everyone quotes when it supports the point he is trying to make, also showed public opinion on the side of the President. Gallup interviewers asked the following question: *"What is your opinion about the action which President Kennedy took to get the steel companies to change their plans about raising steel prices?"*

According to Gallup, 58 percent of the people showed a favorable reaction as opposed to only 22 percent unfavorable. At the same time, 68 percent said that they felt the President should also take similar action to restrain labor unions from asking for wage increases. This poll was taken of a cross section of people, but even when tabulated by occupation groups, a surprising 63 percent of labor unions said that the President should also act to restrain labor.

The first Presidential "popularity" poll after the fracas did show the President's popularity rating down four percentage points, "largely," said the Gallup analysts, "because of the losses he suffered among professional and business people and white collar workers." This drop reflected the first wave of anti-Kennedy feeling in the business community, although a later Gallup Poll asking the public at large whether it felt Kennedy was "antibusiness" showed an unusual 7 to 1 majority as feeling that he was not.

Assessing reaction in the professional and intellectual community is perhaps the most difficult task of all, but generally speaking it would appear that professional economists and the academic community sided with the President. "We've got a situation today which didn't exist twenty-five years ago." said Georgia Tech industrial expert Kennedy Wagner. "A major economic phenomenon in that a six-dollar price rise in steel can affect our whole foreign policy. Whether or not we like it, government has to take action. I might disagree with this decision but not the decision to act." Less critical was Northeastern University President Asa Knowles. "The action was entirely in the national interest." said Knowles. "If he hadn't taken it, the increased steel price would have resulted in high costs to the taxpayers all the way down the line." President Clark Kerr, of the University of California, did not think the President's action indicated that the Administration planned to enter the price-setting business: "This was a specific solution to a specific problem." He also felt it would cause steel executives to give a little more thought to administered prices. "Steel is not really a competitive market." said Kerr. "It's one big company."

Not all economists sided with the President. Milton Friedman, of the University of Chicago, said that it "brings home dramatically how much power for a police state resides in Washington." And another University of Chicago professor, Yale Brozen, was quoted as saying; "Kennedy's action was the greatest display of dictatorial white-fatherness one could imagine. Who is this or any Administration to say what prices should be?" Dr. Raymond Saulnier, President Eisenhower's Chairman of the Council of Economic Advisers, agreed. "I think his action," commented Saulnier, "will go down in the books as the outstanding example of government interference in a business decision in our history."

No doubt, the academic community and the professional economists will be discussing and debating the President's conflict with big steel for years, and supporting statements for both sides, as with any economic issue, will not be hard to produce. However, of all the comments emanating from the academic world, the most interesting one by far was reported by Max Lerner. Immediately following the steel crisis, Lerner spoke at Yale before a student organization which called itself Challenge. Lerner said that one of the things this group was most concerned about was the "military-industrial complex" which President Eisenhower had referred to in his farewell address. Lerner said that, looking at the steel crisis in its broadest context, the students seemed to feel that any President who could take on the steel barons and send them running would also be able to keep the whole military-industrial complex in check, which they felt was the most encouraging thing to come out of the crisis.

Perhaps the most unusual yardstick for measuring public opinion was developed by the New York *Post*. Recalling the President's contrasting the risk of American boys overseas—mentioning that "four were killed in the last two days in Vietnam"—with the pursuit of private power by a "handful of steel executives," the *Post* decided to interview members of the families of two of those servicemen. One had been Staff Sergeant Wayne E. Marchand, twenty-nine, a career soldier. His brother James, a paratrooper, told a *Post* reporter: "We heard the President's speech and we knew he was talking about Wayne. As for myself, I'm pretty bitter that some people are putting money in their pockets while others are paying with their lives." When Mrs. Thelma Anson, mother of Major

Milton D. Britton, who was killed when the observation plane in which he was riding crashed after take-off, was asked for comment by a *Post* reporter, she replied: "He was right. I think every company should make a profit, but we can't go to extremes when boys are dying—or being captured by Commies, which is even worse. I was bitter."

Political Reaction

Despite the Republican Party's historic alignment with big business and vice versa (officers and directors of big steel gave more than $135,000 to Republicans in the 1960 campaign) in the face of the obvious public support for President Kennedy, the Republicans found it difficult to take a position. The first glimmer of hope in the immediate aftermath was the possibility that the Defense Department had violated the law in placing a defense contract with Lukens Steel without the usual sealed-bid procedure. At least two Republican Representatives demanded that the House initiate an investigation of the Lukens' contract, but nothing came of the demands and the issue eventually faded away.

Interestingly enough, behind the scenes there were many Republicans who were delighted at what had happened. One top GOP official quoted in *Newsweek* put it this way: "In the long run, it may well be good for us. This guy Kennedy did a snow job on business. He got businessmen thinking that they had a good friend in him . . . We have nowhere to go for money except to business. I just hope they keep fighting. I'm telling you that our financial bloodstream was drying up . . ." But Republicans were generally silent or evasive in public. As already seen, only a handful of them spoke up in defense of U. S. Steel during the crisis and some who were running for office actually came out against the increase. And the silence continued. William E. Miller, Chairman of the Republican National Committee, even conceded that "probably at first blush, President Kennedy has gained politically over the short run," although Miller felt that in the long run, if steel became a "depressed industry," the Administration would be hurt. Former President Eisenhower at first declined to comment, and House Republican Leader Charles Halleck said: "I haven't quite yet decided what I'm going to say about it." However, Representative Robert Wilson of California, Chairman of the Republican Congressional Campaign Committee, gave a hint as to which way Republicans were leaning when he asked for a "full and frank disclosure of the threats or pressures brought to bear" against the steel companies by the Administration during their clash.

Finally, nine days after U. S. Steel announced its price increase, the Republicans found their position. On April 19, the Joint Senate-House Republican Leadership Committee issued the following manifesto:

We, the members of the Joint Senate-House Republican Leadership, deplore the necessity for issuing this statement, but the issues involved are too compelling to be ignored.

Beyond the administrative operations of the Federal Government, it is a proper function of a President, in fact it is a duty, to help American private enterprise maintain a stable economy. In our free society he must usually find his way by persuasion and the prestige of his office.

Last week President Kennedy made a determination that a 3½ percent increase in the price of steel would throw the American economy out of line on several fronts. In the next 24 hours, the President directed or supported a series of governmental actions that imperiled basic American rights, went far beyond the law, and were more characteristic of a police state than a free government.

We, the members of the Joint Senate-House Republican Leadership believe that a fundamental issue has been raised: Should a President of the United States use the enormous powers of the Federal Government to blackjack any segment of our free society into line with his personal judgment without regard to law?

Nine actions which followed President Kennedy's press conference of Wednesday, April 11, were obviously a product of White House direction or encouragement and must be considered for their individual and cumulative effect. They were:

1. The Federal Trade Commission publicly suggested the possibility of collusion, announced an immediate investigation, and talked of $5,000-a-day penalties.

2. The Justice Department spoke threateningly of antitrust violations and ordered an immediate investigation.

3. Treasury Department officials indicated they were at once reconsidering the planned increase in depreciation rates for steel.

4. The Internal Revenue Service was reported making a menacing move toward U. S. Steel's incentive-benefits plan for its executives.

5. The Senate Antitrust and Monopoly Subcommittee began subpoenaing records from 12 steel companies, returnable May 14.

6. The House Antitrust Subcommittee announced an immediate investigation, with hearings opening May 2.

7. The Justice Department announced it was ordering a Grand Jury investigation.

8. The Department of Defense seemingly ignoring laws requiring competitive bidding, publicly announced it was shifting steel purchases to companies which had not increased prices, and other Government agencies were directed to do likewise.

9. The FBI began routing newspapermen out of bed at 3 A.M. on Thursday, April 12, in line with President Kennedy's press-conference assertion that "we are investigating" a statement attributed to a steel-company official in the newspapers.

Taken cumulatively, these nine actions amount to a display of naked political power never seen before in this nation.

Taken singly, these nine actions are punitive, heavy-handed and frightening.

Although the President at his press conference made it clear that "price and wage decisions in this country . . . are and ought to be freely and privately made," there was nothing in the course of action which he pursued that supported this basic American doctrine.

Indeed, if big Government can be used to extralegally reverse the economic decisions of one industry in a free economy, then it can be used to reverse the decisions of any business, big or small, of labor, of farmers—in fact, of any citizen.

Most disturbing in its implications was the use of the FBI. Since the days of our Founding Fathers, this land has been the haven of millions who fled from the feared knock on the door in the night.

We condone nothing in the actions of the steel companies except their right to make an economic judgment without massive retaliation by the Federal Government.

Temporarily President Kennedy may have won a political victory, but at the cost of doing violence to the fundamental precepts of a free society.

This nation must realize that we have passed within the shadow of police-state methods.

We hope that we never again step into those dark regions, whatever the controversy of the moment, be it economic or political.

It is significant, as many political writers noted, that the Republicans refused to condone the steel companies' action—only their right to make an economic decision. This put them in the politically awkward position of having to defend an act with which they basically disagreed, hence their only argument when and if the issue came up during the coming campaign was to say that they were opposed to the *manner* in which the President had acted. This is the weakest kind of political argument, as the Democratic National Committee was gleefully aware, and it did not take Chairman John Bailey long to come back with a scathing answer. "The question is," asked Bailey, hitting at the basic weakness of the Republican position, "were they for or against the price increase? If they were against it, how would they have protected the public? If they were for it, why not tell that to the people?"

Occasionally a Republican would speak out, but for the most part, once the genuine anti-Kennedy feeling (discussed in the following pages) began to emerge in the business community, the Republicans seemed more and more inclined to remain silent and let the businessman carry the fight. As spring wore into summer, about the only major Republican with any inclination to harp back to the steel crisis was General Eisenhower, who was not running for office. In a long article in the *Saturday Evening Post,* the former President attacked the Administration for forcing the steel companies to retreat by "intimidation." But even Eisenhower hedged on the real issue. "Having no detailed knowledge about the economics of steel manufacturing," he wrote, "I am unable to say whether or not the companies were entitled to the 3.5-percent price increase which brought down on their heads the wrath of the Administration. It seems obvious that the timing of the announcement by Big Steel—coming almost immediately after a major labor settlement—was bad public relations."

The Democrats were remaining discreetly quiet. Former President Harry Truman, speaking with unusual restraint, said matter-of-factly: "He was right, or he couldn't have won. It's as simple as that." There were of course occasional outbursts of crowing, such as the remark by California's Democratic State Vice-Chairman Eugene Wyman, who could not refrain from commenting: "Some people who have jaywalked for years stop when there's a new cop on the beat. Big business, which has been jaywalking all over the country for years, learned there's a new cop on the beat." However, either by instinct or on direct orders from the White House and the Democratic National Committee, the Democrats quickly silenced such remarks. The new cop on the beat was having enough trouble trying to make peace with the jaywalkers.

The President and his aides knew they were on the right side of the issue politically, as almost every political columnist conceded. The businessmen were making a lot of noise, but their discontent—from a strictly political point of view—did not worry the White House. In fact, it is possible the temper tantrum in the business community might even have been welcome—politically. "Let me tell you something," said one Presidential aide. "To win elections you've got to have someone to be against. You've got to have the right enemies. If I were running for office, I'd want to have the Chamber of Commerce oppose me; to have big business oppose me; and if you threw in the AMA, I'd be sure to win."

Such remarks, however, were made in private. In public the Democratic reaction was considerably more restrained. In June, at a Democratic Candidates' Conference in Washington, Ted Sorensen was asked if he would give some guidance on what position Democratic candidates should take on the steel crisis. Here is Sorensen's reply, taken from the transcript of the conference:

I think it is important for all of you to remember if this steel controversy comes up, simply try to remind people of the facts of what actually happened. Cut through all of this oratory about "tyranny," and "usurpation of power." There are only three actions which were actually taken.

The Defense Department met its obligation to the taxpayers to try to purchase steel at the lowest possible price.

The Justice Department met its obligation to law and order by initiating an investigation as to whether a series of simultaneous and identical price rises were the result of monopoly, or the result of coincidence; and no self-respecting antitrust division under any administration, I believe, could have just sat back and watched that happen without doing something about it.

The President of the United States went on the air at his press conference and pointed out why the public interest was concerned with a price rise in steel. According to the Joint Economic Committee, the steel industry alone is responsible for 40 percent of the inflation which has occurred since World War II. Now one of the reasons why the President was certainly justified in doing so was because for the several months preceding that time the steel industry had accepted his help in his efforts to persuade the union to accept a noninflationary wage settlement within the Administration's productivity guidelines. And great pressure was put on the union.

When anyone says, "Is he going to do it to the unions?" bear in mind that he did it to the unions first, to the steel union, and persuaded them to accept that. He already told the United Automobile workers he intends to adhere to that policy wherever possible.

Now, we do not want to be in the position of setting either wages or prices. These are guidelines and they are intended for the guidance of those who are engaged in collective bargaining, which is the way it should be. But I think the President certainly made it clear that the policy of fighting inflation is going to be carried out against whoever tries to buck it.

This was the Democratic position, but due to Republican disinclination to bring the subject up, the Democrats rarely had to defend themselves; whenever they did they stuck pretty faithfully to Mr. Sorensen's "guidelines."

Reaction in the Business Community

Easily the strangest and most interesting reaction came from the business community. It was obvious from the first that businessmen were of mixed feelings about U. S. Steel's action. As already seen, it came on most of them as a surprise and a time when they and financiers alike agreed that the steel market and the economy were not ready for a price rise. Wall Street's first reaction was that the increase made no sense whatsoever, and this feeling was endorsed by many, although not all, businessmen. Of course, most of them were opposed to the Administration's action on general principles, but this did not necessarily mean they approved the particular price increase.

At first, they tended to blame the whole affair on Roger Blough and U. S. Steel. "There's no question that steel is definitely in need of some profit relief," said one executive quoted in *Business Week,* "but there certainly was a better way to present its case. Steel's timing was the key to the whole debacle." An even more significant indication of how top executives felt was given by Richard Wilson, Washington correspondent for the Cowles' publications. "A spokesman of one of the nation's biggest industrial combines, quite equal to U. S. Steel in size, was highly critical Saturday of U. S. Steel's behavior," wrote Wilson. "He thought that it had caused great difficulties for all of industry by forcing the issue of how wide is the power of the White House when, in all realism, it would have been better to leave that matter in doubt. This spokesman said that he knew the opinion at the top level in many big corporations, and that it was universally critical of U. S. Steel for having bungled."

Similarly, *Business Week* said that the majority of business executives polled by its staff agreed that a steel price rise was the last thing needed in the present balance-of-payments situation. There were some who even took the stiff-upper-lip attitude and professed to see a bright side to the crisis. "I really believe some White House advisers were shocked by the aftermath of the price controversy," commented one steelman. "And I do not believe that we are barred in any way from seeking price relief once again, when the market will take it."

Thus throughout the crisis and in its immediate aftermath business seemed to be wavering between the position of one executive who said; "I don't think it's going to be too serious one way or another. I was awfully mad for a couple of days but you get over that," and another who said, almost with a note of panic: "I just figured that this is the way Hitler took over." It is even possible that if they had been left alone to

hink about what had happened and to reflect on the meaning
of the President's words, the majority might have forgotten
he steel crisis, marked it up to the President's quick Irish
emper reacting to what he felt was an open double cross, and
gone back to their former uneasy truce with the Kennedy
Administration. The Gallup Poll had found that 45 percent
of the businessmen polled favored the President, whereas only
34 percent opposed him. This poll was released on May 20.

However, businessmen were not allowed to forget. From
all sides, their favorite opinion leaders were bombarding
hem with dire predictions about the perils of life under a
ocialistic dictator in the White House. If there was any
chance at all of peace between the White House and the business community, it was certainly not being helped by such
molders of business opinion as the *U. S. News,* David
Lawrence, the *Wall Street Journal,* the New York *Herald
Tribune,* and Donald Rogers. These men and publications
kept up a steady fire of anti-Administration dialectic which
he Administration found increasingly difficult to counteract.

For instance, immediately following the crisis, a *Wall Street
Journal* columnist reminded its readers that one of the coun-
ry's worst recessions had followed President Roosevelt's at-
ack on excessive prices and production rates in 1937. "None
of this means, of course," said the *Journal* article, "that the
decline in business was caused entirely by the Roosevelt
moves. It is probable that a recession would have occurred in
any case. There is a real question, however, whether it would
have gone so deep." Similarly, David Lawrence continually
hurled the words, "socialistic" and "Communist" around as
f his cherished, long-held belief that the Democrats were
leading us down the road to Communism was more a reality
han ever. Gradually at first, and then with an almost hysterical burst of hatred, businessmen all over the country began
to cry that the Administration was antibusiness and that
Kennedy was out to get the businessman and reopen the old

war between the Democrats and big business. "Now the die
has been cast," wrote Lawrence in a column devoted in part
to reporting the smoldering discontent and in part to fanning
the flame. Rogers reported that, "in my opinion, after can-
vassing the executives, many of them young men on the way
up in several corporations on several industrial fronts, the
President has lost a great deal of his much-vaunted popularity
since the steel crisis . . . Businessmen now suspect," continued
Rogers, "that the leaders of this Administration do not understand the nature of profits, nor have any respect for the necessity to earn a gain from investment of risk capital."

There was a certain sense of glee in their attack on the
President which businessmen found hard to contain. Barry
Goldwater, expressing a thought that many Republicans and
anti-Democratic business leaders must have shared, told a
conference of the Iron and Steel Institute that the steel
episode may have been a "blessing in disguise" because of the
way in which it exposed "the degree of antibusiness sentiment in the present Administration." As the President continued his efforts to placate business and the Republican press
and business journals continued to scream that he had declared war on business, it was hard not to agree with columnist Inez Robb, who wrote: "It makes an industrious reader
of the business press wonder who declared war on whom, and
who fired the first blockbuster." Miss Robb devoted one of
her New York *World Telegram and Sun* columns to pointing
out that the business spokesmen had actually tossed down the
glove as early as January 1961.

Meanwhile, as the panic continued to build, it was not
helped by reports from investment counselors such as Model
Roland & Company, predicting that in the future steel stockholders might have to expect drastically reduced dividends
as the steel companies would be forced to use what profits they
could manage to squeeze out of their operations for modernization of equipment. Many business executives were big

stockholders in steel and related industries, and the prospect of reduced earnings from stocks which were already wavering and had shown a declining profit-earning capacity hit them where it hurt the most. Finally, on May 28 when the stock market broke, this was the last straw, as far as the businessman was concerned. Many lost sizable fortunes overnight, and in their discouragement—and in some cases downright bitterness—there seemed to be only one logical place to hang the blame: the White House. After the stock market crash, the business community's hostility for the President and his Administration was no longer confined to mumblings in club lounges and locker rooms. It was a major news story, and although at first the White House did not take the grumblings seriously, gradually—as the emotional intensity of the businessman's feelings became more and more apparent—the President, too, became alarmed and began to look on the "Kennedy is antibusiness" cry as a major domestic issue.

CHAPTER 10

"... A Time To Gather Stones ..."

> We have no idea of going around flexing our muscles at everyone.
>
> *—A top Administration official, quoted in the* Wall Street Journal, *commenting on the aftermath of the steel crisis*

In the weeks after the crisis, a great many steel companies held their annual stockholders' meetings. Since most company presidents took the occasion to comment on the price fiasco, as the steel crisis was rapidly coming to be known in the industry, the meetings provided a sampling of the steel industry mood immediately following its clash with the President. Although this mood was sometimes difficult to assess because so many voices were speaking out at once, there was one thing on which every steel executive agreed: the steel industry was still in need of a price increase. This theme was struck by almost every one of them, and it was expressed only two days after the President had successfully rolled back prices, and by the man most responsible for his success— Joseph L. Block, President of Inland Steel. "Steel profits are inadequate," said Block in Japan, "especially when compared with those of other American industries, but we decided we have to balance objectives. America has this balance-of-payments problem and there is the struggle with the Soviet bloc

o we decided a price increase was not in the national inter-
st."

Block repeated this thought in Chicago at a press confer-
nce later in the month after Inland's annual stockholders'
neeting. However, he stressed the fact that the public must
ee the need for increased profits as a means of modernizing
ndustry before prices could be raised. But he hedged on all
questions concerning exactly when prices could be raised. In
televised interview before the meeting, Block also had some
omments about the run-in with the President. He said that
ne felt the President was well within his rights to point out
now the national interest would be affected by a steel price
ncrease, but that the President's methods of bringing pres-
ure to bear on the industry were open to criticism. "I don't
hink the FBI and subpoenas and grand juries should be part
of those methods," Block said. "I've always felt," he added,
'that steel has been made a whipping boy—not only by this
Administration but by others."

Bethlehem Steel's Arthur B. Homer also had quite a bit
o say in late April. At a news conference in which Bethlehem
eported its first-quarter earnings, Homer stressed the fact
hat the steel industry's failure to win a price increase earlier
n the month did not rule out the possibility of a future in-
rease. He also said that during the crisis no one in the Ad-
ninistration contacted Bethlehem, and that he wanted to
nake it clear that his company rescinded the price increase
not because of pressure from the Administration, but solely
because two of its more important competitors had not backed
up U. S. Steel. "After Inland and Kaiser refused to go along,"
aid Homer, "Bethlehem knew that price increases for our
products were not competitively feasible at that time. We
ould not ask our customers to pay higher prices for our steel
han were being paid by the competitors who obtained their
teel from other sources." Although Bethlehem is the nation's
argest shipbuilder, Homer firmly denied that the decision

of the Defense Department to divert steel orders to other companies affected its decision. As for the future, Homer stressed the fact that there was an urgent need for more realistic treatment in depreciation allowances and taxes.

At the Lone Star Steel Company's annual meeting, President Kennedy received a good lacing from the head of the company, E. B. Germany. "The victory of government over steel will be reflected in all other industries for years to come," said Germany. "No company or industry may now raise prices without harboring the fear, and justifiably so, that the Administration may decide to employ the crushing weapons so recently displayed." In Germany's opinion, the President had assumed "dictatorial powers." However, Germany also castigated U. S. Steel. "No incident in my memory," he said, "equals this one for utter disregard of the necessity for giving the public a reasonable, logical and factual explanation before the act."

The annual meeting of Crucible Steel, a company which had not raised prices, was not so heated, but President Joel Hunter said he did not rule out the possibility of a selective price rise sometime in the future, though he felt that a general rise was "remote."

Edward J. Hanley, Chairman and President of the Allegheny Ludlum Steel Corporation, another company which had not raised prices, told his stockholders that in his opinion prices would have been reduced even without any pressure from the White House. "Some of the steel companies, at least which increased prices two weeks ago misjudged their market in some respects," said Hanley. He said that the only other explanation for the move by the top producers was that they really expected to retract some of the boosts later, because of competitive conditions. "In any event," he said, "and most unfortunately, the President and his advisers did not give old fashioned economics a real chance to work. I feel certain that if they had, many of the announced price increases would have been rescinded by now without the help of a Presidential whiplashing on TV, the FBI, the Grand Jury investigation, Senator Gore and Senator Kefauver." Hanley still insisted that Allegheny Ludlum needed higher profits in order to modernize.

Stockholders at Republic Steel's annual meeting were told by President Patton that "we must have adequate profits to help provide the efficient and modern steelmaking facilities that can keep us competitive." Patton also criticized the President for the methods used in rolling back prices, although he conceded that the Administration had the right to try to persuade the companies not to raise prices.

The chorus continued. But the really interesting theme running through the annual meetings was not the consistency with which each company denounced the President and maintained the need for increased profits, but the fact that in announcing their earnings for the first quarter of 1962, every company showed a substantial profit improvement over the same recession-affected quarter of 1961. Even U. S. Steel was no exception. On April 24, Roger Blough met the press for the first time since his televised news conference. This meeting was for the purpose of announcing U. S. Steel's first-quarter earnings, and Blough's principal problem was that he had to explain that U. S. Steel's first-quarter earnings for 1962 were the highest for any quarter since the second quarter of 1961 and that U. S. Steel was still paying a healthy dividend—1 cents a share, as contrasted with only 47 cents a share paid in the same quarter in 1961.

"I wonder if the lay public is not going to feel there is something inconsistent," asked one reporter, "in the urgent need to raise prices recently . . . and the fact that dividends now can be maintained at the same level?" Blough insisted that there was just no margin for reinvestment, and later, in response to another question, stressed that there were thousands of U. S. Steel stockholders who were dependent on their stocks for income and that therefore dividends could not be curtailed. However, he never really seemed to give a clear answer, and at one point was reduced to commenting: "I can appreciate that things are difficult to understand, particularly if I try to explain them."

Unlike most of the other steel company presidents, Blough did not attack the President's action in rolling back prices, and in response to one question, he said that he definitely did not feel the President wanted to determine what prices would be in steel or any other industry. He also emphasized the fact that, despite the need for increased profits, U. S. Steel was not contemplating a price rise at any time in the near future. As for what caused U. S. Steel to back down in its attempted price rise—competition or government pressure—he said: ". . . when some of your principal competitors either don't change their prices or reduce them, you see a very clear instance of the competitive system working, and . . . I would say that this is the area in which you should place the weight."

It was a difficult session for Blough. "The striking thing about the interview," wrote New York *Post* columnist James Wechsler, after attending the press conference, "was the sense that one had been in the presence of a nervous, uneasy, bewildered tycoon—a top-dog who views himself as an under-dog, but who deeply resents the notion that other people are meddling with his business, and who clings to a desperate faith in old maxims. And who, on this lovely April day, probably wished he were on the golf course."

Two weeks later, on a lovely day in May, Blough again had occasion to wish he were on the golf course. This time, it was U. S. Steel's annual stockholders' meeting, reported by those in attendance as one of the noisiest on record. In general the meeting seemed to support Blough, although at times he did not appear to have control. The questioning from the floor was quite rough, and at one point a stockholder asked: "In view of what has happened, wouldn't it be best f you resigned?" Mr. Blough thought that was a matter for the board of directors. However, during the course of the meeting Blough made an interesting observation which reflected the company's efforts to see some brightness in what was generally a dismal experience.

"I want to make it very clear it was not planned this way," said Blough, commenting on the steel crisis, "but we believe that an important public relations gain was made as a by-product of the recent controversy. For years we've been trying to explain the serious profit squeeze, the need to improve the cost-price relationship, and the necessity of more adequate depreciation allowance. I believe we have a far greater understanding today of the part profit plays, not only for the company earning it, but for the economy as a whole. We have seen clear evidence in Washington that our actions have served as a catalyst in generating more widespread understanding that we cannot have a strong American industry without adequate profit."

Blough also thought that U. S. Steel's action had had a beneficial effect on the Administration. "May I add—and I have been in Washington several times since this happened," he said, "and I have had some interesting and clear evidences from some of our friends in Washington—that this whole incident has acted as a catalyst to the thinking there. It had sort of brought people up, and they began to examine what it is that is going to give us employment in this country. What is it that is going to permit this country to compete among nations? It isn't weakened industry—it is a strong industry. How do you get a strong industry except through adequate profits? . . . some of the people down there . . . seem to be telling me a little different story about understanding it than they did before."

All in all, the period immediately following the steel crisis was a difficult one for the steel executives. Despite the brighter side described by Blough, they had suffered a tre-

mendous public relations blow. To counteract it, they had to
stress repeatedly the need for profits—at the same time that
they were announcing high profits and high dividends for the
first quarter of 1962. At the same time, Washington was still
talking tough. The White House had let it be known that
despite the President's willingness to let bygones be bygones
the Administration's policy of controlling inflation at all cost
still stood. At a press conference on April 24, Secretary
Hodges admitted that it might be necessary for the Govern
ment to take action in order to prevent a price increase in
the aluminum industry. To make matters worse, on April 26
a Federal Grand Jury announced indictments against four
steel companies—U. S. Steel, Bethlehem, the Erie Forge and
Steel Corporation and the Midvale-Heppenstall Company—
for price-fixing. The action, unrelated to the recent steel
crisis, was the result of an investigation which had been un
der way since March of 1961. But the public failed to make
the distinction, and the result was a new wave of antibusiness
feeling, not helped by the fact that many commentators took
the occasion to recall the recent scandals in the electrical
equipment industry when several top executives went to jail
for price-fixing.

Add to all this the fact that the stock market was suffering
a sharp decline—one which had started as early as the previous
December but which had been accelerated by the April steel
crisis—and it is easy to see why businessmen were glum and
despondent as only businessmen can be at such times. And it
did not help to have their leading public spokesmen con
tinually reminding them of the "perils" which lay ahead. On
April 20, Henry Gemmill, writing in the *Wall Street Journal*
presented a long analysis of Kennedy's economic policy in
which he concluded that the "steel pattern" would dominate
the Administration's attitude toward business and prices in
the months ahead. The essential elements of this pattern, ac
cording to Gemmill, would be: (1) absolute determination

by the Administration of what a "free market" price should be; (2) the absence of any orderly procedures for submitting price-increase proposals; and (3) enforcement of the price structure by violent, improvised sanctions. An even more dreadful future for the businessman was envisioned by the *U. S. News* in its April 30 issue. According to David Lawrence's publication, nothing less than a full-scale, organized "planned economy" was in the works. "Steel crackdown was one more signal," said the *U. S. News*. "A planned economy, directed from Washington, is what Mr. Kennedy now has in mind. The plan involves vast federal powers, never before equaled in peacetime."

As April wore into May the prevailing mood of the steel industry and business in general was perhaps best expressed by Avery C. Adams, President of Jones & Laughlin, who told his stockholders: "This is a sustained attack on the free enterprise system. It may be an all-out war."

A little over two weeks after the steel crisis, a reporter asked the President, on the telephone, if he was aware of the delayed but now apparent general concern of the business community over his actions during the rollback of steel prices. "Are they aware," he shot back, "of my concern about them?"

The answer was typical Kennedy and goes a long way toward explaining the White House attitude about business discontent, at least in the first weeks after the steel crisis. It is important that this attitude be fully understood. The President and his advisers were not being intimidated by the growing hostility in the business community. They made it clear to everyone who approached them that the basic policy of maintaining economic stability—even if it meant again bringing pressure to bear on both labor and management—would not be altered. The President was aware of the emotional response to the steel incident, but felt that this, too, would pass; that like the Bay of Pigs debacle, it would eventually recede into the background. As for the violent feelings among businessmen, the evidence of which was gradually emerging, the White House staff had no illusions as to its real nature. Despite all his efforts to woo business, the President was fully aware that the truce between big business and the Administration was an uneasy thing at best. Political realists that they are, the New Frontiersmen knew that the main reason the business community had been silent for so long was that it had nothing with which to hit back at the President. Now, suddenly, businessmen had their issue and were returning to form. "Not one of those guys who is making the noise now," said one of Kennedy's lieutenants, "voted for us in 1960, and not one of them is going to vote for us. Who are they trying to kid? We never had them and we aren't going to get them."

White House aides such as Walter Heller stressed how much in common business and government really have. Heller said that he was reminded of this again after attending the Chamber of Commerce dinner and talking with some of the top men in industry such as Edmund Martin. "The trouble," said Heller, "is that when one of these brush-fire wars comes along, everyone automatically slips back into the old clichés about business and government." Heller felt that the cooperation of the two, which had been progressing nicely until the steel crisis, would be restored as soon as the bad feelings had been erased. Regardless of how some members of the Administration might feel about business and businessmen, the President and his closest economic advisers knew that a healthy economy was not possible without a healthy business community, and they intended to continue working toward that goal.

Meanwhile, despite his huffy answer to the reporter, the President was indeed concerned about the hostility which had been aroused. For one thing, the anti-Kennedy mail being

received in the White House was now running in the majority—a rare experience for the New Frontiersmen. It also
seemed that complaints of the businessmen were drowning
out almost everything the President did to publicize his own
program. For instance, he took special pains to air a report of
his 21-man advisory committee on labor-management policy,
because among other things the report recommended some
curtailment of labor's power. But the reaction to the report
was dominated by business complaints that it urged increasing the Government's role in labor-management disputes
affecting the national interest. In a much publicized dissent,
Henry Ford, a member of the committee, said, "It is difficult
to understand how the advocacy of a more dominant government role in collective bargaining . . . can make for more
freedom in the process."

At the same time another report—issued by an emergency
board appointed by the President to help settle a wage dispute
involving 500,000 non-operating railroad workers—helped
confuse the issue. This report made the comment that the
"parties in the dispute spent only four days in face-to-face
discussion" before invoking the Railroad Act—whereas the
advisory committee had reported, in effect, that the Taft-
Hartley procedure should be made more like those in the
Railway Labor Act. However, the emergency board appointed
to consider the railroad labor-management dispute criticized
the speed with which both sides turned to the Government.
The report suggested that the Railroad Act procedures—
which the advisory committee cited as a model—had tended
to stultify collective bargaining in industry.

Such confusing incidents, blown out of all proportion by
the emotional feelings in the aftermath of the steel incident,
combined with the increasing complaints from the business
community, convinced the White House that the time had
come to redouble its efforts not only to persuade business
that he was not against it, but to make another all-out effort

to explain the Administration's labor-management policies. It had been decided that the time and place to make the President's views known would be at the April meeting of the Chamber of Commerce. The President had long been scheduled to address the meeting and told his staff that he planned to aim his talk at the nation as well as at the Chamber.

When he arrived at Constitution Hall, there was restrained applause as he approached the rostrum. Most of those in attendance were obviously hostile, but a certain curiosity was also apparent. This audience had come to see the President of the United States, regardless of the fact that he was a Democrat. Kennedy opened with a mild joke: "I want to congratulate you on your new president, President Plumley—it's nice to have a president from Massachusetts, and we're glad to have him here." He added wryly: "I don't know how widely this view is shared here."

Then he launched into his speech. (See Appendix E.) Within five minutes the audience was restless; people coughed and squirmed until the speech was over, and then applauded coolly. Later one Chamber member commented that the President had made a "good political speech" but had said "not a word" about cutting taxes or government spending. Another asked: "Will this program assure profits?" And a director of the Chamber commented icily that if the President wanted to help business, "he must help lower the tax burden . . . and he must take an equally strong position toward organized labor."

Whether the members of the Chamber knew any more about the President's economic policies after the speech was over is debatable, but no Administration spokesman has ever given a more detailed public explanation of the Kennedy Administration's view of the relationship between government and business. The President concluded on a conciliatory note: ". . . the Bible tells us that 'there is a time for every purpose under the heaven . . . and a time to cast away stones and a time to gather stones together.' [Ecclesiastes: chapter 3, verse 5.] And ladies and gentlemen, I believe that it is time for us all to gather stones together to build this country as it must be built in the coming years."

During the following month the President and his advisers continued to let it be known that the White House felt it was time for gathering stones. For example, on May 8 the President went to Atlantic City, to address a convention of the United Autoworkers. "This Administration," he said, setting the theme of his address, "has not undertaken and will not undertake to fix prices and wages in a peacetime economy. We have no intention of intervening in every labor dispute." The following day, at his press conference in Washington, he was asked to clarify his by now widely quoted remark concerning what his father had said to him about businessmen. (See Chapter 1.) After explaining what his father had actually said, the President tried to toss the whole thing off by commenting: "But that is past. Now we are working together, I hope." The next day a carefully picked delegation from the Administration went down to Virginia for a two-day meeting of top businessmen in Hot Springs. The mood there was primarily uneasy, although some cautious optimism was reported. Generally speaking, the businessmen let it be known that they were confused about the Government's "guideposts"; worried about the profit squeeze; curious as to whether the Government would apply the same pressure to labor as it had to the steel industry in holding the line against inflation; and concerned that "theorists" were pushing the President to the left. The climate was not improved by the fact that on May 11 the stock market took another sharp dip— for the fourth day in a row. The Dow-Jones average fell to the lowest point in almost fifteen months. Most businessmen at the conference seemed to think that the market decline stemmed from the same lack of confidence in prices and profits which was being felt throughout industry itself.

The President continued his campaign. In mid-May there was increased talk emanating from the White House about new efforts to get tax benefits and liberalized depreciation schedules for the businessman. This point was re-emphasized by Walter Heller in a speech made in New York before the State Society of Certified Public Accountants.

A week later the White House Conference on National Economic Issues convened in Washington, and the President opened it with an invitation for businessmen to speak out with their ideas about what was wrong and how to make the economy work. He also had a word to say about business conditions. "I read that the problem really is that business confidence may be somewhat shaken by action of certain public figures. Now, business had a high confidence in the previous Administration, yet there was a recession in 1958 and a recession in 1960. And in 1956, there was a very sharp drop in the stock market before a very good year in 1957. So that doesn't give us the answer to the problem at all . . . What we want," he concluded, "is confidence that we will be able to invest and produce and consume, which is what these basic and successful countries of Europe have had. That is what is going to cause people to reinvest and that's what is going to help make the economy move forward."

Arthur Goldberg and Walter Heller attempted to explain aspects of the Administration's economic program at the same meeting, but—according to the *U. S. News* at least—it ended with the audience as skeptical as ever.

On the other hand, at his news conference on the day after the conference, the President said he felt that in the private— as opposed to the public—sessions of the conference "there was a willingness to forget some of the basic arguments between labor and management and consider some of the new challenges." He also said he hoped for more meetings between labor, management and government in the months ahead.

If the President and his advisers felt they were making any headway, they were certainly discouraged by the report from the annual meeting of the Iron and Steel Institute held on May 24 when Allison R. Maxwell, President of Pittsburgh Steel, leveled a violent attack at the Administration. After reciting all the familiar arguments about the Administration taking us toward a "form of socialism," Maxwell had ended his speech on a note indicating the extent to which the business community in general and the steel industry in particular were still smarting from the President's televised attack.

"In this serious hour in our nation's history," cried Maxwell, parroting the President's April 11 press conference remarks, "we are confronted with grave crises abroad, when our Government is asking servicemen to risk their lives. I am sure you will find it hard, as I do, to accept a situation in which a tiny handful of government officials, in their pursuit of monopoly of power over business and industry, undermine the profit system that has made our nation great, and the very constitutional freedom they have sworn to uphold. By what principle under this Constitution, or by what act of Congress does this oligarchy set prices, malign free citizens, and unleash retaliation against those who do not conform to their decrees against pursuit of private business?" Maxwell asked. "Sixteen months ago," he concluded, "the nation asked this Administration to defend the Constitution and the principles for which it stands. Six weeks ago, we had their answer."

Perhaps the only encouraging note to come out of the meeting was that Roger Blough and Joseph Block firmly declined to comment on Maxwell's impassioned speech and pointedly refused to endorse it, despite the standing ovation Maxwell received.

Whether or not the restraint shown by businessmen such

as Block and Blough would, in the long run, have brought a more rapid truce between business and the Administration will never be known. For, only four days after Maxwell's speech, an event occurred which was to bring the ugly passions of the business community bursting to the surface as if a painful and poisonous boil had been lanced. On May 28— Black Monday—the stock market crashed. From that point on and during most of the summer of 1962, the businessman's hatred for the Kennedy Administration constituted a serious national crisis for the Administration. As already seen, the business feelings against the Kennedy Administration prior to the market crash were nearly uncontrollable. Two weeks before the crash, when the market was heading down, a high Administration official who had previously held a top job in business, visited home and reported that he was almost physically assaulted by his former associates. "You — — —!" they cried. "You're to blame for the market collapse—you and the rest of the Kennedy crowd." He added: "They turned on me as if I had personally cost them money. I can imagine what they were saying after Black Monday this week." He was right, although even he might have been stunned a little at the vehemence of some of the remarks made about the President and his advisers in the weeks immediately following the crash.

An analysis of precisely what caused the crash of 1962 is outside the scope of this book. In only five and one half hours, the market suffered a paper loss of $20.8 billion and there was nearly 10 million shares worth of trading. It was the greatest loss in history; double the loss of the blackest day in 1929. Actually, most of 1961 had witnessed a bull market, and as early as May—one year before the crash—U. S. News correspondents covering a convention of market analysts in Richmond, Virginia, reported that a great many market experts were wary of what was happening. The thinking at the convention was summed up by one analyst: "It can't go on.

Actually, I am afraid this market is already 1929 all over again, except for the fact that much less of the stock is being bought on credit."

The bull market had continued throughout 1961, and had then leveled off at an all-time high in December. During the winter and early spring of 1962, the market started to drop, taking a fairly abrupt dip at the time of the steel crisis. A brief rally followed that, but it dipped again and continued to plunge until the break on May 28. Regardless of what caused it all, the important point here was that many business people held the President and his advisers directly responsible. They argued that the President's action in the steel crisis had shattered the confidence of the public as well as the businessman and that this lack of confidence eventually resulted in a panic on Wall Street. This view, incidentally, was shared by former President Eisenhower, who at first said that irresponsible spending programs of the Administration had caused the crash. Two months later, in the *Saturday Evening Post,* he wrote: "By this time, most economists . . . are agreed that while there were other important elements in the general market situation presaging a decline in stock prices, the action against big steel did help trigger the near panic of selling . . ."

Administration economists, of course—as well as a great many neutral economists—do not agree. The position of the Administration on the role of the steel crisis in the stock market crash was stated by Walter Heller, who said that as a result of the President's action during the steel crisis, the investor had become convinced that inflation was no longer a way of life and that he did not need to hedge against it in the market. Hence, to that extent, the Administration's firm decision to roll back steel prices did play an important part in the 1962 crash, although it is questionable whether the "lack of confidence" arguments put forth were as important as most businessmen seemed to believe.

CHAPTER 11

The Great "Kennedy-Is-Antibusiness" Crusade

I MISS IKE—HELL, I EVEN MISS HARRY!
—*Legend on business cards circulated by businessmen in Texas*

Before discussing the summer of 1962 feud between the Kennedy Administration and the business community—a feud sparked by the steel crisis and blown into a major domestic issue by the stock market crash—a word should be said about the position of organized labor in the post-crisis period. During the crisis union officials were of course emphatic in their denunciation of big steel, charging that the company's double cross of the President proved what the unions had been saying all along—you couldn't trust big business. In addition, the steelworkers let the White House know that if the President failed to roll back steel prices, the Administration's "guideposts" policy was dead, as far as labor was concerned. When Kennedy's strong action against Big Steel was successful, labor was naturally pleased and perhaps even a little happy to see the big companies take such a public beating. But in the immediate aftermath most union officials were under no illusions that the Administration's attack against the steel companies spelled good news for labor. As a result of the pressure Kennedy had put on the steelworkers during the wage negotiations, the unions were aware, even before the steel crisis, that the President meant what he said about his intention to maintain price stability. But after the crisis—especially with the cries of persecution coming from the business community—labor knew that the President would be more than ever obliged to prove that his efforts to hold back inflation would also be directed against labor's wage demands. "Kennedy is already committed to being just as tough on us if the occasion arises," said one union official.

Although less vocal in their criticism, many union leaders saw much the same threat that business leaders saw in the President's display of power. One AFL–CIO official said that Kennedy's power play demonstrated the ability to dictate terms in any situation viewed by the President to involve the national interest. "The question now," he said, "is when and how government will use the new price-and-wage power." A union head said: "Instead of just being a participant, government is now the first party in the council. Labor and management will now figure the Government is ready to use force to get what it wants, so that they had better go along."

In the following weeks the Administration continued to demonstrate that its efforts to maintain price stability were not directed at business alone. At a press conference in mid-June, the President publicly urged the flight engineers' union to submit to arbitration its dispute concerning a third man in the cockpit rather than go out on strike, as the flight engineers threatened to do. Similarly, the Administration continued to oppose one of labor's pet long-range goals—the 35-hour week. Arthur Goldberg explained the Administration's position to the ILGWU convention in emphatic terms, saying, "It is my considered view that the general reduction in the work week at the present time would be to impair adversely our present stable price structure by adding increased costs that industry as a whole cannot afford to bear. The result would be that our goods would be necessarily higher priced, would be less competitive at home and abroad, and the result would be more unemployment instead of less unemployment." The mood of labor was suggested by the fact that, despite Goldberg's speech at the convention, the ILGWU delegates, who were already enjoying the 35-hour week, voted to support its adoption throughout the nation.

More important than labor's opposition to strong government intervention in labor-management disputes and their differences with the Administration on the question of the 35-hour week, was a basic disagreement with the Administration's policy that wage increases must be kept within the "guideposts" of productivity increases. For instance, in his report to the United Autoworkers Convention on May 6, Walter Reuther said: "A healthy balance between capacity and demand requires a shift in the present distribution as between labor income—wages and salaries—and nonlabor income—profits, interest and the like. Wages and salaries, at least in the immediate future, must increase faster than our normal potential for increasing productivity . . ."

After a telephone conversation with Walter Heller, Reuther issued another statement the following day, attempting to reconcile his earlier statement with the President's position. "The historic policy of the UAW with respect to wages and prices," said Reuther, ". . . commits us to achieve wage increases and fringe benefits out of the great productivity of the American economy and not out of the pockets of consumers through higher prices. This UAW policy on collective bargaining is in conformity with and supports the efforts of the President to achieve a stable price structure."

The two statements taken together, although suggesting that the UAW supported the Administration's policy in so far as it was "noninflationary," can hardly be said to be in conformity with the Administration's position. The UAW feels that labor is entitled to salary and fringe benefit increases *greater* than the increase in productivity warrants, whereas the Administration proposes that labor keep its demand within productivity gains. The UAW's objective is noninflationary because it proposes that industry absorb the cost—thereby shifting the present distribution of wages and profits—rather than pass it along to the consumer in increased prices. Obviously, businessmen anticipated future trouble from labor and were going to have to be shown anew that the Administration would be just as tough on the unions as it had been on U. S. Steel.

Despite labor's friction with the Administration concerning its labor-management policies, its protests were never as violent as those of the business community. In addition, the President was genuinely concerned about the stock market crash and whether it would shake public confidence to the extent that consumers would postpone purchases. On June 6 he called a special White House meeting to discuss the economy. Included were Secretaries Dillon and Hodges, and Heller, Sorensen and John Kenneth Galbraith, Harvard economics professor, author of *The Affluent Society* and Kennedy's Ambassador to India, who happened to be home for a medical checkup. The possible courses of action discussed included a tax cut and various pump-priming measures.

The President also continued his efforts to try to persuade businessmen to develop a better understanding of government's problems. At a meeting of the Brookings Institution's public conference for business executives and their public affairs fellows on June 7, the President said that he hoped those present would act as "ambassadors of goodwill" between Washington and the business community. He complained of the "stereotypes" which continued to hamper the dialogue between Government and business and prevented the discussion from ever getting into the sophisticated and technical problems which faced the American economy. Four days later the President was to expand on this theme in one of the most controversial episodes of the Kennedy-business feud—the President's Yale commencement address.

Just as he had elected the Chamber of Commerce meeting as the place to present a full-dress statement of the Administration's labor-management policy, he now decided that the Yale commencement exercises would be the place to set forth his reaction to the outburst of business hostility. As the commencement loomed up on his appointment calendar, Kennedy was becoming somewhat exasperated and impatient with the businessman's attitude. How, he would ask ayone who brought up the subject, could any sane businessman be alarmed and angered because he had been deprived of the painful privilege of paying $6 a ton more for the steel he used? Why was the Administration's "government intervention" so much more wicked in principle than the similar "governmental intervention" of Richard Nixon and the Eisenhower Administration during the steel strike of 1959–60? That time, the President would point out, there had been a long and crippling strike, a wage rise, and by government request, no price rise. In the recent steel crisis there had been no strike, a very moderate wage increase, and no price rise—again by government request—although admittedly more sternly requested. To this the President would add his own long list of actions designed to help businessmen and then ask why they should throw such a tantrum just because he had been a little harsh with Roger Blough for the sake of the American economy as a whole and American business in particular.

Such was the President's mood during this period—"not yet fighting mad, but . . . both impatient and mocking" was Joseph Alsop's description. It was a mood in which he could not resist reminding Federal Reserve Board Chairman William McChesney Martin of the advice Martin had given him early in the year—that the best way to convince the businessman of the Administration's good intentions would be to submit a blanced budget and work out a quick, noninflationary steel settlement. Both of these things had been done, the President noted to Martin, and yet, for all this, "everyone went mad up there [in New York]."

For the Yale speech, the President called on just about everyone around him for assistance. Assignments went to Arthur Schlesinger, Jr., McGeorge Bundy, Heller and Galbraith. This group developed a working draft which was then turned over to Ted Sorensen for final polishing. On the plane to New Haven, there were more revisions, with the President, as is his custom, making several last-minute additions. It was perhaps best summed up by a sentence which Kennedy omitted ("inadvertently," an aide said) but which was later quoted by *Newsweek:* "This Administration is not going to give way to a general hostility to business merely because there has been a single temporary disagreement with an industry, nor will the future belong to those who ignore the realities of our economic life in a neurotic search for unending reassurance."

The President opened the speech with some typical Kennedy humor. He referred to General De Gaulle's occasionally acknowledging America to be the daughter of Europe, and said that he was pleased to come to Yale, the daughter of Harvard. "It might be said now," he added, "that I have the best of both worlds, a Harvard education and a Yale degree."

The speech was long and touched on many aspects of the economy, but the section dealing with the President's attitude concerning business—especially his much-quoted reference to the "myths" which he felt were obstructing the dialogue between business and government—should be read in full. (See Appendix F.) The speech was not meant to be challenging; some aides insisted it was an olive branch. Nevertheless, it brought a heated response which rocked the White House somewhat, considering how anxious the President had been to restore peace and quiet.

The President had hardly finished his closing remarks at Yale when the kind of "political debate" he had most wanted to avoid erupted. The "myth" theme of his speech caused both businessmen and politicians to hit back hard; these "great truths" cannot be shrugged off as myths, was their reaction. For instance, regarding myth number one—"that Federal deficits create inflation and budget surpluses prevent it"—Senator Harry Byrd said: "The President and his advisers appear to be trying to prepare the country for a long series of deficits. They talk about borrowing in times of so-called recession and paying back in times of recovery. In reality, they don't pay the debt back . . . They overlook the fact that they are imposing on future generations the cost of interest payments which even now amount to ten cents out of every tax dollar paid. And this interest will be paid over and over again as we borrow more money simply to make interest payments."

Senator Barry Goldwater was even more caustic. "I am sure," he said to the Senate, "that every member would be happy if we could solve our public debt problem through the expediency of 'mythology.' Wouldn't it be nice if we could forget that nine-point-four billion which we must pay each year in interest on the national debt? We might just get the President to call it a 'myth' and write the whole thing off."

As for myth number two—"that government is big, and bad . . . and steadily getting bigger and worse . . ."—Harlee Branch, Jr., President of the Southern Company (a holding concern for four major power companies), provided the following rebuttal: "I don't know any responsible person who claims that government is bad merely because it is big. However, it is my impression that if the President had selected a pre-World War II year as the starting point to compare the growth of federal government with other sectors of the economy, he probably would have arrived at quite a different conclusion. The Federal Government grew tremendously during World War II . . . What we need to be concerned with, as the President pointed out, is not the size of government, but the necessity and effectiveness of many governmental expenditures and activities and particularly those involving competition between government and its citizens . . ."

Myth number three—"lack of confidence in the national administration"—also came in for a counterattack. "Kennedy hasn't reassured anyone," said Robert M. Bacon, a general partner in E. F. Hutton & Company in San Francisco. "The stock market reflects the degree of confidence the average businessman has in the Administration . . . It's the same old problem. Kennedy wants full employment, wants to continue to spend money and create deficits—and doesn't think deficit financing is important. He's made a gesture toward keeping wages down, but it's only a gesture."

Even Joseph Block of Inland Steel was critical of the Yale speech. "I don't agree necessarily that the things he pointed out as myths are myths," said Block, "but the time is always present when we should examine our beliefs and policies . . . I'm afraid a lot of people will take it as a combative speech. And I think it was a little combative when he said these things weren't 'myths.' When you say 'Let's re-examine,' that's right; but he has gone beyond that."

The week of June 11 was a big week in the feud, and the amount of time the President spent worrying about the business community is indicative of the energy applied to economic problems during the months of April, May, June and July 1962. Following his Yale speech, the President flew back to Washington to attend a meeting with a group of businessmen which included Roger Blough, Henry Alexander, Alan Sproul, former President of the Federal Reserve Bank of New York, Thomas J. Watson of IBM and Crawford Greenwalt, President of du Pont. Secretary Dillon and Undersecretaries

Fowler and Roosa were also present. The President gave each of the businessmen a copy of his Yale speech. The group had been formed as a result of the meeting between Blough and the President on the Tuesday following the steel crisis.

Any temporary calm which the President might have achieved with this highly publicized meeting was more than offset two days later by a speech Solicitor General Cox made at Harvard. He suggested that the trouble during the steel crisis had not been the result of the President's action, but because there had been no prescribed procedure for asserting the public interest in wage and price decisions. Cox's feeling—in line with his thinking on the problem after the President had brought him into the steel conflict with his midnight telepone call to Tuscon—was that the President's action had had too much of an *ad hoc* flavor, the implication obviously being that legislation was needed to prevent such action as U. S. Steel took, thereby making it unnecessary for the President to act as he did. This is precisely what the businessman feared most: a formal "plan" that would permit the Government to control both wages and prices "in the national interest."

The Cox speech whipped the simmering discontent into a still brighter flame. In return, the White House irritation and impatience zoomed; this produced more heat in the business community. The argument ran back and forth, with first one side seeming to have the initiative and then the other; both sides, by this time, were beginning to show the effects of the argument. In a deft assessment of the White House mood during this period, Alan Otten, one of the *Wall Street Journal's* most perceptive reporters of the Washington scene, wrote: "A counterpoint of irritation and anger is beginning to run through the reassuring tunes the Kennedy Administration has been singing to business. The new melody connotes increasing frustration over businessmen's refusal to believe the White House really has their best interest at

heart. At times the key is muted. 'How stupid can they get?'
At times it builds into an irate, 'They should see what we
could do if we really tried.' "

Actually, as more and more commentators noted during
this period, the essential conservatism of the Administration's
economic policies made the businessman's increasing hostility
all the more ironic. "This is a paradox of a high order,"
commented Bernard D. Nossiter, an economic writer for
the Washington *Post*. "Nearly every fresh announcement
from the White House enunciates a policy rooted in orthodoxy, and each evokes a louder outcry from business . . ."
It was becoming clear that the real argument was not over
economics but over power. The reaction of the business
community, so the press thesis went, was primarily due to
the businessman's realization that his power to manage was
slowly being diminished in many areas, of which pricing was
only the most recent and most dramatic example. There
was of course some truth in this, if one assumed that increased
action on the part of the Administration to fight the Cold
War, stabilize the economy, halt inflation, solve the balance-
of-payments problem and spark economic growth, automatically resulted in diminishing the power of the businessman
to control events and the economy. The President's point was
that the complex problems facing America in its present
international situation called for complex responses, some
of which affected the economy—*and that these responses were
not necessarily antibusiness.*

However, some businessmen would not listen. If this was
indeed a struggle for power, they clearly felt that they were
winning. One with contacts throughout the entire upper
echelon of big business stated that a number of businessmen
had said to him, in effect: "Now we've got him [the President]
where we want him. He'll be sorry this ever happened before
we get through with him." This attitude was confirmed by
Columnist Marquis Childs. Drew Pearson also reported that

businessmen now felt the President was on the run. "It's a rout," a prominent industrialist told Pearson.

If it was a rout, the President was not showing any signs of panic; he even found time for a quip or two in the heat of battle. While speaking to a group of Peace Corps volunteers in the Chamber of Commerce building in Washington, he remarked that he had "never expected to get such a warm reception in this building." At his press conference that same day (June 14), a questioner mentioned reports that businessmen had said they now had the President where they wanted him, to which he replied: "I can't believe I am where big business wants me."

Kennedy also showed that he could be philosophical about the beating he was taking. "I know that when things don't go well, they [the businessmen] like to blame the President, and that is one of the things which Presidents are paid for." It was also at this press conference that the President made his public effort to persuade the flight engineers not to go out on strike. He opened with a long discussion of the economic implications of the strike, and closed by urging the engineers "to reconsider their actions, and either submit this case to arbitration or agree with the carriers on some other means of settling their dispute without an interruption of operation." In response to a question, the President added that if the flight engineers did not meet his request, the Government would have to consider what further action would be proper. In the business community's state of mind at that time, it was hard to determine whether this statement—reaffirming as it did the Administration's intention to be just as tough on labor as it had been on the steel industry—soothed fiery feelings or only worked them up to a greater heat. It clearly indicated that the Government intended to follow through on its announced policy of intervening in *all* labor-management disputes when the Administration felt the public interest was involved.

In response to another press conference question, the President voiced mild disagreement with Cox's speech at Harvard, and stressed again his own view that "this is a free economy . . . in the final analysis, we have to attempt to work out the solutions on a voluntary basis."

The situation promised to get worse before it got better. By late June and early July, the "hate Kennedy" mood in the business community had almost reached a state of hysteria. Some White House aides admitted that they had under-estimated the depth of this feeling, but as the summer of 1962 began, there was little doubt that the country was going through something it had not experienced since the days of Franklin Roosevelt when a great many people—enraged by a Wall Street revolt—turned on the President and his family with frightening ferocity.

An example of how business' fear and suspicion worked can be seen in the reaction to an incident in late June. In line with the Grand Jury investigations into possible price-fixing in the steel industry, subpoenas went out asking for the itemized expense accounts of all steel executives having any-thing to do with setting prices—an understandable, if sensi-tive, request, considering that a great deal of the evidence used in the indictment of electrical equipment industry exec-utives for their clandestine price-fixing meetings had been obtained from old expense accounts. Considering the emo-tional state of the business community, any action taken by the Grand Jury would naturally be considered as "anti-business." But so jumpy were the businessmen that the attempt to seek this sort of information kindled an immediate rumor that the Kennedy Administration was striking back at steel by starting a top-secret investigation into its executives' expense accounts.

Such was the mood of business, and there were signs that this mood was beginning to spread, although a Gallup popularity poll taken at the height of the "hate Kennedy" campaign showed the President with a still solid 71 percent, a figure topped by General Eisenhower only once—in March of 1957. Still, as in the 1930's when the anti-Roosevelt jokes ranged all the way from his dog to the members of his family, the Kennedy jokes were becoming bitter and personal and directed almost as much at the Kennedy family as at him. There was even a revival of the aged New Deal joke which asked if FDR, Harry Hopkins and Henry Wallace were in a sinking boat, who would be saved? Answer: The country. Paradoxically, the President was, at one and the same time, being damned as a dictator (". . . A Frank Hague in Ivy League clothes," said one sputtering Republican who also compared him to Hitler and Caligula) and as an ineffectual Chamberlain ("The Thinking Man's Coolidge" . . . "The most dynamic President since Ike").

Buttons began to appear emblazoned with the letters SOB, from the initials of the "Sons of Business Society" and showing a mournful hound in the doghouse. Ohio Republican Representative William H. Ayres, who created the society, sent $100, raised from the sale of the buttons, to Harvard, suggesting that the money be used to start a scholarship for a student to study "What makes the economy tick." A "New Frontier Coloring Book" showed the Liberty Bell wrapped in chains with a caption: THIS IS OUR NEW NATIONAL SYMBOL. IT IS CALLED THE SECURITY BELL. In the San Francisco *Chronicle*, columnist Art Hoppe wrote of "Just Plain Jack— the heartwarming story of a lovable Irish family and their struggle to prove that running a country can be fun."

Most of the jokes making the rounds failed to bring a laugh in the White House, but even some pro-Kennedy Democrats seemed to be telling them with relish. Some examples:

● Did you hear that they're opening a new restaurant in New York? It's called the Forum of the Twelve Kennedys.
● They've changed the name of the New Frontier; now it's called One Man's Family.

- Richard Nixon was telling his California audiences: "I'm getting into shape for the campaign by jumping into my pool every day—with my clothes on."
- Caroline Kennedy certainly is a nice kid. But that's the last time we should let her plan a Cuban invasion.
- Union leaders are worried because Kennedy's handling of the Presidency has set the on-the-job training program back at least four years.
- The Kennedy rocking chair is the symbol of the New Frontier; you get the feeling of moving but you don't go anywhere.

Dissatisfaction with the Administration's economic policies was not the only thing bothering people during the summer of 1962. Suddenly the small irritations—Robert Kennedy's swimming pool and Jacqueline Kennedy's high social life, etc.—bubbled to the surface in an emotional outpouring heightened by frustration over the stock market and other day-to-day crises. By mid-July, the anti-Kennedy mood had become so pronounced that the editors of *Newsweek* felt it rated a cover story. In making a survey of the national mood, it found that, broadly speaking, the anti-Kennedy sentiment fell into five major categories: the steel case; the stock market; the President's advisers; the President's family; and the Administration's legislative program.

It was emotional, hysterical—at times almost irrational—but underneath was a genuine disturbance, especially in the business community. As later Gallup Polls showed, the business community was not quite as upset as the strange anti-Kennedy flare-up in late June and early July suggested, but still there was a basis of truth in all the excitement. The remark of one Chicago executive quoted by Edwin Darby, financial editor for the Chicago *Sun-Times,* expressed the real reaction of many businessmen. "I voted for Nixon," this man said, "but when Kennedy won I wasn't upset. I thought he'd do a good job in the foreign area, and that of course is paramount. I didn't fault him particularly over the Cuba fiasco. I felt that came so soon after he was in office that it had to be blamed in part on the old Administration. But the way he went after the steel companies was too much for me. I don't trust him any more."

Administration spokesmen who maintained that the people doing the loudest crying had never been for Kennedy and never would be were probably right, but that did not tell the whole story. It is true that most of the dissenters had, like the Chicago executive, voted for Nixon and might not support Kennedy in the future. It is also very likely that many businessmen had made their peace with the new Administration and might well have gone through the four years of the Kennedy rule reasonably content. In short, the Administration's economic policies and the President's sincere efforts to woo the businessman and prove that he was not anti-business had actually begun to produce results until the steel crisis shattered the truce. After that, any hopes that the hatchet might be buried were shattered by the stock market crash.

Administration officials most concerned with the problem went through several phases in their feelings about the reaction of businessmen: at first they discounted it as a natural reflex reaction to the steel crisis; then they became angry and irritated at the businessman's apparent unwillingness to hear the Government's side of the case; then they became a little alarmed—especially after the stock market crash—that perhaps the situation had gotten out of hand; then a period of frustration set in caused by an inability to communicate with the businessman; finally came resignation and the hope that eventually the storm would blow over and that when it did Washington and business would once again be able to attack the problems facing both of them. All these attitudes and reactions were reflected in the week-to-week moods of the President, and early Summer—at the height of the anti-Kennedy crusade—found him resigned and philosophic. By mid-July, he felt that the surge of criticism had passed its peak. "These things come and go in great waves," he told a *Newsweek* correspondent.

This feeling was supported by the attitude of the businessmen who were being invited to the White House. On July 12, the President was host at a luncheon which included Elliott V. Bell, Editor and Publisher of *Business Week,* and Sidney Weinberg, a Wall Street banker who has always been active in the Republican Party. Those who attended the luncheon said there was no evidence of hostility in the White House dining room, and Andy Hatcher said the President thought the meeting had been "very useful" and that he planned more of them. The following morning, H. Ladd Plumley, President of the U. S. Chamber of Commerce, paid a visit to the White House, and after his meeting with the President told reporters that he felt there had been a thaw in the feud— although at a luncheon the same day Plumley was drawn into admitting that he still did not feel the President had grasped the problems foremost in the minds of business. Nevertheless, in the weeks that followed, it became increasingly evident that the business community was calming down. And, strangely enough, by September 1, when the political campaign shifted into high gear, the complaints were virtually muted. As for the campaign itself, the question of the steel strike and the issue of business confidence were rarely mentioned—except by Dwight Eisenhower and Barry Goldwater, neither of whom were actually running for office.

Eisenhower seemed especially intent on making a campaign issue out of the business confidence crisis. "The Administration seems almost driven to alienate major elements of the business community," the former President told Republican members of Congress at a pre-campaign meeting held at the Sheraton-Park Hotel in Washington. "Even in its speeches, which are publicly advertised as friendly toward business, menacing language somehow has to appear. Indeed, the official Administration posture can be interpreted only as: 'Business, get friendly—or else!' "

Although the Republican National Committee at first endorsed the former President's views, by the time the campaign actually got under way Ike was virtually alone in his efforts to make the steel crisis and Kennedy's presumed antibusiness attitude a campaign issue. The reason for this was obvious: despite all the earlier efforts of Republicans and many voices in the business community to make it an issue, the public had shown no signs that it was responding. Two Gallup polls, announced in August, told the story. On August 8 one gave the public response to the question: *"Do you think business conditions in this country would be better or worse today if a Republican President were in office?"* The answers: Better —17 percent; Worse—24 percent; About the same—46 percent. Even more revealing was the poll released on August 17, in which people were asked: *"Do you think President Kennedy is 'antibusiness'?"* To this the response was: Yes—14 percent; No—65 percent. When broken down on a party basis, the poll showed Republicans answering: Yes—24 percent; No— 53 percent. Even more significant, when broken down on an occupational basis the poll showed "business and professional people" answering: Yes—19 percent; No—68 percent! Of course, this category included small businessmen, lawyers and doctors, etc. Only a month and a half earlier, Marquis Childs had written that in a personal poll of fifty bankers, he found the almost unanimous view that Kennedy's policies were harmful to business. This view no doubt reflected the feeling in the financial community and on Wall Street, but the Gallup Poll probably came much closer to reflecting the view of the average businessman—to wit, that the President was not antibusiness despite the strenuous efforts of Republican politickers and some active Republicans in the business community to make him appear so.

In the opinion of at least one pollster, the steel crisis actually influenced more voters in the 1962 elections than the Cuban crisis, which seemed to dominate the campaign, and the President's stand in the steel crisis helped the Democrats much more than the Republicans. Professor Ithiel D. Pool of the Massachusetts Institute of Technology's Political Science Department said, after the election, that polls he conducted for Simulmatics Inc., showed that the voting tendency was along class lines—"the 1930's all over again." Less than half of those making over $15,000 a year voted Democratic this time as compared to two years ago. "Business votes for Democrats have all but vanished," said Professor Pool, "but the lower income vote has more than filled the gap." In comparing the steel crisis and the Cuban crisis, Pool came to the conclusion that: "The differential effect of the steel price issue changed more votes than did the Cuban crisis, which was more pervasive in its effects and crossed all class lines."

What caused the sudden collapse of the Kennedy-is-antibusiness crusade after its July peak? There were a number of reasons for the businessman's finally getting his temper under control, ranging perhaps all the way from the calming effects of a summer vacation to the fact that one simply cannot sustain intense hostility in the face of mounting evidence that one is in the minority. But there were also some specific influencing factors which helped restore the truce, however uneasy, between business and government.

In the first place, the efforts of the President and his aides to develop a serious "dialogue" could not have failed to affect businessmen. Despite their emotional state, sooner or later it had to become obvious to them that the President's efforts to help business were genuine and that he was as eager for a healthy, prosperous business community as they were. Once this became evident, the differences narrowed down to an economic debate. Several business leaders, such as Roger Blough, Joseph Block, Henry Ford, Sidney Weinberg, Hal Korda and David Rockefeller, helped to restore the peace, and full credit must be given to these men. In the middle of the summer, *Life* magazine published an exchange of letters between Rockefeller, President of the Chase National Bank, and President Kennedy. "Naturally, nobody could agree with both David Rockefeller and the President about what ails the U. S. economy and about the cure," *Life* said. "But everyone who reads their letters will be in a better position to discuss the subject concretely and seriously. This is what the President wants every citizen to do, and *Life* prints the two letters in lieu of an editorial."

In addition to help such as this, the President was getting some unwanted help from another source—Congress. In the closing days of the 86th Congress, the conservative coalition, made up of Southern Democrats and the majority of Congressional Republicans, combined to defeat the bulk of the Administration's legislative program, most of which was opposed by big businessmen and the financial community. This also tended to calm down many executives. At the same time, in August, Congress passed legislation providing for a tax credit averaging 7 percent, which, although not as liberal as the bill first proposed by the Administration in 1961, was supported and signed by the President. Under the legislation, corporations, in many cases, get more of a tax break in dollars than they will have spent on an investment, which Treasury officials feel encourages investment. The bill was passed despite the opposition of an unusual conservative-liberal bloc. The conservatives objected to the Government "subsidy" to business as a reward for investment; the liberals objected because the incentive was not great enough.

Just a month earlier, the Treasury Department announced the long-awaited revision of tax depreciation regulations.

According to the President, the new depreciation schedules —the first in twenty years—would provide a reduction in tax liabilities amounting to a $1.5 billion "tax cut" for the first year. The potential increase in depreciation allowances, according to the Treasury Department, could run as high as $4.7 billion. Despite grumblings from business, especially the steel industry, that the new schedules were not liberal enough and that the net result would be to give industry lower profits to explain to the stockholders, most businessmen agreed with one steel industry executive who said: "We've been asking for larger write-offs for years so that we can modernize and cut costs, so it isn't likely that we won't use those additional write-offs merely because they will reduce reported earnings." When looked at in the hard, unemotional light of the board meeting, businessmen had to agree that both the tax credit legislation and the new depreciation schedules would help their investment picture. At the same time, business liked the Administration's readiness to consider a tax cut. When Walter Heller outlined the Administration's attitude toward a tax cut at a meeting of businessmen held at Hot Springs in October, one businessman was heard to comment: "I support Heller's tax policies. I think he's really beginning to listen to us."

However, there can be little doubt that of all the specific factors influencing the rise and fall of the Kennedy-is-antibusiness crusade, the most important were the condition of the stock market and the general state of business. A chart of the stock market for 1962 could almost be attached to the foot of the business community's bed and be read as a fever chart, so accurately did it trace the emotional illness of the patient during this period. As we have seen, after a slight rise in prices immediately following the steel crisis, the market started straight down and kept going down through Black Monday on May 28 and well into the following month. On June 22 it hit its lowest point, with the Dow-Jones industrials reading 539.19. However, by early July it was climbing again and continued steadily upward during July and August, pausing long enough for a slight relapse in September and October before starting up again. By the end of November, the market had scaled to well above the point to which it had descended on May 28—and it was still climbing.

By the end of the third quarter, most estimates of business conditions pointed to a good year for 1962. In November, *The New York Times* reported that dollar profits were headed for a record high. The steel industry was a glaring exception to this otherwise rosy picture, and even many industries reporting record high profits were still talking about a "profit squeeze."

Another factor influencing the businessman's attitude was the fact that despite frequent charges of Federal reprisals, there was very little evidence that the Administration was actually taking action against the steel companies after prices were rescinded in April. The Federal Trade Commission's re-examination of a 1951 consent order forbidding steel companies to fix prices, and Representative Celler's investigation—completely faded into the files. There was no longer any talk around the Justice Department of breaking up U. S. Steel. Senator Kefauver, of course, continued to press his investigation and in September his subcommittee attempted to bring a citation for contempt of Congress against four steel companies for refusing to supply information. However, the companies were getting used to fighting Kefauver and they announced that they intended to fight the contempt citation all the way to the Supreme Court, an action on which it could take years to get a decision. Most members of the Kefauver staff were frankly not very optimistic.

Last but not least it should be pointed out that although most businessmen finally ran out of steam in their criticism of the President, this did not necessarily mean that they had changed their minds about his Administration. It simply meant that many of them probably decided that they were wasting their time yelling that the Administration was anti-business. And perhaps some—but certainly not all—even began to doubt whether it was really true. Finally, after Labor Day, there was increased talk of a Berlin crisis, and in October came the Cuban crisis which completely silenced any scattered complaints still emanating from the upper echelons of big business. It has never been fashionable to complain about business conditions when men are being put in uniform.

As for steel prices, in October, Kaiser Steel lowered its price $12-a-ton, and some of the major companies doing business on the West Coast—including U. S. Steel—followed suit almost as fast as they had raised to $6-a-ton back in April. Kaiser said that the price decrease had nothing to do with the hold-the-line policy urged by the President in the spring, that the company had been considering the move for two years. "This action proves," said Senator Kefauver, who was investigating steel prices long before the ides of April 1962, "the correctness of the position which I have held for several years, that the price of steel is too high."

Perhaps Kefauver was right. In October, U. S. Steel and the industry lowered prices on stainless steel in the East about 2 percent, and in December the mill base price at U. S. Steel's Fairless Works was reduced $1-a-ton. Despite complaints that the tax credit and new depreciation schedules would not help the industry out of its jam, the steel companies appeared to be pushing ahead with new construction, regardless of sagging prices. In December, Bethlehem announced that it would build its long-anticipated new plant in the Chicago area, although Bethlehem and the entire industry was still operating way below full capacity. According to the *Wall Street Journal,* other companies were making similar moves. President Glossbrenner of Youngstown estimated that his company would spend 15 to 20 percent more on capital improvements in 1963 than in 1962. "From what I hear," he said, "most of the steel companies will be doing the same thing. They're all in the same boat; it's toward better quality and lower costs."

By the fall of 1962, the steel crisis appeared to be a thing of the past, but it obviously was one of those national eruptions that will never really die. Whenever men gather to discuss public affairs, the Government and the office of the Presidency, the steel crisis of 1962 cannot help but be raised. The issues were too great and were never really settled, and the discourse of Democracy thrives on such crises.

PART III

THE IDES OF APRIL

CHAPTER 12

Conclusion

> How far would I go? I believe our system of checks and balances, our whole constitutional system, can only operate under a strong President. The Constitution is a very wise document. It permits the President to assume just about as much power as he is capable of handling. If he fails, it is his fault, not the system's. I believe that the President should use whatever power is necessary to do the job unless it is expressly forbidden by the Constitution.
>
> —*Senator John F. Kennedy, quoted by James M. Burns* in John Kennedy: A Political Profile

Although both sides in the steel battle took positions behind hastily erected barricades of economic statistics, the conflict was not an economic one. The obvious fact that U. S. Steel could use more profits does not completely explain Roger Blough's disturbing the calm that warm afternoon in April any more than the Administration's desire to hold back inflation, protect its labor-management policy or even assert the national interest, completely explains the President's furious reaction. The U. S. Steel Company needed a price rise, but (as seen in Chapter 8) there are definite weaknesses in the company's economic case and it is hard to believe that the profit situation alone justified such an open affront to the President and his economic program.

But what did? A complete explanation of the company's sudden move will probably remain locked in the company archives or in the files of a few top executives of U. S. Steel until future historians or biographers are given access to the necessary documents on which to reconstruct the past. For the present, Roger Blough is sticking to his position that the need for more money with which to modernize equipment was the sole reason. President Worthington has said, explaining his company's action: "We looked at the costs of the fourth quarter of 1961, and the first quarter of 1962, and we looked ahead to the prospects down the line. We have to invest four hundred million in physical properties every year just to stay even. Adding it all up, it was certainly high time we got going."

"But did you have to do it now?" Washington *Post* financial writer Joseph A. Livingston asked a high official of U. S. Steel at the time of the price rise, adding, "if you had to do it, couldn't you have waited two or three months until the excitement over the labor contract died down?"

"Joe," the official replied, "have you ever known of a good time to raise steel prices? Every time we've raised prices we've been criticized, investigated or threatened with investigation."

"Any time is a bad time to raise steel prices," Livingston admitted, but added that "some times are worse than others. And this is the absolute worst time."

So the whole country thought, but not Roger Blough. As he has since explained: "When would there have been a better time to test the market? . . . from the competitive angle in a highly competitive industry, one of the best possible times we could elect to increase prices would be one not expected by the rest of the industry." From that point of view, U. S. Steel certainly could never have picked a better time.

Still, the explanations offered by U. S. Steel do not satisfy. They don't seem to tell the whole story; something appears to be missing. Take the question of profits, for instance.

In a free economy, of course, there is no such thing as an "ideal" level of profits. Everyone wants as much as the traffic will bear, and as long as they keep within the law it is generally conceded that they have a right to seek it and that not too much harm can come from this, because competition and demand will eventually force a realistic price. In the last decade, industrial profits have been "squeezed down" 8 percent to 4.5 percent of the Gross National Product. If 1960 corporate profits, after taxes, had kept pace with the economic growth of other sectors of the economy over the last decade, they would have been about $18 billion higher than they were —some $41 billion, instead of $24 billion. There are many economists who will agree that the long-range profit picture has not been good, but ironically enough, at the time when U. S. Steel chose to act, the short-range profit picture, at least, was quite healthy. According to a spring 1962 issue of *Fortune,* economists summed up the situation this way: "Profits are pretty good in some industries, not so good as that in many, not too bad in most, and very good in very few."

It is agreed that the steel industry, because of competition from other products and modern and more efficient foreign steel mills, was one in which the profit picture was "not so good," but even in the steel industry there were bright spots. According to a First National City Bank survey, net profits in the 4th quarter of 1961 compared with the 4th quarter of 1960, were up 70 percent in the iron and steel industry (although U. S. Steel showed a drop of 19 percent during this period). As a result, it might seem that U. S. Steel's view of the industry's profit picture was a subjective one; that, whereas everything Worthington and Blough might say about the "profit situation" being critical in their company, might be true, it was not necessarily true for other companies. In an article on corporate profits in the May 1962 issue of *Fortune,* obviously written just about the time the steel storm was gathering, the magazine surveyed the profit situation generally and then commented on the glum attitude taken by Worthington. "In the face of these developments," said

Fortune, referring to the fairly optimistic surveys of the First National City Bank, "Mr. Worthington of U. S. Steel may seem to be too gloomy. Some of his remarks may be put down to his company's poor showing in 1961, and the fact that the steel industry was in the middle of wage negotiations when he spoke . . ."

In other words, when U. S. Steel officials said that the company needed a price increase to rescue it at a time of financial crisis, they meant it. But the company executives responsible for the decision made a serious miscalculation when they decided to go ahead and raise the prices across the board; the miscalculation was in thinking that the rest of the industry was in the same bind and would join in, as it had in the past. Based on past experience, U. S. Steel naturally expected even companies with good profit structures—such as Inland and Armco—to go along whether they needed the extra profits or not.

In 1957, Blough had said: "There isn't certainly any steel company in the first ten or in the first twenty that couldn't require us to change our prices overnight simply by taking action which is different than the action we take." Five years later, Inland proved his point, but the mystery is: Why did Blough not foresee this? *Fortune* pointed out that even prior to U. S. Steel's action, Bethlehem had foreseen that Inland would not go along with an across-the-board price increase, and that was one reason why Bethlehem was opposed to an increase—right up to the very day U. S. Steel made its announcement.

Inland was concerned about the plant Bethlehem was planning to build in the Chicago area. In addition, Inland had been able to absorb most of the cost increases of the previous wage contract, and as late as November of 1961, Joseph Block told the Controllers Institute of America that he opposed a price rise, offering as his objection the fact that an increase "would further weaken the American steel industry's competitive position in relation to foreign producers . . ." Block insists that the White House reaction had nothing to do with Inland's decision not to raise prices. The reasons, says Block, were three: (1) that it was not the time to raise, with steel orders being canceled because of the wage settlement; (2) that an aura of price stability had been established by the wage contracts; and (3) that a price rise at that time was out of keeping because many of the smaller companies—including some Inland subsidiaries—had not signed their wage contracts.

Inland's independence and unwillingness to go along did not bring the company any bouquets from the steel industry. As one steel executive quoted in the *Wall Street Journal* said later: "I'd tell you what I think of Inland, but you couldn't print it." Incidentally, many businessmen, in the privacy of their clubs, were saying the same things about U. S. Steel and Roger Blough.

If Bethlehem was able to foresee Inland's position, why wasn't U. S. Steel? And why wasn't Roger Blough able to foresee the extent of the President's reaction? The answers to these questions are not easy, and some which have been suggested are not very complimentary to the executives of U. S. Steel. Both Administration officials and businessmen said that only sheer "stupidity" could explain U. S. Steel's action, and especially its timing. One columnist described the leadership of the steel industry as having completely lost touch with reality; another politely suggested that some business leaders suffer from a "mentality gap." Even *Fortune,* in its first reaction said the price increase was "not necessarily a piece of good sense."

Such charges are pretty strong, but perhaps the explanation suggested indirectly by Clarence Randall in *The New York Times'* Magazine is more palatable. And if true, the results would be the same. In the article, "Business, Too, Has its Ivory Towers," Randall discussed at length the ways in which a modern corporation official gradually gets cut off, and then completely isolated, from the outside world. It begins when as a coming young man he is invited to join a "snug, well-heeled little group" which has rented a private car attached to the end of the commuter train, and becomes complete when the executive is chairman of the board, surrounded by men who rarely have ideas different from his. In the meantime he has gone from club car to private limousine, to private plane, to private luncheons at the "club within a club," and to golf foursomes carefully made up by his secretary from a group which seldom includes more than six different players—usually all executives like himself. "It is not their physical withdrawal as such that is significant," says Randall, "but that of which it is the symbol—namely their intellectual divorcement from the tumult of outside thought. Preoccupied with the complex affairs of their own corporations, they cut themselves off from the sources of facts and ideas by which mass judgments are formed in our country. Their thinking on the great questions is borrowed and the opinions they hold are seldom tested by controversy."

Randall says that he knows whereof he speaks because he behaved pretty much as the others did when he was an executive in the steel industry—that it was not until his retirement that he began to change. Most important, he concludes that the typical isolated executive of the kind he describes is not equipped to meet many of the problems facing society or even his corporation. "In times of crisis," says Randall, "such an officer is not ready to face sudden storms of public opinion."

Keeping in mind this isolated, inbred type of executive, it becomes easier to understand how the heads of a large corporation might have acted unwisely, even on a matter concerning their own industry—such as a judgment as to whether the rest of the industry was in exactly the same position. It also makes it easier to understand another proffered explanation for the debacle—that an increased profit margin was urgently desired in the steel industry not just to raise funds for reinvestment but to put it in the same league with General Motors and other profit leaders who can look for a 20-percent-profit return when operating at a normal rate, as compared to the steel industry's 12 percent. To board executives of a giant corporation who see the game as a clash between profit-and-loss statements, stock dividends and the relative standings in the annual rating of the top U. S. corporations, it might actually appear that they are "losing" the game despite the fact that their annual statements show profits running into billions of dollars.

It is even more understandable how such isolated executives could have misjudged the reaction in Washington. This is not to suggest that U. S. Steel did not realize that it had picked the worst possible time to raise its price; in fact, if one explanation is correct, it was possibly the best time, but not for the reasons Blough gave. To understand the full implications of Blough's timing, it is necessary to go back to the 116-day steel strike of 1959 which was eventually settled early in 1960 by Richard Nixon's intervention. For several weeks, Nixon met with both labor and industry leaders and at one point was forced to tell industry representatives that if they did not give in they might face compulsory arbitration, Federal wage and price controls, possibly even plant seizure. As he put it: "You are running the risk of destroying the free competitive system."

The steel industry finally gave in on terms recommended by Nixon, which amounted to concessions to the steelworkers totaling about 40 cents an hour over a two-and-a-half-year period. (Blough said then that this increase was "less inflationary" than others in the past, whereas in the spring of 1962 he said he did not agree that the current 10-cents-an-hour increase was "noninflationary.") The strike was settled, and Nixon—who was considered the number one Republican Presidential candidate—and Secretary of Labor James Mitchell received credit for a major political victory.

However, the settlement did not pass into the history books without a few ugly comments, and the loudest charge of all was that there had been a "deal." Walter Lippmann said the strike "had been settled by a political fix," and even President Eisenhower's Secretary of Agriculture Ezra Taft Benson has since written that Nixon "came out of it resembling a cat with political cream all over his whiskers." In his book, *Cross Fire,* Benson wrote: "At the first Cabinet meeting in 1960, early in January, I questioned the steel settlement. It seemed to me inevitable that the settlement would cause steel prices to rise, if not in 1960 at least in 1961 or 1962, and this would in turn affect other industries in which labor unions would feel impelled to fight for similar increases. Any way I looked at it, the steel settlement seemed written in political ink."

It did to almost everyone else too. The main charge was that Nixon had managed to convince the steel companies that a concession to labor, combined with a decision not to raise prices in 1960, would help the Republicans at the polls that year. The implication was that a price rise would be all right in 1961: that if a Republican was President, there would be no objection; if a Democrat was in, he would be out to get the steel companies anyway, so what difference would it make?

The only trouble with this scheme was that 1961 brought a recession, which made it impossible for the steel companies to raise prices. However, in the opinion of some observers, the steel companies began as early as the summer of 1961 to prepare for a price rise the following year. That July, Conrad Cooper attacked the Administration's labor-management policy as leading to "government controls of virtually all major bargaining, a steppingstone to the establishment of national wage and price policies." Similarly, when the President wrote the steel companies in September of 1961, although the companies did refrain from raising prices, Blough and most of the other officials replied with a letter which distinctly left the door open for a future price increase. And despite the steel leaders' obvious understanding that labor's wage restraints in 1962 meant they were expected to hold prices down, U. S. Steel leaders continued to talk about price increases while the negotiations were going on.

It should be said that as far as the 1962 wage negotiations were concerned, if U. S. Steel and the industry had been planning since 1961 to announce in 1962 the price rise it felt it was justified as a result of the settlement achieved by Vice-President Nixon, the pronounced efforts on the part of the Administration to hold back labor put the industry in a difficult position. In the first place, it is possible that the businesslike manner in which the Administration let it be known that it expected labor to observe its "guideposts" took the steel companies by surprise. They may very well have been guilty of believing their own propaganda and assuming that a Democratic Administration would never put the pressure on labor. But the net result was that the Kennedy Administration was in the position of working for the steel companies in the wage negotiations.

What could steel do? The industry could hardly make a flat public statement that it planned to raise prices, because that would enable labor to ignore the Administration and increase its demands; and steel—we are assuming—was still seeking a price rise to which it felt it was already entitled as a result of the 1960 settlement. It could perhaps go quietly to the Administration and say that a price rise was coming no matter what, but considering the Administration's closeness to the labor unions, the word would certainly get back to the unions; furthermore, the Administration could hardly keep it quiet because of the position it would be put in with labor. In addition, if 1962 was to be the year to raise prices, it was essential that it be a good year, and all the economic forecasters were predicting a good year *only if a steel strike was averted.* Consequently, it was essential to the steel companies that a strike be avoided, and any hint to the unions that a price rise was on the way might very well have inspired wage demands which the companies would not meet; which in turn might have produced the dreaded strike.

Hence the temptation to let the Administration hold the unions down so that the 1962 rise would actually be related to the 1960 settlement and not a 1962 increase was understandable—and understandably risky. The evidence that it actually was such an outgrowth is almost conclusive. As one steel executive said in the *Wall Street Journal:* "The industry could absorb the cost increase going into effect under the new labor contract. But absorbing that plus the preceding 40 cents is another matter." And it should be remembered that in the statement announcing the price increase, U. S. Steel President Leslie Worthington emphasized that it was a "catch-up" adjustment which was necessary regardless of what the 1962 contract called for. On U. S. Steel's behalf, it should be further emphasized that Roger Blough maintains that he had warned the Administration that a price rise was possible—first by never committing U. S. Steel to hold prices down, and second by such statements as the one made in the *U. S. News* "interview" of February 26. (See Chapter 2.)

But the problem was that the Administration had insisted that the "public interest" also be represented at the bargaining table; industry was no longer dealing with just the labor unions, but with the office of the Presidency. As one Administration official has put it: "The key to the whole steel crisis was that when you are dealing with the President of the United States, complete candor is expected."

The steel companies did not feel that they could go to the President and state their case frankly, but as it turned out that probably would have been the best thing for them to do. President Kennedy knew all about the deal in 1960. As a practical politician, he would no doubt have tried to live with it, despite the fact that it would hurt his program. He of course would have fought it publicly, but some Administration officials say that if the steel companies had shown more candor, the worst they could have gotten out of it would have been a fact-finding board. And even President Kennedy says that something could have been worked out if only the steel companies had not attempted to confront the Presidency with an open challenge.

But for reasons still known only to themselves, the executives of U. S. Steel chose to do it the way they did. And even allowing for the isolation of their paneled boardrooms, their manner of announcing the increase must be viewed as a calculated move. No matter how you look at the steel crisis, it is hard not to come to the conclusion that Roger Blough and U. S. Steel knew exactly what they were doing by picking the time they did. By doing so, they achieved several things, all of which, from their point of view, appeared both desirable and attainable:

● They would achieve a price increase which they needed and which would have been "justified" by the wage concessions of 1960;

● They would publicly dramatize the fact that industry was not going to permit government intervention in labor-management negotiations, and that they would not permit the President of the United States to set prices;

● Politically, it would produce friction between labor and the Administration, pull the rug out from under the Kennedy victory for having achieved a "noninflationary" settlement, and for the record, place the price increase—and any inflation which might result—in a Democratic Administration which presumably had six more years in office;

● Offset the dismal annual report which the company was about to release, by holding out to stockholders the possibility of increased profits in the future as a result of higher prices.

This would also help stabilize the price of U. S. Steel stock, which had become shaky on the stock market.

Roger Blough, of course, pleads political naïveté and has continually denied that there was any political implication in his company's move, and he could hardly do otherwise. But the evidence seems irrefutable that U. S. Steel had a two-fold purpose in its act: in addition to the economic motives, it decided to confront the Administration with a deliberate challenge to its wage-management policy. Although *Fortune* denies that there is any direct evidence for this theory, it does admit its existence and refers to it as an attempt by Blough to act as a "business statesman." For the sake of his company, the industry and the nation, so the theory goes, Blough was seeking a way to break through the bland harmony that had prevailed between government and business and to break the "jawbone" method of control which government was exercising over the industry.

But just as U. S. Steel made some serious economic miscalculations, it also made some serious miscalculations concerning a power play such as the one it appeared to be attempting. In the first place, the position of the company itself had changed considerably from the last time it had been involved in an across-the-board price increase. Since 1958, the company's tonnage of steel shipped had fallen considerably below the level of 1950, and it also had been unable to hold its percentage for the market. By 1961, it had only 25.4 percent, as compared with 30.1 percent in 1955. A decline in profits had accompanied the loss in its share of the market; in 1957 it earned 9.5 percent net on every dollar of sales, whereas by 1961 it was earning only 5.8. On profits, compared to percentage of worth, the drop was from 14 percent in 1957 to 5.8 percent in 1961. In 1961, Inland earned $55 million on sales of $725 million, while U. S. Steel was only earning $190 million on sales of $3.3 billion. "U. S. Steel," said a large steel company sales vice-president, "has by far the largest and most comprehensive sales force, advertising operation and technical service of anyone in the industry. They seem to do all the things the book says you should do to maintain your share of the market. But it keeps going down."

In short, when U. S. Steel moved to lead the industry into a major fight with the Government in 1962, it was leading from weakness and not from strength. It was making a difficult and unpopular move which it felt had to be done, but which the company was not strong enough to pull off alone. And, ironically, several of the other companies were strong enough so that they did not need to go along in the face of violent Presidential and public opposition. As a result, a crippled giant and a wavering band of followers who had been called into battle by surprise—and in some cases reluctantly— found themselves facing a well-organized, quick-moving and powerful adversary who managed to rally public opinion to its side almost before the crippled giant was aware that the battle had begun.

U. S. Steel's most serious miscalculation was its failure to estimate the intensity of the President's reaction. This was the crux of the entire crisis, and many reasons have been suggested for Blough's miscalculation. There is one argument that nothing in his nearly twenty-five years of experience with the Government would have led him to anticipate the President's anger. Time and again in his career he had seen the Government clash with big steel—and lose. Similarly, the President and Secretary Hodges had spent nearly a year trying to woo him and other leaders of industry, and the President had been especially cordial and conciliatory during the fight with the business council. Even if the President did get angry, so the argument goes, Blough had no reason to believe that White House anger would make any difference; the steel industry had weathered White House anger before and no doubt could do it again. Twelve times since World War II, steel had raised prices, and after the sound and fury of politics had subsided, steel had experienced nothing except perhaps a little embarrassment.

A very sophisticated version of the Blough-had-no-reason-to-expect-the-President's-reaction theory was suggested by Richard Austin Smith in his *Fortune* article, "Behind U. S. Steel's Price Blunder." It is an interesting thesis and cannot be ignored. According to Smith, one possible explanation for U. S. Steel's ignoring the reality of the situation was founded in the company's corporate psychology. "The company's outlook on the world," says Smith, "had been profoundly influenced by the fact that back in the twenties it was adjudged a 'good trust.' This judgment, handed down by the Supreme Court in a four to three decision, permitted big steel to escape dismemberment at the hands of the Justice Department, but at the price of the aggressiveness that produced big, strong companies out of split-up empires like Standard Oil. U. S. Steel was left intact, but it was inhibited from trying to obtain a larger share of the total market for steel. This somewhat dulled the corporation's competitive instincts." The result was that U. S. Steel gradually evolved an approach to business and pricing not unlike that of a public utility; at times, for instance, it even refrained from raising prices when it could have. On the other hand, this habit of thinking like a public utility led to a certain insensitivity to the market and a tendency to look inward. Consequently, it was able to justify a price increase simply on the ground that now it needed one, just as when a public utility can justify a need for a price increase, one is usually forthcoming.

Of course, if such thinking did govern the board of directors, it is understandable that a sudden angry reaction to their efforts to raise prices would naturally come as a shock. However, the only trouble with this corporate psychology, as Austin points out, is that U. S. Steel is not a public utility. Its actions must still stand the test of the market place and are still subject to scrutiny in Washington, and any thoughts that it is above the battle, as public utilities are, can only be attributed to an isolation even more confining than that which Randall described.

No matter what the explanations are, if Roger Blough and his colleagues had been paying attention to public affairs, they should have been able to foresee the President's reaction. The March 30, 1962, issue of the *Wall Street Journal* suggested that a steel price increase would be met with opposition in Washington, and if ever a President had forewarned potential antagonists that he intended to utilize fully the powers of his office in the pursuit of his objectives, it was John F. Kennedy. Back in 1960, after Vice-President Nixon had arranged a settlement of the disastrous 116-day steel strike, Senator Kennedy said: "Had the President seen fit to use more vigorously the powers of his office at an earlier date, thousands of steelworkers and their families would probably not have lost millions of dollars of wages." A few months later, in a speech before the National Press Club, Kennedy, as the leading candidate for the Democratic presidential nomination, outlined his concept of the Presidency. It has since become a widely quoted speech because in it he set forth for the first time his views on the powers of the presidential office—a subject which he returned to again and again during the campaign. "What do the times demand for the next four years in the White House?" the Senator asked in his Press Club speech. "They demand," he answered, "a vigorous proponent of the national interest—not a passive broker for conflicting private interests." During the early days of his Presidency it also became widely known that Kennedy had been much taken with a book by Richard Neustadt, *Presidential Power: the Politics of Leadership,* a book which contained an approach to power to which the new President had obviously given some thought: "If he wants it for the future, he must guard it in the present."

The most obvious fact concerning presidential power which U. S. Steel failed to appreciate was not just that the President would react in the manner he did, but that when presented with such a challenge he was *forced* to respond. Not only was his economic program endangered, and in his opinion the national interest as well, but more important still—his Administration was challenged in such a way that if he had done nothing, his ability to provide the kind of leadership he felt necessary for the 1960's would have been seriously weakened. The President built his case around the national interest and his economic goals, but he actually fought back to preserve the power of his office and the integrity of his leadership. Some critics of the Administration's action even maintain that the President's primary mistake was in not making it clear to the public that the real issue was the affront to his office, rather than either the national interest or the preservation of his economic program.

Whether or not it was a mistake is debatable, but the President made the decision to build his public case on the threat to the national interest and his economic program, and once having chosen to fight, he could not afford to lose. In a year-end television interview, Kennedy was asked to comment on some suggestions that in retrospect perhaps he would not have acted as vigorously as he did. The President replied that there was an issue of good faith involved and that he was forced to make an effort to roll back prices. And he added: "Now, supposing we had tried and made a speech about it, and then failed. I would have thought that would have been an awful setback to the office of the Presidency. Now, I just think, looking back on it, that I would not change it at all. *There is no sense in raising hell, and then not being successful. There is no sense in putting the office of the Presidency on the line on an issue, and then being defeated.* Now, an unfortunate repercussion of that was the strong feeling that the Government might interfere in a good many labor-management matters or that it might interfere in the whole question of the free enterprise system. It was regrettable that the general conclusion was drawn in this particular incident. Given the problem that I had on that Tuesday night, I must say I think we had to do everything we could to get it reversed." (Author's italics.)

When the President is presented with such a challenge, he is forced to make an immediate response. Often, to delay too long in reaching a decision is to lose the first battle, and if the President had remained silent too long, it is possible that *all* the steel companies would have joined the parade before he had a chance to state the Administration's case. He reacted immediately, decisively and along a broad front.

There are many who say his reaction was too great and that the situation did not warrant such an "awesome display" of presidential power. And it should be stressed that criticism of the President did not come solely from the business community or the pro-Republican press. One of the most critical commentaries on his action appeared in the liberal weekly *The New Republic,* and was made by an associate professor of law at Yale University, Charles A. Reich. It was Reich's opinion that although he felt the action of the steel companies was "ill-considered and inflationary," the President's accomplishment in "forcing the companies to their knees is one we may come to rue." After discussing in detail the methods used by the President—none of which were illegal, Reich conceded that "the President has no right to force his economic policies on an unwilling industry *without legislation* . . . Freedom has little meaning if it only allows action that 'responsibility' conforms to the President's idea of the national interest. He can set national goals and urge others to follow, and in areas of his constitutional authority, like foreign policy, he can command obedience. But in the area of economics, private business and the public have the right to act according to their notions of the public good until the people's elected representatives decide otherwise." Finally, says Reich, even allowing that everything he had said about President Kennedy's methods and objectives had been wrong, "his victory is still disquieting. It demonstrates how much power government has today. Such power, no matter how wisely exercised, is hardly any less frightening because the victim forced to surrender was a group of corporate giants and not a small business or a private citizen."

A comment should be made about Professor Reich's curious remark that "private business and the public have a right to act until the people's elected representatives decide otherwise." By "elected representatives," Reich of course meant Senators and Representatives, but one wonders how the professor could overlook the fact that the President is also the representative of all the people and a much more "representative" one than the Congress. If it is granted that holding the price line was *in the public interest,* it should not be forgotten that the President *is* the people's representative and will have to answer for his action in the steel crisis at the polls in 1964— which Roger Blough and the executives of U. S. Steel will not.

In determining whether the President did or did not overstep his authority in the steel crisis, some thought must be given—as in all cases involving the use of presidential power— to the objective the President was trying to achieve. Professor Reich and others may be frightened at how much power resides in the office of the Presidency, but the hand-wringing over its existence is not going to make it go away any more than hand-wringing will diminish the equally frightening power which exists in our large corporations. In a country as big and powerful as the United States, concentrations of power are inevitable and they are everywhere—in the Presidency, in Congress, in bureaucracy, in industry, in labor, in the statehouses, in the communications media, etc. In determining how wisely this power is being used, the purpose for which it is unleashed, whenever it is unleashed, cannot be overlooked. There will of course be those who argue that this is in effect saying that the ends justify the means—and it is, to which there should be no objection as long as in a country of laws the means are kept within the law.

As for the objective for which his power was unleashed, the President's policy of holding back inflation and stabilizing the wage-price spiral has been endorsed by almost every major public figure in both political parties and included in every lofty statement of national goals which has been written in recent years.

Back in March of 1959, when President Eisenhower was urging the steelworkers and the steel industry to come up with a noninflationary wage settlement, he told a news conference: "Here is a place where labor and management must show statesmanship on both sides. And frankly, I would expect as a measure of their statesmanship, that there is no advance in the price of the commodity the public has to pay. And the reason I say this is so," Eisenhower continued, "is this: while this is a matter between the steelworkers and the steel companies, the whole public is affected by everything they do . . . If we are going to retain the methods and procedures that belong properly in a free economy . . . we must do it in such a way that the price is not compelled to go up."

Similarly, "Goals for Americans," the report of Eisenhower's Commission on National Goals, said: ". . . The inflation that accompanies the war and has continued in the years since the war has elevated the national concern for price and wage stability . . . How can we, then, give the necessary direction to our economic organization? Obviously, government participation has been and will be essential." [1]

"Decisions for a Better America," prepared by the Republican Committee on Program and Progress in 1960, said: "Inflation is the particular enemy of small business . . . Reces-

[1] Pp. 158–159.

sion is an equally dangerous enemy . . . Wise national economic policies will seek to steer between these dangers." [2]

The Rockefeller Panel Report, "Prospect for America,"
said: "Business and labor must exercise restraint, the former
in its pricing policies, the latter in its wage demands." [3]

And even the Republican platform for 1960 promised the
"use of the full powers of government to prevent the scourges
of depression and inflation." [4]

In short, there is probably no national domestic issue on
which there was such unanimity of agreement as the need to
control the wage-price spiral and to curb inflation. Hence
even those who were uncomfortable about the sudden flash
of White House lightning must concede that it was turned
on in a worthy cause.

Having considered the objective for which the "awesome
power" was unleashed, let us now take a look at the "power"
itself. The White House maintains that when all is said and
done, its weapons boiled down to three, each of which should
be examined:

(1) Most important, the President went on television and
delivered a blistering attack against the steel companies in an
attempt to rally public opinion to the side of government.
This can hardly be called revolutionary; President Eisenhower had spent a great deal of his press conference television
time railing against inflation and had once threatened both
labor and management that he would take his case to the
people if a noninflationary wage settlement was not reached
in 1959. According to Eisenhower Cabinet Secretary Robert
Keith Gray, Nixon and Mitchell achieved their settlement
in 1959 with only two weapons—"the prestige of the President
and the threat that he would take his case to the Congress and

2 Pp. 123–124.
3 P. 271.
4 P. 9.

the people if he could not get a settlement with a minimum of inflation built into it." [5]

(2) The Administration organized its legal machinery in an attempt to determine whether the steel companies—and U. S. Steel in particular—were violating the antitrust laws. This, again, is nothing new. The Justice Department, the Federal Trade Commission and the Congress had been keeping a watchful eye on the steel industry for years, and Congressional investigation committees in particular had let it be known that what they call "administered" pricing is at best a questionable practice skirting the borders of the antitrust laws, and that any pronounced trend in this direction would be subject to increased government attention. The defenders of the steel companies argued that "follow-the-leader" pricing had been the practice of the industry for some time, but as Senator Kefauver had repeatedly pointed out, something new had been added to steel pricing in recent years: the increasing of prices by the major producers at about the same time, by the same amount to the exact same level, despite the fact that the demand for steel is weak and the steel mills are operating far below capacity. Consequently, when the Government is presented with dramatic new evidence of identical increased pricing at a time when the market is soft, it is obligated to take action.

Before leaving this point, it should be said that despite the Administration's public position that it did not go too far in its dramatic initiation of the antitrust investigations, in private, many officials in the Administration felt that perhaps there was too much of a public flurry and that possibly the price could have been rolled back solely by the President's public appeals combined with Inland's decision. This was not the immediate reaction in the Administration, but it began to gain favor during the summer when the emotional state of

---

[5] *Eighteen Acres Under Glass*. Doubleday, New York, p. 292.

the business community became more and more obvious.

(3) The Department of Defense announced that it would purchase steel from companies which did not raise prices. Under the law, the Department of Defense is obligated to seek the most favorable price for its purchases, and as long as it had an alternative—steel available from domestic mills at lower prices—the Department had no choice but to consider shifting contracts. As for existing contracts, the standard escalator clause dictates that the price of steel involved in a contract will be the price at time of delivery. However, the Government has thirty days in which it can cancel the order if the price is increased between the time the contract is signed and the steel is delivered. According to the Defense Department, the twenty or so officials charged with reviewing contracts would have been negligent if they had not been studying alternative purchases, as long as some steel companies had still not raised prices. If all companies had increased prices simultaneously, the Department's counteraction would be limited, because there are restrictions on the purchasing of foreign steel.

All in all, the White House felt that, contrary to popular belief, the weapons it had for dealing with such a dispute were actually quite feeble, and except for the incident involving the FBI, the Administration showed no regrets at anything it had done. However, some members of the Administration have publicly conceded that the FBI agents could have waited until morning.

In defense of the agents, Robert Kennedy has since commented that "no one from this department enters anyone's office without their express permission . . . nothing was done in the steel case differently from hundreds of other investigations. One of the primary functions of the FBI is to make preliminary investigations in antitrust cases. In these or any other preliminary inquiry, search warrants or subpoenas

are not used . . . FBI agents are carefully trained to make
courteous inquiry into such situations . . . no one is under
any compulsion to answer agents' questions unless they wish
to. No documents or records need be made available to
agents . . . No steel executive made any complaint or report
to us that the agents were anything but courteous. One
Southwestern executive complained to a newspaper, but
when we sought the specifics of the complaint from him he
was unable to supply them."

When the dust settled, it had to be conceded that the incident was somewhat exaggerated. After all, the one reporter
most irritated by the FBI intrusion—John Lawrence—said
later that he prevented a nocturnal visit merely by telling
them he had nothing to say. If the "police state" were actually upon us, it is unlikely that the government "Gestapo"
agents could be put off merely by telling them that one had
nothing to say.

The essence of the Kennedy performance was that virtually
overnight the President and his task force had been able to
organize every last bit of ammunition available for the struggle and fire it almost simultaneously. The force of the volley,
combined with the fact that the steel companies had taken a
position behind a very shaky steel market, routed the enemy
before a second volley even had to be fired. As late as Friday
morning, there was more than one Kennedy lieutenant who
did not believe the first volley was enough, and the ammunition was running pretty low for a second strafing. But, in a
situation confused by a break in its own ranks, steel had to
retreat. Or, as *Fortune* put it: "When the increase was rescinded under competitive pressure from the other companies, credit went to Kennedy"—a credit soon followed by
the deafening flashback of criticism.

Included in this criticism is the charge that the President,
too, miscalculated; that the price rise would have stuck re-

gardless of what he did and that his sudden show of force was responsible for an unnecessary alienation of the business community. This may be true, but the White House argues that it was impossible to tell what would have happened if no action had been taken. As already seen, U. S. Steel's move would have been a severe blow to the President's leadership position even if the price increase had been rescinded voluntarily. And who can be sure that the other companies, even Inland, would not have gone along if the White House had not turned on the heat? They always had in the past. Who can be sure that Inland alone could have forced the retreat? "Inland could have been beaten," said one steel executive interviewed by *Business Week,* "even in the Chicago market. And support from Kaiser wouldn't have mattered."

As for foreign competition eventually forcing prices down, the best advice the White House had was that foreign prices are even more tightly "administered" than U. S. prices. It was very possible that most foreign prices would have been raised by about the same amount, as Roger Blough himself later suggested in an article in *Look.*

But the President's critics are right on one point: just as Blough miscalculated in underestimating the extent of the President's reaction to the price increase, the President miscalculated in underestimating the extent of the business community's reaction. Whether he would have softened his retaliation if he had anticipated the reaction will probably never be known, but it can be said with certainty that Kennedy was genuinely disturbed at the intensity of that reaction during the summer, and no doubt would just as soon have avoided it.

Despite the sound and fury, many people involved believe that much good came out of the crisis—and this includes members of the business community as well as members of the Administration. Both Roger Blough and Joseph

Block saw positive gains from the crisis. In Block's opinion, there were good results in three areas: the education of the public in the difficulties facing the steel industry; the demonstration that the industry is still competitive; and the storm of resulting protest which may make the Government hesitate to use coercive powers in the future. Block felt that at least some Administration officials agreed that the Government might have gone too far, and became more sympathetic to the industry's position. He is probably right.

As to what the Administration would do if a situation such as the steel crisis should develop again, talks with various Kennedy lieutenants in the Labor and Treasury departments and the Council of Economic Advisers produced conflicting views: one said that the methods used to stop the steel industry might be used again if and when a price situation ran contrary to public interest; others pointed out that the steel industry holds a unique position in the American economy, and the manner in which its price rise was announced made it an unusual case. These people cannot visualize such an incident reoccurring.

Despite conflicting opinions, most Administration officials involved agreed with the latter opinion. But they did point out that the "guideposts" set forth in the President's economic report applied to both wage demands and prices—a fact of which few businessmen were aware. The labor "guideposts" stated that wage increases and fringe benefits should more or less match the increase in the output per man hour of the entire economy—not just the industry getting the increase—in the postwar period. According to the report, this has been between 2.6 and 3.5 percent a year. If the industry is short of labor or one in which labor wages are unusually low, then labor should seek more than this average; if the industry is suffering from unemployment or if wages are unusually high, then the union should settle for less than the average.

For the businessman, the "guideposts" established for him

were less clear. According to the report, prices should rise if productivity in his industry is lagging, and prices should be cut if productivity is about at the national average. However, prices should rise faster if the industry needs higher profits to attract capital from outside—not from its own earnings—to expand capacity for an increased demand; or if costs for items other than labor are rising. Prices should fall more rapidly if the lack of demand for the product shows capital should leave the industry; or nonlabor costs have fallen; or excessive market power has given the industry profits well above those earned on investments in industries of the same risk.

Despite their existence, the business "guideposts" have not been pressed to nearly the same degree as the labor "guideposts," and in fact, very few businessmen are aware of them. Despite the President's success in rolling back steel prices, Administration officials do not feel that the problem of how to cope with business pricing in the future has been solved, by any means. However, one official has sketched out conditions under which the President *might* repeat his steel actions: a price increase in a "basic" industry when the rise is uniform among leading producers and covers a broad range of products, made with careful deliberation and in the face of a falling demand.

As Bernard Nossiter (in the Washington *Post*) said of the above hypothetical case: "This description of a possible Administration move against a price action implies that nothing would have happened had the steelmakers raised prices by different amounts on different products over a period of several months." One Administration official has acknowledged that if steel had used this nibbling approach, "it would have posed a very tough question for us."

The President continues to maintain that he would not have reacted to the steel price increase in the way he did if his leadership had not been challenged. "The steel situation won't happen again," he has said. "That was a personal thing."

And this is the essence of the steel crisis. The most serious miscalculation on the part of U. S. Steel was a simple one and one that big business is often guilty of making: Roger Blough and his executives seemed to overlook the obvious fact that the President of the United States is still a human being, and no human being enjoys a public affront. "U. S. Steel picked the wrong President to double-cross," said one White House aide. But to paraphrase Roger Blough's comment about the right time to raise prices, one can only ask: Who is the right President of the United States to double-cross? From George Washington to Dwight Eisenhower, any President would have reacted pretty much the same as Kennedy—although some with more vigor than others. The "awesome power" of the Presidency is available to any man elected to the office; it's there to be used, and the American people know that and expect their President to use it. Any man or group of men who choose to challenge that power do so at their own risk; it behooves them to remember that the man who sits in the office of the Presidency of the United States is subject to the same hopes, fears and emotions that reside in his fellow citizens. Despite all the howling about the "demagogic tactics" displayed by the White House during the steel crisis, the President's reaction was a very human one, and it was not the first time—and it probably will not be the last—that our giant corporations have demonstrated their inability to understand human emotions.

Appendices

A. Statement by U. S. Steel Announcing Price Increase, April 10, 1962.

PITTSBURGH, PA., April 10—For the first time in nearly four years, United States Steel today announced an increase in the general level of its steel prices. This "catch-up" adjustment, effective at 12:01 A.M. tomorrow, will raise the price of the company's steel products by an average of about 3.5 percent—or three-tenths of a cent per pound.

Since our last overall adjustment in the summer of 1958, the level of steel prices has not been increased, but if anything, has declined somewhat. This situation, in the face of steadily mounting production costs which have included four increases in steelworker wages and benefits prior to the end of last year, has been due to the competitive pressures from domestic producers and from imports of foreign-made steel, as well as from other materials which are used as substitutes for steel.

The severity of these competitive pressures has not diminished; and to their influence may be attributed the fact that the partial catch-up adjustment announced today is substantially less than the cost increases which have already occurred since 1958, without taking into consideration the additional costs which will result from the new labor agreements which become effective next July 1.

Nevertheless taking into account all the competitive factors affecting the market for steel, we have reluctantly concluded that a modest price adjustment can no longer be avoided in the light of the production cost increases that have made it necessary.

If the products of United States Steel are to compete successfully in the market place, then the plants and facilities which make those products must be as modern and efficient as the low-cost mills which abound abroad and as the plants which turn out competing products here at home.

Only by generating the funds necessary to keep these facilities fully competitive can our company continue to provide its customers with a dependable source of steel, and to provide its employees with dependable jobs. But the profits of the company—squeezed as they have been between rising costs and declining prices—are inadequate today to perform this vital function. Our annual report, published last month, shows clearly the effect of this squeeze.

In the three years since the end of 1958, United States Steel has spent $1,185,000,000 for modernization and replacement of facilities and for the development of new sources of raw materials. Internally, there were only two sources from which this money could come: depreciation and reinvested profit. Depreciation in these years amounted to $10 million; and reinvested profit, $187 million—or, together, only about two-thirds of the total sum required.

So, after using all the income available from operations, we had to make up the difference of $388 million out of borrowings from the public. In fact, during the period 1958–61, we have actually borrowed a total of $800 million to provide for present and future needs. And this must be repaid out of profits that have not yet been earned and will not be earned for some years to come.

During these three years, moreover, United States Steel's profits have dropped to the lowest levels since 1952; while reinvested profit—which is all the profit there is to be plowed back into the business after payment of dividends—has declined from $115 million in 1958 to less than $3 million last year. Yet the dividend rate has not been increased in more than five years, although there have been seven general increases in employment costs during this interval.

This squeeze, which has thus dried up a major source of the funds necessary to improve the competitive efficiency of our plants and facilities, has resulted, inevitably, from the continual rise in costs over a period of almost four years, with no offsetting improvement in prices.

Since the last general price adjustment in 1958, there have been a number of increases in the cost of products and services purchased by the corporation, in state and local taxes and in other expenses, including interest on the money we have had to borrow —an item which has jumped from $11.5 million in 1958 to nearly $30 million in 1961.

And from 1958 through 1961, there have been industry-wide increases in steelworker wages and benefits on four occasions amounting to about 40 cents an hour, and, also, increases in employment costs for other employees. These persistent increases have added several hundred million dollars to the employment costs of United States Steel, without regard to future costs resulting from the new labor agreement just negotiated.

In all, we have experienced a net increase of about 6 percent in our costs over this period despite cost reductions which have been effected through the use of new, more efficient facilities, improved techniques and better raw materials.

Compared with this net increase of 6 percent, the price increase of 3½ percent announced today clearly falls considerably short of the amount needed to restore even the cost-price relationship in the low production year of 1958.

In reaching this conclusion, we have given full consideration, of course, to the fact that any price increase which comes, as this does, at a time when foreign-made steels are already underselling ours in a number of product lines, will add—temporarily at least —to the competitive difficulties which we are now experiencing. But the present price level cannot be maintained any longer when our problems are viewed in long-range perspective. For the long pull, a strong, profitable company is the only insurance that formidable competition can be met and that the necessary lower costs to meet that competition will be assured.

Only through profits can a company improve its competitive

potential through better equipment and through expanded research. On this latter phase we are constantly developing lighter, stronger steels which—ton for ton—will do more work and go much further than the steels that were previously available on the market. They thus give the customer considerably more value per dollar of cost.

As more and more of these new steels come from our laboratories, therefore, our ability to compete should steadily improve. But the development of new steels can only be supported by profits or the hope of profits.

The financial resources supporting continuous research and resultant new products, as well as those supporting new equipment, are therefore vital in this competitive situation—vital not alone to the company and its employees, but to our international balance of payments, the value of our dollar, and to the strength and security of the nation as well.

B. Change in Unit Employment Costs in the Steel Industry, 1958–1961.

Changes in employment cost per unit of output reflect the extent to which changes in hourly employment cost are offset by changes in output per-man-hour. While employment cost per hour of all wage and salaried employees in the basic iron and steel industry rose from 1958 to 1961, there was an equivalent increase in output per man-hour. As a result, employment cost per unit of steel output in 1961 was essentially the same as in 1958. This was achieved with only a small increase in the percent of capacity utilized by the industry.

This statement is based on the following:

Percent change
1958 to 1961

Employment cost per-man-hour	+ 12.8
Output per-man-hour	+ 12.6
Employment cost per-unit-of-output	+ 0.2

The above figures are derived primarily from data published by the American Iron and Steel Institute. The man-hours cover all persons employed. Employment costs include wages, salaries and supplements such as contributions to social security and private pension, health and other programs. Output is based on detailed information on the production of pig iron, ferro-alloys, and 39 classes of steel-mill products, with carbon, alloy, and stainless steel products considered separately. To form an overall output measure, these are combined in terms of their relative unit labor requirements; for example, a ton of alloy steel counts more in the index than a ton of carbon steel.

Percent of capacity utilized was 60.6 for 1958, as published by the American Iron and Steel Institute. An estimate of 64.6 for 1961 was made by the Bureau of Labor Statistics based on estimated total capacity and production.

C. Statement by the Secretary of Commerce, Luther Hodges, Thursday Afternoon, April 12, 1962.

Ten days ago, I congratulated both the steel industry and the steel union for their statesmanship in reaching an early agreement that appeared to serve the public interest. It was my feeling that a major obstacle to further economic recovery had been removed.

The price increase announcements by U. S. Steel and other major steel companies change this picture completely. Tuesday evening a handful of men said, in effect, that Steel comes first, the United States of America second.

I am shocked and disappointed at this totally unexpected development. We have in this country, and I hope we will always have, a free economy. Subject to anti-trust laws and public services requiring regulation, any firm or industry is free to set prices as it sees fit. It is free to make mistakes, and I believe the steel industry's mistake is a tragic one. Its action is a disservice to the country and to the business community as a whole.

It is against the best interests of business—overall—because the public will be so antagonized by this development that all business may lose favor in the public eye. I trust this will not happen.

It is "anti-business"—because it may initiate a round of inflation which can only be harmful to business generally, especially small business.

It is "anti-business"—because it will give enouragement to those who contend that it is not possible to get responsible action on a voluntary basis, and that only compulsion and regulation will work.

The country had every right to expect price restraint by the steel industry in light of our international situation, in light of the moderate labor settlement just concluded, and in light of the pressing need to avoid obstacles to further economic recovery. The President, speaking for all the American people yesterday, expressed their keen disappointment that such price restraint was not forthcoming.

As a former businessman, and as the Cabinet member charged with responsibility to help achieve a healthy business condition, I am confident that the business community as a whole is disturbed by this development. They were expecting and hoping for price stability in this basic industry. Now they are troubled.

I recognize the need for adequate profits and have frequently spoken out on this subject. The national interest is best served, however, if such profits result from high levels of production rather than high unit profits. I am concerned that the steel price increase will mean lower total production in this basic industry if buyer resistance develops—both at home and in our foreign markets. And I am concerned about the demand for the products of all industries if the price spiral should begin.

Despite this provocation by the leading steel companies, I call upon American industry generally to do everything possible to hold the price level. Our economic recovery requires it; our international balance of payments situation requires it; our future economic growth and prosperity require it.

D. Statement by the Secretary of Defense, Robert McNamara, Concerning Steel Procurement, April 13, 1962.

The President has expressed his concern over "actions of U. S. Steel and other leading steel corporations increasing steel prices by some $6 a ton." I too am shocked by this wholly unexpected and, in my judgment, unjustified development. It strikes a blow at the President's program to maintain price stability based on a national wage policy which limits wage increases to productivity gains.

But my primary concern is with the grave and far-reaching consequences that this action may have on the security of the United States. Our military budget has already been increased to an all-time high, in order to meet the increased dangers that confront us. As I reported to the President on Wednesday, if this price increase fans out across other sectors of our economy, it can further increase the cost of our national defense in excess of $1 billion a year.

It is not only the effect of this price increase on our military budget that concerns me, however. A matter of even greater concern is the effect of our forces and bases overseas. National security demands that our military forces and the forces of our allies be deployed around the world, wherever freedom is challenged. The U. S. military operations overseas today cost us some $3 billion a year in foreign exchange. We have to earn that $3 billion each year in the export market. We cannot expect to maintain our forces overseas if our trade balance does not improve. It will not improve if a new round of price increases is set off by the action of U. S. Steel. These price increases will make it harder to sell our exports abroad, and will stimulate imports from abroad.

At the President's direction, therefore, and as a matter of

prudence, we are assessing the impact of the price increases on defense programs and procurement policies, and we are examining possible alternative sources and alternative materials. To minimize the effect of the price increase on defense costs I have today directed that where possible procurement of steel for defense production will be shifted to those companies which have not increased prices. I understand that similar action is being taken by other governmental agencies.

Further, I have noted that while iron and steel prices have increased by 90 percent since 1947, the prices of nonferrous metals have increased by only 40 percent. Therefore, we are particularly studying the possibility for replacement of steel by other materials including the potential of increased research and development in this area.

E. Address of the President to the United States Chamber of Commerce, April 30, 1962.

I want to take advantage of your presence in the Capital to convey my thinking about the present and future relationship of government and business, and to penetrate the dust of controversy that occasionally rises to obscure the basic issues and the basic relationships.

Almost all of the great nations of the world have their financial and political capitals located in the same city—London, Paris, Rome, Madrid and the others. Our founding fathers chose differently, in an effort to isolate political leaders from the immediate pressures of political life and national life, but this has placed a special obligation upon all of us, to speak clearly and with precision, and to attempt to understand the obligations and responsibilities which each of us face.

The foundation of the Chamber in April of 1912 marked a turning point in the relations between government and business, and there are some who say that the events of April of 1962 have also marked a turning point in the relations between government and business. I hope that this is so, in the sense that both sides will have new emphasis upon the obligation to understand each other's problems and attitudes.

In 1960 I do not think it wholly inaccurate to say that I was the second choice of a majority of business men for the office of President of the United States, and when I approached the White House the cheers of members of the Chambers of Commerce around the country were not overwhelming or deafening.

But in almost every major problem that I have encountered since assuming this responsibility, I have been impressed by the degree to which the best interests of the national government and the country are tied to the enlightened best interests of its most important segments.

But I have also been impressed that all the segments, including the national government, must operate responsibly in terms of each other, or the balance which sustains the general welfare will be lost.

As President my interest is in an economy which will be strong enough to absorb the potential of a rapidly expanding population, steady enough to avert the wide swings which bring grief to so many of our people, and non-inflationary enough to persuade investors that this country holds a steady promise of growth and stability.

My specific interest at this time is in maintaining a competitive world position that will not further stir the gold at Fort Knox.

As business men, your interest is profits or the maintenance of an adequate margin of return on your investments. To the extent that you want to protect your profit margins, our interests are identical, for after all we in the national government have a large stake in your profits. To the extent that you must raise your prices to make these profits, our interests at home and abroad stand in delicate balance.

Union leaders interests lie in the rate of return on labor for their members. To the extent that their efforts are devoted to securing equitable wages for their workers, our interests are identical, because we must have consumers to absorb our vast productive capacity, and as this year has reminded you the national government also lives off personal income taxes. To the extent that their efforts take the form of demands which will not upset the balance which has thus far stemmed inflation in this Administration, our interests are in concert. These areas where conflict exists between what I would call private interests and the general welfare must be met, and it seems to me by assumption of responsibility by all of us who care for our country.

We have many burdens in Washington—we do not want the added burden of determining individual prices for individual products. We seek instead an economic climate in which an expanding concept of business and labor responsibility, an increasing awareness of world commerce and the free forces of domestic competition will keep the price level stable and keep the government out of price-setting.

If American business does not earn sufficient revenue to earn a fair profit, this government cannot earn sufficient revenues to cover its outlays. If American business does not prosper and expand, this government cannot make good its pledges of economic growth. Our foreign policies call for an increase in the sale of American goods abroad, but it is business not government who must actually produce and sell these goods.

Our domestic programs call for substantial increases in employment, but it is business not government who must actually perform these jobs. While government economists can point out the necessity of increasing the rates of investment, of modernizing plant and productivity, while Washington officials may urge responsible collective bargaining and responsible wage-price decisions, we also recognize that beneath all the laws and guidelines and tax policies and stimulants we can provide, these matters all come down, quite properly in the last analysis, to private decisions by private individuals.

It is easy to charge an administration is anti-business, but it is more difficult to show how an administration, composed we hope of rational men, can possibly feel they can survive without business, or how the nation can survive unless the government and business and all other groups in our country are exerting their best efforts in an atmosphere of understanding, and I hope cooperation.

We have worked to establish the responsible view that we take of our role in the economy, and I do not think the record of our decisions, taken in totality, has been one to suggest that we are not responsive to the problems of business. I will point to our efforts in the field of inflation, to the balance of payments, to the transportation policy, for example, recently enunciated, as tenders of this concern. I expect to be able to point out soon to more realistic income tax guidelines on the depreciable lives of business assets, and to the 8 percent tax credit for investment in equipment and machinery, which has been proposed and is now being considered by the Senate.

I do not regard the vigorous enforcement of the anti-trust laws, for example, to be anti-business. These statutes, most of which have a long historic past antedating the life of the Chamber of

Commerce, are based on the basic premise that a private enterprise system must be truly competitive if it is to realize its full
potential. And it is natural in these important basic industries
in which one or two companies may control over fifty percent of
the total national production, that the government should be
concerned that the realities of competition exist, as well as their
appearance. But this is in the interest of business, and you know
quite well that nearly every action taken by this government,
and previous administrations, in the field of anti-trust actions,
or actions by the Federal Trade Commission have been based
upon complaints brought by business men themselves. This is in
the interest, therefore, of business, as well as of the general public.

When I talk of the public interest in these matters, I am not
using a rhetorical phrase. It costs the United States three billion
dollars a year to maintain our troops and our defense establishment and security commitments abroad. If the balance of trade is
not sufficiently in our favor to finance this burden, we have two
alternatives—one, to lose gold, as we have been doing; and two,
to begin to withdraw our security commitments.

This is the heart of the issue which has occupied the attention
of so many of us in recent months, of our efforts to persuade the
steel union to accept a non-inflationary wage agreement—and to
persuade the steel companies to make every effort to maintain
price stability.

In the competitive contest for world markets, upon which the
balance of payments depends, our record since the end of the
Korean War has not been wholly satisfactory, I am sure, to any
of us. From the end of the Korean War, our export prices rose
about 11 percent, while average export prices in the Common
Market held steady. There were significant wage raises during
this period, as we know. Indeed our wage levels in the large manufacturing industries rose 30 percent in the United States but they
also rose 58 percent in the same period in France and Germany.
But their output per man-hour increased sufficiently so that their
costs per unit of output rose less than ours. During this period,
our gold stocks declined by five and one half billion dollars, and
the short-term dollar claims of foreigners, a potential call on our

gold stock, rose by an equal amount, 11 billion dollars in the past few years.

I do not mean to say that we have priced ourselves out of world markets. Our merchandise exports of over 20 billion dollars testify that we have not. And our comparative price performance has improved in the last two or three years. But if we are to stem the gold outflow, which we must by one means or another, eliminate the deficit in our balance of payments, and continue as I believe we must to discharge our far-flung international obligations, we must avoid inflation, modernize American industry, and improve our relative position in the world markets.

Never in the fifty-year history of the Chamber of Commerce has its dedication to a vigorous economy been more in the national and international interest than it is today. This Administration, I assure you, shares your concern about the cost-profit squeeze on American business. We want prosperity and in a free enterprise system there can be no prosperity without profit. We want a growing economy, and there can be no growth without the investment that is inspired and financed by profit.

We want to maintain our national security and other essential programs and we will have little revenue to finance them unless there is profit. We want to improve our balance of payments without reducing our commitments abroad, and we cannot increase our export surplus, which we must, without modernizing our plants through profit. We can help through new trade policies that increase the business man's access to foreign markets, particularly to the expanding markets of nearly 200 million people which we will have in Western Europe.

And I want to salute the United States Chamber of Commerce for its historic endorsement of the new Trade Expansion Bill. We can help by making more realistic the income tax guideline on the depreciable lives of business assets, a move long called for and needed, and now being carried through. I recognize that many of you would like, as I would, to have far more rapid depreciation schedules. I can assure you that we are limited only by the fact, which you must recognize, that these depreciation changes will, in their early years, mean a loss of governmental revenues. If we wish to bring our budget as closely as possible to balance as far as the economy permits, we do not feel able to relinquish at this time these sources of revenue in toto. But we should look ahead to the maximum extent possible, as we have already done in textiles, and as we are now examining in steel, and we are quite conscious of the competitive advantages which rapid depreciation gives to the Western European manufacturers. We are looking ahead now to make these depreciation schedules more realistic.

We can help, if Congress will pass the pending bill by granting an 8 percent tax credit for investment in equipment and machinery, and those of you who do not feel that that is sufficient, and it may well not be, must recognize that this particular provision, limited as you may feel it is, will cost the government in the next fiscal year one billion, 800 million dollars in tax revenues if it is accepted by the Senate. And I believe in the form that it is in it will result in far more stimulus to business for every dollar of tax revenue foregone than the more familiar alternatives that many of you might have preferred.

I recognize that some of you are opposed to some of the revenue measures which we have recommended to balance revenue losses which we incur from the tax credit. But we cannot responsibly forego such a large amount of our budget unless we consider alternate means of recouping that loss. We take these steps only for budgetary reasons, and in the case of tax havens abroad in order to make less advantageous the flow of American capital into other countries and to place enterprises there on a fair competitive basis with American companies here which must pay the taxes which they do not.

We can also help by creating a climate of collective bargaining in which increased wages are held within the appropriate limits of rising productivity, a rising productivity that will also provide for investments in modernization, for profits, and even we hope lower prices, to stimulate increased purchasing.

And may I add at this point that when an administration has not hesitated to seek Taft-Hartley injunctions for national emergencies, has successfully urged moderation on the steel workers and other unions, has expressed a firm and continuing opposition to the 25-hour week, or anything less than the 40-hour week, and has gone on record against featherbedding and racketeering and road blocks to automation, it surely does not need to be asked whether it will invoke the national interest wherever it believes it to be threatened.

In addition, this Administration can help alleviate the business man's cost-price squeeze through new transportation policies aimed at providing increased freedom of competition at lower cost to the shipper, through fiscal and monetary policies aimed at making more capital available at less cost, and through a whole host of other policies on patents, productivity and procurement.

But perhaps most important of all are our efforts which are aimed at creating conditions of high employment, and what is most important I know to all of you, high capacity utilization. For when the economy is expanding, profits generally are expanding, and not at the cost of a consumer. But when the economy is slack, we not only have unemployment but profits are inevitably slack. Just as there can be no prosperity without profits, so are profits hinged to prosperity. With the high fixed costs of modern production and business organizations, few American business firms can earn an adequate profit on an inadequate volume. Profits have been under pressure since early 1957 because the economy has been operating below capacity since 1957. To restore profits to an adequate level, to maintain an adequate level of employment, we must restore the economy to full activity.

In short, our primary challenge is not how to divide the economic pie, but how to enlarge it. To fight now over larger slices of the existing pie, by seeking higher margins on lower volume, or higher wages ahead of productivity, can only weaken our effort to expand the economy of the United States.

The recovery of the past year has already raised our total output rate by 50 billion dollars. Corporate profits by 13 billion. Personal income by 32 billion. Employment by 1 million 200 thousand. And industrial production by 13 percent. And this upswing is continuing. Housing starts rebounded vigorously last month. Retail sales are rising. Consumer intentions are encouraging. Business plans an 11 percent increase in its investment in new plant and equipment. And construction awards are at an all-time high. I am convinced that our economy in 1962 will break all records in production, employment and profits. But we must, of course, always do better.

For had we achieved these goals of full employment and high capacity, I am confident that none of the events which made this last month so memorable would have taken place at all. And if we can now join in achieving these goals, I am confident that they may never need to take place again.

I realize that we shall not reach these goals overnight, nor shall we achieve them without inconvenience, some disagreement, and some adjustments on every side—among labor, business and the government.

But the Bible tells us that "there is a time for every purpose under the heaven . . . . a time to cast away stones and a time to gather stones together." And ladies and gentlemen, I believe it is time for us all to gather stones together to build this country as it must be built in the coming years.

Thank you.

F. Excerpts from the President's Remarks at the Yale Commencement Exercises, June 11, 1962.

... As every past generation has had to disenthrall itself from an inheritance of truism and stereotype, so in our own time we must move on from the reassuring repetition of stale phrases to a new, difficult but essential confrontation with reality.

For the great enemy of the truth is very often not the lie—deliberate, contrived and dishonest—but the myth—persistent, persuasive and unrealistic. Too often we hold fast to the clichés of our forebears. We subject all facts to a prefabricated set of interpretations. We enjoy the comfort of opinion without the discomfort of thought.

Mythology distracts us everywhere—in government as in business, in politics as in economics, in foreign affairs as in domestic policy. But today I want to particularly consider the myth and reality in our national economy. In recent months many have come to feel, as I do, that the dialogue between the parties—between business and government—is clogged by illusion and platitude and fails to reflect the true realities of contemporary American society.

I speak of these matters here at Yale because of the self-evident truth that a great university is always enlisted against the spread of illusion and on the side of reality. No one has said it more clearly than your President Griswold: "Liberal learning is both a safeguard against false ideas of freedom and a source of true ones." Your role as university men, whatever your calling, will be to increase each new generation's grasp of its new duties.

There are three great areas of our domestic affairs in which, today, there is a danger that illusion may prevent effective action. They are, first, the question of the size and the shape of government's responsibilities; second, the question of public fiscal policy; and third, the matter of confidence, business confidence or public confidence, or simply confidence in America. I want to talk about all three, and I want to talk about them carefully and dispassionately—and I emphasize that I am concerned here not with political debate but with finding ways to separate false problems from real ones.

If a contest in angry argument were forced upon it, no Administration could shrink from response, and history does not suggest that American Presidents are totally without resources in an engagement forced upon them because of hostility in one sector of society. But in the wider national interest, we need not partisan wrangling, but common concentration on common problems. I come this morning to ask you to join in this great task.

Let us take first the question of the size and shape of government. The myth here is that government is big, and bad—and steadily getting bigger and worse. Obviously this myth has some excuse for existence. It is true that in recent history each new Administration has spent much more money than its predecessor. Thus President Roosevelt outspent President Hoover, and with allowances for the special case of the Second World War, President Truman outspent President Roosevelt. Just to prove that this was not a partisan matter, President Eisenhower outspent President Truman by the handsome figure of $182 billion. It is even possible something of this trend may continue.

But does it follow that big government is growing relatively bigger? It does not—for the fact is for the last 15 years, the Federal Government—and also the Federal debt—and also the federal bureaucracy—have grown less rapidly than the economy as a whole. If we leave defense and space expenditures aside, the Federal Government since the Second World War has expanded less than any other major sector of our national life—less than industry, less than commerce, less than agriculture, less than higher education, and very much less than the noise about big government.

The truth about big government is the truth about any other great activity—it is complex. Certainly it is true that size brings dangers—but it is also true that size also can bring benefits. Here at Yale which has contributed so much to our national progress in science and medicine, it may be proper for me to mention one great and little-noticed expansion of government which has brought strength to our whole society. The new role of our Federal Government as the major patron of research in science and in medicine. Few people realize that in 1961, in support of all university research in science and medicine, three dollars out of every four came from the Federal Government. I need hardly point out that this has taken place without undue enlargement of government control—that American scientists remain second to none in their independence and in their individualism.

I am not suggesting that federal expenditures cannot bring some measure of control. The whole thrust of federal expenditures in agriculture have been related by purpose and design to control . . . as a means of dealing with the problems created by our farmers and our growing productivity. Each sector, my point is, of activity must be approached on its own merits and in terms of specific national needs. Generalities in regard to federal expenditures, therefore, can be misleading—each case, science, urban renewal, education, agriculture, natural resources, each case must be determined on its merits if we are to profit from our unrivaled ability to combine the strength of public and private purpose.

Next, let us turn to the problem of our fiscal policy. Here the myths are legion and the truth hard to find. But let me take as a prime example the problem of the federal budget. We persist in measuring our federal fiscal integrity today by the conventional or administrative budget—with results which would be regarded as absurd in any business firm—in any country of Europe—or in any careful assessment of the reality of our national finances. The administrative budget has sound administrative uses. But for wider purposes it is less helpful. It omits our special trust funds; it neglects changes in assets or inventories. It cannot tell a loan from a straight expenditure—and worst of all it cannot distinguish between operating expenditures and long term investments.

This budget, in relation to the great problems of federal fiscal policy, is not simply irrelevant; it can be actively misleading.

And yet there is a mythology that measures all of our national soundness or unsoundness on the single simple basis of this same annual administrative budget. If our federal budget is to serve, not the debate, but the country, we must and will find ways of clarifying this area of discourse.

Still in the area of fiscal policy, let me say a word about deficits. The myth persists that federal deficits create inflation and budget surpluses prevent it. Yet sizable budget surpluses after the war did not prevent inflation, and persistent deficits for the last several years have not upset our basic price stability. Obviously deficits are sometimes dangerous—and so are surpluses. But honest assessment plainly requires a more sophisticated view than the old and automatic cliché that deficits automatically bring inflation.

There are myths also about our public debt. It is widely supposed that this debt is growing at a dangerously rapid rate. In fact, both the debt per person and the debt as a proportion of our gross national product have declined sharply since the Second World War. In absolute terms the national debt increased only 8 percent, while private debt was increasing 305 percent, and the debts of state and local governments increased 378 percent. Moreover, debts, public and private, are neither good nor bad, in and of themselves. Borrowing can lead to over-extension and collapse—but it can also lead to expansion and strength. There is no single, simple slogan in this field that we can trust.

Finally, I come to the problem of confidence. Confidence is a matter of myth and also a matter of truth—and this time let me take the truth of the matter first.

It is true—and of high importance—that the prosperity of this country depends on assurance that all major elements within it will live up to their responsibilities. If business were to neglect its obligations to the public; if labor were blind to all public responsibility; above all, if government were to abandon its obvious—and statutory—duty of watchful concern for our economic health—if any of these things should happen, then confidence might well be weakened and danger of stagnation would increase. This is the true issue of confidence.

But there is also the false issue—and its simplest form is the assertion that any and all unfavorable turns of the speculative wheel—however temporary and however plainly speculative in character—are the result of, and I quote, "lack of confidence in the national administration." This I must tell you, while comforting, is not wholly true. Worse, it obscures the reality—which is also simple. The solid ground of mutual confidence is the necessary partnership of government with all of the sectors of our society in the steady quest for ecnomic progress.

Corporate plans are not based on a political confidence in party leaders but on an economic confidence in the nation's ability to invest and produce and consume. Business had full confidence in the Administrations in power in 1929, 1954, 1958, and 1960—but this was not enough to prevent recession when business lacked full confidence in the economy. What matters is the capacity of the nation as a whole to deal with its economic problems and its opportunities.

The stereotypes I have been discussing distract our attention and divide our effort. These stereotypes do our nation a disservice, not just because they are exhausted and irrelevant, but above all because they are misleading—because they stand in the way of the solution of hard and complicated facts. It is not new that past debates should obscure present realities. But the damage of such a false dialogue is greater today than ever before simply because today the safety of all the world—the very future of freedom—depends as never before upon the sensible and clear-headed management of the domestic affairs of the United States. . . .

Sources

Because of the desire of many of the participants in the steel crisis to speak "off the record," I will not list the names of those who granted me interviews for the purpose of developing this account of the crisis.

The coverage of the crisis by several leading newspapers and magazines was extremely valuable. These include: *The New York Times,* the Washington *Post,* the *Wall Street Journal, Time, Newsweek,* and *U. S. News & World Report.* The chronology of events which appeared in *The New York Times* on April 23, 1962, was especially valuable. In addition, the following magazine articles were extremely helpful:

Blough, Roger M.: "My Side of the Steel Price Story," *Look,* January 29, 1963

Burck, Gilbert: "The Private Strategy of Bethlehem Steel," *Fortune,* April 1962

Graham, Robert E., Jr., and Bauman, Jacquelin: "Corporate Profits and National Output," *Survey of Current Business,* November 1962

Porter, Frank C.: "Steel's Long, Deep Sleep," *The New Republic,* January 5, 1963

Randall, Clarence B.: "Business, Too, Has Its Ivory Towers," *The New York Times Magazine,* July 8, 1962